# The Long War over Party Structure

A long-standing debate in American politics is about the proper structure for political parties and the relative power that should be afforded to party professionals versus issue activists. In this book, Byron E. Shafer and Regina L. Wagner draw systematically on new data and indexes to evaluate the extent to which party structure changed from the 1950s on, and what the consequences have been for policy responsiveness, democratic representation, and party alignment across different issue domains. They argue that the reputed triumph of volunteer parties since the 1970s has been less comprehensive than the orthodox narrative assumes, but that the balance of power did shift, with unintended and sometimes perverse consequences. In the process of evaluating its central questions, this book gives an account of how partisan alignments evolved with newly empowered issue activists and major postwar developments from the civil rights movement to the culture wars.

Byron E. Shafer is Hawkins Chair of Political Science at the University of Wisconsin, Madison. He was formerly Mellon Professor of American Politics at Oxford University from 1984 to 2001. He has written on numerous aspects of the structure of American politics, and he has attended all national party conventions for both parties from 1980 onward.

Regina L. Wagner is Assistant Professor of Political Science at the University of Alabama, Tuscaloosa. Her work focuses on political representation, gender and politics, legislative politics, and political parties. She received her PhD from the University of Wisconsin, Madison, in 2018.

# The Long War over Party Structure

## Democratic Representation and Policy
## Responsiveness in American Politics

**BYRON E. SHAFER**
*University of Wisconsin*

**REGINA L. WAGNER**
*University of Alabama*

**CAMBRIDGE**
UNIVERSITY PRESS

# CAMBRIDGE
## UNIVERSITY PRESS

University Printing House, Cambridge CB2 8BS, United Kingdom

One Liberty Plaza, 20th Floor, New York, NY 10006, USA

477 Williamstown Road, Port Melbourne, VIC 3207, Australia

314-321, 3rd Floor, Plot 3, Splendor Forum, Jasola District Centre, New Delhi - 110025, India

103 Penang Road, #05-06/07, Visioncrest Commercial, Singapore 238467

Cambridge University Press is part of the University of Cambridge.

It furthers the University's mission by disseminating knowledge in the pursuit of education, learning and research at the highest international levels of excellence.

www.cambridge.org
Information on this title: www.cambridge.org/9781108718868
DOI: 10.1017/9781108753517

© Byron E. Shafer and Regina L. Wagner 2019

First published 2019
First paperback edition 2022

A catalogue record for this publication is available from the British Library

ISBN 978-1-108-48491-6 Hardback
ISBN 978-1-108-71886-8 Paperback

# Contents

v

# Figures

# Tables

# Preface

Political parties are generally recognized as the great intermediary institutions of democratic politics. They are *intermediary* because they connect the social base for politics with the operative institutions of government. Yet they become *institutionalized* in a way that most other intermediaries do not because they are intended explicitly to manage this connection. In doing so, however, they always partially transform public wishes in the process of transmitting them. Sometimes this transformation is modest, a kind of side payment for necessary activity. Other times, it is much more substantial, shaped strongly by the operational character of the intermediary institutions that perform the activity. Either way, the crucial body in this transmission is expected to be the political party.

That is the grand theoretical justification for a concern with party structure and with the specific arrangements – offices, incentives, preferences – that constitute that structure and by which this mediating process occurs. Moreover, for much of American political history, this has not been a simple "academic" matter. Instead, there has been a kind of open war over the appropriate structure of American political parties, and hence over the implications of alternative structures for democratic representation. In effect, there have been two fronts to this war. One front was theoretical, involving the proper standards for judging political parties as intermediary institutions. The other front was intensely practical, involving struggles over the policy rewards of American government. Though unlike the situation in some other realms, theoreticians and practitioners were often intensely aware of each other.

A potted history of this two-front war could run all the way back to the Founders, who thought a great deal about what was for them the unhappy

xi

prospect of political parties as crucial intermediaries.[1] This history would pause with the Jacksonians, who usually receive credit for launching the organized parties with their strong internal structures that came to dominate nineteenth-century American politicking.[2] The story would pause again with the Progressives, who took up both the intellectual and the empirical efforts to make intermediation work differently, that is, in a more participatory manner and on a volunteer basis.[3] And it would be brought up to date in a most surprising fashion when political scientists began to survey party fortunes in the immediate postwar world – and discovered that the reported demise of organized parties had been grossly overstated.[4]

At that point, 130 years after the initiating efforts of the Jacksonians and 80 years after the countervailing efforts of the Progressives, the two grand alternative models of party structure were alive and well on the American political landscape:

- There were still what we shall call "organized parties," built upon the tangible rewards – opponents would call these the "spoils" – of governmental policy. Such rewards became the central incentive for political activity; the operational result was a hierarchy of long-serving party officeholders. Seen from below, these individuals rose

---

[1] Most succinctly in the "Farewell Address" from President George Washington, his statement declining a third term, collected in James D. Richardson, ed., *A Compilation of the Messages and Papers of the Presidents* (Washington, DC: Bureau of National Literature, 1897–1913), Vol. 1, 205–216.

[2] For the birth and maturation of the organized party system, Joel H. Silbey, *The American Political Nation, 1838–1893* (Stanford: Stanford University Press, 1991). For that story in the words of the politician commonly viewed as most influential in this creation, Martin Van Buren, *Inquiry into the Origin and Course of Political Parties in the United States* (New York: Hurd & Houghton, 1867).

[3] On Progressivism, Richard Jensen, "Democracy, Republicanism, and Efficiency: The Values of American Politics, 1885–1930," Chap. 6 in Byron E. Shafer and Anthony J. Badger, eds., *Contesting Democracy: Substance and Structure in American Political History, 1775–2000* (Lawrence: University Press of Kansas, 2001); for the coming of an alternative party model, Richard L. McCormick, *The Party Period and Public Policy: American Politics from the Age of Jackson to the Progressive Era* (New York: Oxford University Press, 1986); and for the extension of that model through the twentieth century, James W. Ceaser, "The Development of the Presidential Selection System in the Twentieth Century," chap. 5 in James W. Ceaser, *Presidential Selection: Theory and Development* (Princeton: Princeton University Press, 1979).

[4] Most especially in Alan Ware, *The Breakdown of Democratic Party Organization, 1940–1980* (Oxford: Oxford University Press, 1985), and David R. Mayhew, *Placing Parties in American Politics: Organization, Electoral Settings, and Government Activity in the Twentieth Century* (Princeton: Princeton University Press, 1986).

up from localized social organizations. Seen from above, they could be put into the field as the metaphorical "machinery" that waged election campaigns and coordinated policy making.

• Yet, there were also numerous examples of what we shall call "volunteer parties," likewise built around governmental policies but now conceived more as abstract and general programs. These again provided the central incentives for political activity, but this time by mobilizing those who cared intensely about one or more of these substantive domains. For them, pursuit of such programs was its own reward. The operational result – at least ideally and often initially but not always in perpetuity – was open and shifting networks of issue activists, built and rebuilt as candidates and issues changed with the times.

But almost at the very point when scholars were rediscovering the continued vitality of two alternative models for party structure, the balance between the two shifted in a major way. A mix of party systems dating to the 1830s and amended but not transformed from the 1880s onward met the cataclysmic combination of major social change and sweeping institutional reform, once more joining intellectual concerns about properly democratic intermediation with institutional moves to restructure that process in the real world of practical politics. The best-known result was a comprehensive reworking of the mechanics of presidential selection. Yet these presidential reforms were only the most visible product of a collection of institutional changes reaching well beyond them. If this larger complex of reforms was more geographically and temporally dispersed, it was also procedurally more far-reaching, leaving few states without recurrent and lasting impacts from a comprehensive reform surge.

At first, one associated result was the flowering – really the re-flowering – of scholarly work on the differential contribution of various forms of internal partisan organization.[5] In short order, however, this result turned opposite and ironic. The long scholarly tradition of analyzing differences within American party systems at the grand level largely died away, in tandem with the alleged disappearance of the great historical distinctions

---

[5] See, among many, Austin Ranney, *Curing the Mischiefs of Faction: Party Reform in America* (Berkeley: University of California Press, 1975); William J. Crotty, *Political Reform and the American Experiment* (New York: Thomas Y. Crowell, 1977); and Nelson W. Polsby, *Consequences of Party Reform* (New York: Oxford University Press, 1983).

between organized versus volunteer political parties. Or so the dominant narrative ran. By the late 1960s and early 1970s within this narrative, the forces championing autonomous participation, volunteer parties, and a fluid politics had routed the forces associated with social connection, organized parties, and representational stability – and come to dominate American politics.

This apparent resolution was assumed to be both general and permanent. An unsurprising but unfortunate corollary was that scholarly work in the immediate area began to die away. If political parties, headquartered in fifty otherwise diverse states, were now reformed in theory and similar in practice, there seemed little more to say. We take this to be an unhappy resolution, unhappy as befits a study of the long war over party structure on both empirical and theoretical grounds. Empirically, the details of a much-reported triumph by the volunteer model were more impressionistically asserted than systematically demonstrated. Yet the resulting balance between party types mattered – and still matters – even just on its own terms. Which is to say: if systematic investigation confirms this triumph, how general was it? Or, said the other way around, how much of the alternative (organized) model actually survived?

Theoretically as well, an alleged triumph by one of the two main models was taken, implicitly and – we think – incorrectly, to imply that an understanding of party structure in American politics no longer mattered in the terms that had been so central to the long-running debate. Yet even if that were true, the practical adoption by individual states of one model rather than the other did go on to affect both the degree of ideological polarization between the active parties and, even more consequentially, the nature of the ties between party activists and their own putative rank and files – and these effects were continuing, still, to make their contribution to policy responsiveness and democratic representation in American politics. Accordingly, this filtering effect has to be the larger focus (and hence the larger contribution) of an effort to return in a systematic fashion to these once-fundamental questions about the operational nature of American politics.

From one side, the dominant narrative, asserting the end of the long war and the homogenization of American party politics, would by itself suggest the need to return to the issue of organized versus volunteer political parties; to address this distinction with the kind of systematic indicators that are capable of tracing its evolution across all the postwar years; and, most especially, to consider some contributions of the modern result to the shaping of political representation in the United States. Even if this narrative were entirely correct (which it is not!), implications for democratic responsiveness would remain both omnipresent and subtly insistent in the modern world – magnified, of course, by whatever the changing balance in party types turned out to be.

Yet this narrative could also be false, and in two fundamentally different ways, each with its own implications for democratic responsiveness. In the first, the situation that serious researchers uncovered in the 1960s – a world where organized parties, despite previous obituaries, had survived surprisingly well – might still hold in the 2010s, rebalanced no doubt and ever-elusive in its measurement, but continuing to make important contributions to American democracy. Alternatively, the dominant narrative could be more or less completely misleading in the polar opposite fashion. The 2000s were to bring a small but persistent body of new work arguing forcefully that the alleged triumph of volunteer parties had never had the behavioral consequences claimed by their proponents.[6] Recast in the analytic terms used here, this work implied that the participatory reforms associated with that triumph had in practice served to *resurrect* what was nothing less than a modern incarnation of the old organized-party model.

Either contrary result would push implicitly in the same theoretical direction: back toward a set of classical – time-honored – questions about party structure and policy responsiveness. Together, those possibilities have set the stage, we think, for a return to what was long one of the major issues, both theoretical and practical, in American politics. This involves the internal structure of US political parties and the implications of this structure for the larger nature of democratic representation. In historical terms, we now possess better evidence than was ever available at the height of this war through which to confront arguments about the true evolution of conscious party reform. In contemporary terms, we can finally ask in a systematic fashion about the representational and policy impacts of an alleged behavioral triumph.

In that light, how is the active party linked to its rank and file under organized versus volunteer systems? This is perhaps the crucial aspect of *democratic representation*, and hence the operational nub of political intermediation. What then happens to the policy preferences of party

---

[6] Most pointedly, Marty Cohen, David Karol, Hans Noel, & John Zaller, *The Party Decides: Presidential Nominations before and after Reform* (Chicago: University of Chicago Press, 2008); and Seth E. Masket, *No Middle Ground: How Informal Party Organizations Control Nominations and Polarize Legislatures* (Ann Arbor: University of Michigan Press, 2011).

activists – the operative party elite – when one structural model largely supplants the other? This is in turn the crucial contribution to *policy responsiveness*. What is a changing balance of party types doing to partisan policy alignments overall? This is the question of how parties organize policy demands, and it is the second key aspect of democratic representation. And lastly, what is this changing balance doing to different *policy domains*, both those that have attained overall partisan alignment and those that have not? This is the second key contribution to policy responsiveness.

Those are the questions that we propose to address in *The Long War over Party Structure: Democratic Representation and Policy Responsiveness in American Politics*. Chapter 1 begins this effort by way of a small set of scholarly landmarks. These address what party structure is, the alternative forms it can take, and the representational implications of adopting one or the other of two great alternatives. The chapter moves to a systematic effort to convert previous work on the topic – varied and impressionistic but always circling back to the same central concerns – into a set of indicators that can be followed systematically. With that accomplished, Chapter 1 closes by setting out the actual distribution of organized and volunteer parties in the fifty states across the postwar period, 1950–2010. Within this description, the year 1970 does indeed prove to be a critical change point, in effect the formal triumph of the volunteer model.

Chapter 2 turns to an effort to demonstrate the impact of these alternative structures (and of the changing balance between them) on American politics, most especially with regard to policy responsiveness and democratic representation. The hunt begins in the policy domain that has long been the bedrock of the modern party system, namely social welfare. Fortunately, the relevant literature comes prepackaged with hypotheses about how party structure interacted with welfare preferences, even if they were initially created for other purposes. When these hypotheses are largely sustained in our inquiry, albeit as elucidated in some new ways, social welfare can go on to provide an analytic template for asking about the impact of organized and volunteer parties in other major substantive domains. The chapter closes with one of these others, the domain of civil rights.

Chapter 2 suggests that the choice between organized and volunteer structures did filter policy preferences in notably different ways, though not necessarily the ways that their proponents intended. The resulting list of impacts proves to be imposing: affecting overall partisan alignments, the manner of their arrival in American politics, the degree of ideological polarization between the active parties, the size of the gap between party activists and their rank and file, and the behavior of specific populations inside all of this. So Chapter 3 cannot escape going in search of the rest of the major policy conflicts that have characterized postwar American politics. The first element in this involves the policy domain of cultural values. Yet once that is available, it proves possible to move to a more comprehensive level, using social welfare and cultural values jointly to isolate the major *ideologies* in American politics during this period, namely liberalism, conservatism, populism, and libertarianism. The chapter closes with the fourth of the four substantive domains usually regarded as central to policy conflict in the United States in the postwar years, namely foreign affairs and national security.

Chapter 4 returns to our underlying concern with the filtering effect of party structures, reorganized and presented in two ways. In the larger of the two, this chapter puts the four major domains of postwar policy conflict back together and considers their evolution as a collective whole, in common with the evolution of the comprehensive ideologies that accompanied these individual domains. Yet the chapter also attends to the variety of generic ways in which party structure can shape this evolution. These include its impact on individual partisan populations, on overall partisan alignments, and on ideological polarization within these alignments, along with the manner in which all of these evolve from one era to another.

In the end, however, an attempt to resuscitate a major perspective on democratic representation can hardly announce that this resuscitation is complete, much less that the long war is over, and thus that history has ended. So there must be an Afterword, addressing a major new twist on the argument about links among party structure, policy responsiveness, and democratic representation. No analysis can be definitive about a hypothesized future, but it is possible to close with some of the major questions that a fresh look at prospective impacts would involve – most especially the prospect that party activists have ultimately defeated the reformers, restoring control over superficially participatory parties and pulling their activist components further than ever from the voting rank and file. Much more work would have to be done before anyone could confirm or dismiss the accuracy of this latest salvo in the long war, but the Afterword suggests that successor scholars with similar concerns could indeed do such work.

\* \* \*

The obvious wisecrack about the intellectual roots of this project is that it begins with the decision by Andrew Jackson, as implemented most centrally by Martin Van Buren, to create the organized Democratic Party in response to being denied a presidential nomination in 1824. Its direct roots are more mundane but still hardly linear. One of us (Byron) wrote a thesis prospectus involving party structure and its differential impact on policy outcomes – a prize-winning proposal, he said proudly – but then ended up writing a very different doctoral dissertation. The other of us (Regina) wrote her very first graduate paper on – what else? – the differential impact of party structures, focused on the United States but with a comparative hook. Yet she too then went off in a different direction, with a doctoral dissertation on the interaction of gender, party, institutional rules, and local cultures in American politics.

Several years later, we were working together on other projects when we began to return to an old common interest. The first step in converting a mutual curiosity about party structure into something real was to collect and organize the available indicators, to see if the dominant narrative had any patterned reality. When it did – organized parties survived a good deal longer than the received wisdom would suggest, but there was a huge shift toward volunteer parties around 1970 – we then went in search of actual policy impacts from this shift. The search began with social welfare, the ostensible base of the New Deal party system. When these appeared, somewhat to our surprise, we expanded the focus to include the other major domains of postwar policy conflict, namely foreign affairs, civil rights, and cultural values.

By then, we were generating papers and giving conference presentations. For these latter, the annual meetings of the American Political Science Association and the biennial conferences of the Policy History Association were particularly helpful. We thank the latter in particular for some conscious intellectual support.

Specific individuals also made distinctive contributions. Shannon Johnson, currently in Washington School of Law at American University, created the measures that underpin the Afterword to this volume. Monica Busch, currently in graduate school in the Department of Political Science at the University of Wisconsin, came to the project late, but early enough to create and manage the index. Byron benefited from extended conversations with Alan Ware of Oxford University and Richard Johnston of the University of British Columbia. Regina benefited from insights into the inner workings of R from Bradley Jones, research associate at the Pew Research Center, and from a variety of thoughts on different aspects of the project along the way from Elizabeth Sawyer, also currently in graduate school in political science at the University of Wisconsin.

When the time came to move this project from manuscript to published work, Sara Doskow at Cambridge University Press took it under her wing and adeptly managed that particular transition, all the while urging us to sharpen the argument in several key regards. Danielle Menz at Cambridge then held all the specific pieces in line on the way to a final product. We thank both of them. Formal classes on research design often suggest a kind of synoptic approach to the research enterprise. We think that many serious projects are more likely to look like this one, emerging from a latent curiosity and progressing through one result that leads to another.

# Party Structure in Theory and in Practice

## *Organized Parties, Volunteer Parties, and Their Evolution*

At an abstract level, it is easy to make an argument for the virtue of an effort to isolate and examine the impact of party structure. Political parties are the great intermediary institutions of democratic politics. Yet they inevitably transform and not just transmit public wishes. It is hard to imagine how their internal structure would not be central to that transformation. So the effort to unpack these influences should be inherently virtuous, that is, intrinsically connected to question of policy responsiveness and democratic representation. Yet the moment this effort shifts to the operational level, embedding a theoretical argument in the practical details of American politics, problems surface, likewise inherently.

Intermediary institutions are by definition connected to much else in the political process. Citizens have social backgrounds that shape the demands falling upon state parties in a powerful way. Pennsylvania will be an industrial state and Iowa a farm state whichever party model each approximates. Issues of the day go on to impinge on those parties with a force that their internal structure can mitigate but rarely dismiss. There are wars, recessions, and disasters, along with partially autonomous social movements, and these are unlikely to confine themselves to states with only one party type. Voters themselves acquire partisan identifications that may in fact be reciprocally shaped by life in an organized or volunteer party but are rarely altered by party structure alone at any single point in time.

And always in the background, interacting with all such social forces while offering a historically remarkable stability, is the US Constitution as governmental framework. In other words, we are trying to tease out the influence of an omnipresent factor – party structure – that is nevertheless rarely the single dominant influence on political outcomes. On the other hand, these challenges do at least come almost prepackaged, with a nearly inescapable way of proceeding. The first step is to create defensible measures of the presence and distribution of organized and volunteer parties across an extended period of time, that time being the years from 1950 to 2010 for our purposes. This is the task of Chapter 1.

Thereafter, with policy responsiveness and democratic representation as the focus, it becomes necessary to apply these measures and search for distinctions between them with regard to public preferences and their transmission. The good news here is that the American National Election Study (ANES) now includes sixty years of survey evidence on policy preferences, and these do permit the creation of scales tapping partisan representation in major policy domains across the postwar years. Within them, it is additionally possible to isolate specific preferences by political era for the four key partisan populations in such an analysis: Democratic activists, the Democratic rank and file, the Republican rank and file, and Republican activists. That is the task of Chapters 2 and 3.

Underneath all of that, the two leading questions are simple enough to ask, if devilishly tricky to resolve. How are active partisans related to their rank and files in organized versus volunteer parties? And what do these activists contribute to the ideological positioning of the two party types in the process of managing partisan affairs? Chapter 4 brings back the answers that are contributed (and scattered) along the way, assembling them into a small set of larger and recurring impacts.

First, least common but most dramatic when they actually appear are differences in the overall partisan alignment of major policy domains. The question here is whether alternative party models go so far as to *align* the four main partisan populations in fundamentally different ways. This is a high standard of impact, yet it is met at various times with various policy domains, and when it is, the differential contributions of party structure stand out.

Second, more reliably present are contributions from party structure to the behavior of the active parties, that is, the aggregate populations of activist Democrats and activist Republicans. The key consideration here is the nature and scope of *partisan polarization*, both the distance between the active parties and the degree to which one or the other set of party activists shapes it disproportionately. Party structure proves to be reliably enmeshed in these activist divisions.

Third and most consequential is the question of how an active party relates to its own rank and file. There are periods and issues in which active parties sit cheek by jowl with their partisans. These, however, are rare: there is usually some distance between party activists and their rank and file, a distance that changes by political era and by policy domain. Despite such variation, the evolution of this *representational gap* tends to be additionally shaped by party type. This is the most theoretically apt measure of representational difference by party structure as well as the least confounded by other factors that also effect the transmission of preferences.

Last but most common are impacts limited to single partisan populations – Democratic or Republican, activist or rank and file – each of which is fully capable of major policy shifts without any echoing impact from its opposite numbers. Differences in party structure almost always distinguish such shifts additionally, and the postwar period comes close to offering all the logical possibilities: Democratic activists moving (leftward) on their own, Republican activists moving (rightward) with the same autonomy, Democratic rank and files standing to the left of their own active parties, Republican rank and files standing to the right of theirs, all four populations polarizing simultaneously, and activists polarizing while their rank and files stay put.

The effort in Chapter 1 to set up this analysis begins in the first section with a quick summary of the relevant literature from the mid-twentieth century, when the topic returned as a major analytic concern. Relevant indicators, producing the essential scale, will be gathered and analyzed in the section after that. Next, it becomes important to demonstrate that these concrete indicators and their composite scale can be linked convincingly to the rich but impressionistic literature from which they grew. All that accomplished, the chapter can go on to trace the actual distribution of organized and volunteer parties in the American states across the postwar period, 1950–2010. This proves to be largely a familiar story, now systematically supported but with fresh nuances and an enlarged reach. Chapters 2 and 3 can then turn to its democratic impact.

## THE POSTWAR SCHOLARLY BACKDROP

The strong political parties of the nineteenth century, built around the spoils of politics – jobs, contracts, and favors – and mounting army-type campaigns to maintain control of those spoils, were a revelation when they appeared.[1] The Jacksonians brought them to life as an institutional

---

[1] Silbey, *The American Political Nation.*

form; the years after the Civil War brought them a level of fungible resources never previously seen. Yet those years also brought a chorus of disenchantment, whose members saw the need for some institutional alternative. Their dissent from the organized model of party structure had both theoretical and practical roots. The high costs of corruption associated with this organized model,[2] along with the insulation from politics that followed for those not among the social groups supplying party retainers,[3] caused the Progressives to go to war on existing arrangements by way of a fresh and comprehensive alternative.

Their volunteer model valorized an educated and disinterested citizenry, and it quickly acquired a phalanx of associated reforms that were intended to bring the model into being and buttress it thereafter. Major elements within this alternative structure included the secret ballot, civil service, and primary elections, though the full panoply would become voluminous.[4] Yet what resulted was hardly a rapid transformation but rather a long incremental conflict between (a) differing approaches to party business, (b) differing constituencies seeking to shape public policy, and at bottom (c) differing conceptions of democratic politics – featuring two models with distinctive internal arrangements at the center of these ongoing struggles in the fifty states.

At the same time, the long war over party structure was implicit evidence of the degree to which both scholarly theorists and practical politicians continued to believe that the internal arrangements of political parties mattered to policy responsiveness and democratic representation. Anecdotal reports on the intensity of the battle, usually accompanied by rhetorical arguments about its consequences, were readily available.[5] Yet systematic evidence for the truth of these beliefs remained in surprisingly short supply. In what ways did party structure matter? Where did it matter? When did it matter? The main purpose of this chapter, then, must be to assemble the systematic indicators, ideally leading to the creation

---

[2] Mark W. Summers, *The Era of Good Stealings* (New York: Oxford University Press, 1993).

[3] Arthur S. Link & Richard L. McCormick, *The Progressives* (Arlington Heights, VA: Harlan Davidson, 1983).

[4] Alan Ware, *The American Direct Primary: Party Institutionalization and Transformation in the North* (New York: Cambridge University Press, 2002), follows the fortunes of the most stereotypical reform device, the public primary election.

[5] For example, Edward J. Flynn, *You're the Boss: My Story of a Life in Practical Politics* (New York: Viking Press, 1947). The jacket proclaims, "This is the story of the man who has ruled politics in the greatest Democratic county north of the Mason-Dixon line – New York's Bronx – for a quarter-century and has never lost a local election there."

of a defensible scale, which would permit cataloguing the comparative progress of two alternative models and then searching for the actual impact of organized versus volunteer political parties.

There was a general sense among those who studied these developments impressionistically and through specific historical cases that the onward march of party reform and its volunteer model was the dominant story of the ongoing war. Official party structures of the traditional kind – fully developed, fully staffed, fully resourced, and effectively hierarchical – reliably seemed less common than they had once been, and they occasioned more comment in places where they did exist. Yet there was little historic benchmarking of a systematic sort through which to back up – or dissent from – this general sense – that is, until a set of major efforts toward just such a picture began to appear in the mid-twentieth century, with results that occasioned some surprise.

Efforts to think about the intermediary structure of American political parties in the postwar world usually begin with the work of James Q. Wilson. In a crucial early article from Wilson and Peter B. Clark, the authors set out a theoretical framework for linking incentive systems with structural impacts.[6] Within this framework, Clark and Wilson argued that the crucial maintenance activity of any organization was to mobilize and distribute incentives, that all such incentives had consequences for individual behavior, and that changing the nature of these incentives would thus alter institutional (and not just individual) activity. They then classified their incentives in three general categories: *material*, the most tangible and fungible; *solidary*, the most social and associational; and *purposive*, the most substantive and ends related: "If the behavior of organizations is closely related to their incentive systems, the dynamics of organizational change may be predicted by knowing the circumstances under which incentive systems change."[7]

A dozen years later, Wilson took this theory onward, applying it to the full range of organizations regularly involved in American politics in the book-length *Political Organizations*.[8] Yet his crucial elaboration for our purposes, focusing the theory on political parties, came in chap. 6, where Wilson tied his three categories of incentives to what were in principle three types of party structure: "The Machine," "The Purposive

---

[6] Peter B. Clark & James Q. Wilson, "Incentive Systems: A Theory of Organizations," *Administrative Science Quarterly* 6(1961), 129–166.
[7] Ibid., 149.
[8] James Q. Wilson, *Political Organizations* (New York: Basic Books, 1973).

Party," and "Solidary Parties." Each featured different patterns of recruitment, different operating priorities, and different contributions to policy outputs. Yet while this analytic schema had room for all three party types, there was from the first an underlying dichotomy in Wilson's further argument, one based on the first two polar types. In turn, these generated his ideal-typical participants, the "professionals" and the "amateurs":

A decentralized party structure will, among other things, use a variety of appeals to enlist members. And for each kind of incentive, there is a corresponding organizational style and pattern of internal control, though perhaps not a characteristic strategy. ... A political machine is a party organization relying chiefly on the attraction of material rewards. These rewards include patronage jobs, preferents, economic opportunities, and finally, exemptions. ...

This does not mean that considerations of policy are entirely absent from materially induced party organizations. One policy in particular is of great importance – namely, whether or not the candidate is prepared to take care of his supporters if elected. And publicly, policy is much discussed. ... Partly, this is ammunition being passed out to workers so that they in turn can use it on voters, most of whom receive nothing of material value directly from the party but whose questions and concerns need to be dealt with.[9]

While at the other end of the continuum:

By "amateur" is meant a person who finds an enterprise – here, politics – intrinsically rewarding because it expresses a commitment to a larger purpose. Though an amateur is not indifferent to considerations of partisan and personal advantage or unmoved by the sheer fun of the game or the opportunities to meet people and wield influence, he is distinctive in that he takes the content of public policy and the outcomes of government seriously.

Because establishing the proper relationship between means and ends is vital to the amateur, he is concerned with devising mechanisms to ensure not only that the right ends are selected, but also that they are selected for the right reasons and that effort toward them on the part of political leaders is continuous and sincere. Accordingly, political amateurs in this country, and perhaps generally, are vitally interested in mechanisms to ensure the intraparty accountability of officeholders and party leaders. ... The concern for policy implies a concern for mechanisms, such as intraparty democracy, to ensure that the correct policy is followed. In addition, a chance to participate in making decisions is in itself an important incentive for members of amateur clubs.[10]

By the time Wilson was applying this theoretical argument to the available alternatives for American politics, he believed that the effort had gained urgency because the balance of party types in the United States

---

[9] Ibid., 97, 100.    [10] Ibid., 106–107.

was in fact shifting decisively, from material incentives and hierarchical organization to purposive incentives and the volunteer party:

The chief consequences of these trends have been a change in the process of candidate selection and in the nature of electoral appeals. Party organizations composed of persons motivated by material rewards have a strong interest in winning an election, for only then will their rewards be secured. Provided there are competitive parties, candidates, at least at the top of the ticket, will be selected and electoral appeals fashioned so as to attract votes from the largest possible number of citizens. When the organization consists of members motivated by purposive rewards, the candidate selected must be one that can attract their enthusiasm, even if he cannot attract voter support, and the appeals issued must be consistent with their preferences, even if voters find them repugnant.[11]

Alan Ware was a second scholar who shared this sense of a crucial turning point in the structural character of American party politics. So, not long after the publication of *Political Organizations*, Ware began a book-length attempt to unpack the specifics of this transition, away from material incentives and an organizational hierarchy among formal officeholders and toward purposive incentives and their social networks among issue activists. *The Breakdown of Democratic Party Organization, 1940–1980*[12] features a lament in its opening pages about the absence of wide-ranging and systematic data on party structures nationwide – a dilemma that we attempt to begin addressing in the subsequent pages of this chapter:

[E]ven those aspects of party organization which could be illuminated by the data pose a problem for the researcher, because so little material of this sort was collected by our predecessors. This means that anyone who wishes to trace, say, the decline in recruitment to party organizations will find hardly any material with which to compare profiles of contemporary organizations.[13]

In an effort to capture this change with sufficient richness to talk about it operationally, Ware focused on three very different locales: New York City, once the stereotypical home of a Democratic Party machine; Denver, a voluntaristic culture that had nevertheless generated a Democratic Party capable of coordinating multiple campaigns; and the East Bay in California, self-consciously hostile to organized politics but producing a network of reform Democratic clubs that performed many of the same

---

[11] Ibid., 115.
[12] Alan Ware, *The Breakdown of Democratic Party Organization, 1940–1980* (Oxford: Oxford University Press, 1985).
[13] Ibid., 9.

functions in all but name. Careful and rich consideration of these arche-
typically diverse parties convinced Ware – as they would convince
Mayhew in his counterpart national survey – that the demise of material
incentives and hierarchical structures had been overstated:

> The main thrust of our argument differs from a popular contemporary view. For
> we claim that in the 1940s and 1950s, the parties were not becoming so weak that
> complete collapse in the 1960s was inevitable. Far from being in continual decline
> since the height of the New Deal, in some respects the parties actually had a brief
> revival about the middle of the century.[14]

Yet what Ware described as an "Indian Summer" for organized parties
did finally come to an end. The late 1960s and 1970s threw up a set of
further challenges to these continuing structures, and it was these challenges that would ultimately bring about the demise of old structural
arrangements. Leading stresses on the old order still varied from place
to place: fratricide in New York, reform in Denver, extremism in the East
Bay. But despite their idiosyncratic starting points and regardless of the
particular mix of stressors that fell upon these differing incarnations
of old-time party structure, the result was generalized, sweeping, and
qualitatively different. This result was given further impetus – a further
shove – in Ware's argument by the explicitly anti-party issues of the time:

> There can be little doubt that what happened to the Democratic Parties in America
> between the early 1960s and the late 1970s was truly extraordinary. Within a few
> years, most of them were transformed.
>      ... [T]here are two important respects in which issue conflicts did harm the
> Democratic parties. First, they helped to make issue-oriented activists much more
> skeptical about the value of party; what emerged in the 1960s was issue-activism
> which was not party-oriented, as it was in the 1950s, but which was prepared to
> use party institutions for realizing objectives as, and when, they seemed useful. ...
> Secondly, the issue conflicts actually revived long-standing anti-party sentiments
> in America, sentiments which were minority ones in the amateur Democratic
> movement of the 1950s, but which became more apparent in the late 1960s.[15]

At about the same time that Ware was deep-mining his three major
cases, David R. Mayhew, in *Placing Parties in American Politics*,[16] was
taking the opposite tack. Working on essentially the same problem,
Mayhew began by accumulating any and all available reports of party

---

[14] Ibid., 42.    [15] Ibid., 241, 246–247.
[16] David R. Mayhew, *Placing Parties in American Politics: Organization, Electoral Settings, and Government Activity in the Twentieth Century* (Princeton: Princeton University Press, 1986).

politics in the fifty states and their major localities, whether historical or journalistic. From these, he fashioned a data set that was encyclopedic if still inevitably impressionistic and nothing like a random sample. Like Ware, he lamented the absence of anything even vaguely resembling systematic data on his central phenomenon, party structure. Yet in adopting the opposite strategy in the face of that problem, Mayhew argued that good accounts of the operative nature of politics in major areas almost always revealed its structural principles or, when they did not, reflected the simple fact that such principles were more or less nonexistent:

One reason for supplying the close documentation on traditional and other sorts of electoral organization ... is to show that it can be done. Good observers are capable of noticing organization, describing it, and telling what it does. This is important: it produces a suspicion that writers who give detailed accounts of nominating politics without discussing organization are dealing with places that do not have much organization to discuss.[17]

Asking "What if the more fundamental policy-related distinction in the American party sphere of the last century or so has indeed had to do with structure rather than competition?"[18] Mayhew turned to defining his central focus as clearly as possible, so that it could be applied to distinguishing among the state party systems that surfaced from good descriptive accounts. For this, it was the notion of a traditional party organization (TPO) that was specified, elaborated, and mobilized:

Finally, the special term *traditional party organization* is needed since no other has quite the right meaning. ... [I]ts acronym TPO will be used interchangeably in the following chapters to refer to any organization at the level of county, city, city ward, township, or other local jurisdiction about which all five of the following statements can be made:

1) It has substantial autonomy ...
2) It lasts a long time ...
3) Its internal structure has an important element of hierarchy ...
4) It regularly tries to bring about the nomination of candidates for a wide range of public offices ...
5) It relies substantially on "material" incentives, and not much on "purposive" incentives, in engaging people to do organizational work or to supply organizational support.[19]

In search of the distribution and evolution of these TPOs, Mayhew came to much the same conclusion as Ware: that the many previous reports of the death of organized parties had been overstated. Like

---

[17] Ibid., 143.  [18] Ibid., 5.  [19] Ibid., 19–20.

Ware, however, Mayhew also concluded that the era of the TPOs was indeed coming to a close as the 1960s gave way to the 1970s. Accordingly, a major side benefit to pursuing party structure at that time and in this manner was that it affirmed and reinforced what many authors had treated as a key turning point in the long war over party structure:

The late 1960s is a good time to inspect because it both closes and samples fairly well a long twentieth-century span between the second and third of three major periods of structural change in American parties – the first being the Jacksonian period, the source of the nineteenth century's characteristic system; the second, the Progressive period, during which national, state, and local parties were substantially overhauled with the effect of producing a hybrid twentieth-century system; and the third, the last decade and a half or so, during which local party organizations have decisively declined and telecommunications processes, candidate organizations, and capital-intensive party organizations have become central features of distinctive new electoral politics.[20]

### MEASURING PARTY STRUCTURE

To retreat to basics: the problem common to previous students of the nature and impact of party structure has been that measures that fully satisfy the theoretical distinction between organized and volunteer parties, tapping most especially the nature of internal party careers and the scope of internal party resources, were available only as rare snapshots of a particular place at a single point in time. Or, said the other way around, they were not available nationally at any time, much less regularly across time. As a result, analysts could not check the contribution of party structure to policy responsiveness and democratic representation in anything other than an impressionistic fashion, much less track continuity and change in that contribution in any objective and systematic way.

Formally, this problem is opposite to the one often found in tracking the evolution of public opinion. There, the latent variable in question cannot in principle be measured directly. By contrast, here, the analyst knows exactly what an ideal measure of the latent variable would look like. It remains "latent" only because the relevant direct indicators never were (and never will be) collected. In the end, however, the solution to both problems is the same: collect and analyze a sufficient array of

[20] Ibid., 7.

alternative indicators with face validity, that is, with direct substantive connection to the phenomenon being examined. Search for some major element of commonality among those indicators. Check the resulting measure – the embodiment of this commonality – against the impressionistic works that gave original impetus to the whole effort. And use this systematized measure to pursue the theoretical matters at issue.

With the notion of organized versus volunteer parties, the analyst does at least begin with some inescapable touchstones for isolating the relevant indicators. From one side, these come out of the histories of intraparty warfare. While battles over the specifics of reform are often part of some larger story in these accounts, the structural preferences of the two sides, organized versus volunteer, tend to be clear.[21] From the other side, there have been a variety of self-conscious reform agendas, essentially grocery lists for reform. These have been assembled by organizations reliably dedicated to the volunteer perspective.[22]

Our reading of both sources, historical and taxonomic, suggests that diverse conflicts in the long war tended to be pitched on a small set of recurrent battlefields. Moreover, with rare exceptions, the preferences of organized versus volunteer parties were immediately clear. Most happily for our purposes, concrete indicators are available for most of these in the modern world, some of which meet the further requirement of covering the entire period from the 1950s to the 2010s. They include the following:

## Appointment Powers
- *Merit Systems:* The ability to make personnel appointments was central to organized parties. The first direct and most fundamental challenge to this ability was the coming of civil service, that is, of generalized merit systems.
- *Unionization:* The other great constraint on the ability to make personnel appointments came later, from the rise of labor unions specializing in public employees, which became the great institutionalized competitor to the official party in this regard.

[21] Alan Ware, *The American Direct Primary*, spreads its reform net much more widely than its title might indicate. On the municipal level, Edward C. Banfield & James Q. Wilson, *City Politics* (New York: Vintage, Books, 1963), pulls a variety of reform proposals together, most especially at chap. 11, "Reform," again in a manner where it is not difficult to distinguish the organized from the volunteer position.

[22] As with the program of the National Municipal League, addressed comprehensively in Frank Mann Steward, *A Half-Century of Municipal Reform: The History of the National Municipal League* (Berkeley: University of California Press, 1950).

### Financial Regulations
- *Transparency of Party Finance:* Organized parties reliably took the view that management of their resources was an internal matter – they should be judged on their performance – while public openness about political finance was often central to the reform drive.
- *Regulation of Campaign Contributions:* Organized parties took the view that the raising of funds was likewise an internal matter – a natural part of coalition building – while limitations on contributions from organized interests were often central to the reform ethos.

### Voting Strictures
- *Ballot Forms:* The traditional party-column ballot was a central product of the strong-party era. The office-block alternative sought to shift public attention away from party attachments and toward candidate qualifications.
- *Ticket Provisions:* If parties could make nominations internally, they naturally wished to follow with a straight ticket – encouraging voters to accept the total product while accepting collective responsibility for it – while the reform approach favored disaggregating offices and encouraging individualized attention to them.

### Institutional Mechanics
- *Institutions of Nomination:* The classic arrangement for nominations to public office under organized parties involved making those nominations *through* the official party structure, most often in convention. The reform alternative was nomination by public primary election.
- *Institutions of Policy Making:* Afterward, organized parties wanted it to be (their) elected officials who made the resultant public policy. Reformers continued to want an augmented public role, to the point of permitting citizens to legislate directly by way of the referendum.

### Partisan Limitations
- *Partisan Endorsements:* The endorsement of candidates was a central activity of organized parties – why else would a party exist? – while a ban on such endorsements was often part and parcel of the drive for party reform, a conflict at its most intense with judicial elections.
- *Participatory Structures:* For organized parties, a concomitant to the fact that nominations should be internal and policy made by their nominees was that political participation should belong to party members. Conversely, volunteer parties wished to use open and participatory processes to recruit both activists and voters.

The initial source for measures of most of these was the *Book of the States*, first published by the Council of State Governments in 1935 and produced annually since that time.[23] They were then supplemented and cross-checked through materials available from the National Conference of State Legislatures.[24] As it turns out, all of these indicators are positively correlated, while there is no theoretical reason for using them other than through a directly additive measure, so the resulting scale bids to become the principal measure of party structure used here.

Within it, states can vary from 0, taking the position associated with organized parties on every indicator, to 10, taking the position associated with volunteer parties on every indicator. In the immediate postwar years, there were indeed states falling at every position on the resulting scale, while at no point in subsequent years did any of these ten indicators reverse the direction of their individual relationships or cease to scale collectively. Over time, an increasing share of states would move toward the higher (the volunteer) end of the scale, and this movement – the changing distribution of organized versus volunteer parties in the American states – is a substantive finding in its own right, one to be pursued in the remainder of Chapter 1.

Before that, however, it is desirable to have some further test of the construct validity of this scale, that is, some external standard for validating our fresh measure, over and beyond its internal consistency. The fundamental question here is whether a scale crucial to all that follows can be shown to align substantively with previous major efforts at measuring what is meant to be the same general phenomenon. In other words, does it produce results sufficiently similar to those found by key predecessors who did not have the advantage of multiple indicators and an ongoing scale? Three of these analyses are in fact sufficiently detailed in their specifics to permit the structural classification of political parties in all fifty states in a manner that is at least empirically grounded, and hence comparable, making them stand out as potential cross-checks for construct validity.

Among the three obvious candidates for such an exercise, one has already been introduced in detail. This is David R. Mayhew, *Placing Parties in American Politics*. Its central organizing concept, the "traditional

---

[23] The first edition was *The Book of the States* (Chicago: Council of State Governments and American Legislators, 1935). The most recent version was *The Book of the States: 2016 Edition* (Lexington, KY: Council of State Governments, 2017).

[24] Accessed through their website at www.ncls.org.

party organization" or TPO, has been central to our own definition of organized versus volunteer parties. Moreover, Mayhew is willing to go on and scale state parties on the strength and generality of their TPOs:

In the ensuing sketches, each state is given a score gauging the prominence of TPOs in its politics in the late 1960s on a 1-to-5 scale. In principle, the score for each state is an average of scores for each of its lower political units (counties in most states) weighted appropriately according to population size, ... In practice, given the evidence, it is impossible to be anywhere near so exact. My fallback procedure is to circumvent the arithmetic and make scoring judgments about states as wholes, basing them on whatever evidence there is but staying as close as possible to the logic of positing scores for locales and then weighting and averaging them. Scoring by states makes sense: states have in fact varied as states in the prominence of their TPOs.[25]

A widely referenced predecessor is Daniel J. Elazar, *American Federalism; A View from the States*.[26] While Elazar's main mission was to understand the operation of American federalism from the bottom up – through what he called "The States as Systems within a System" – this enterprise required categorization of the individual states according to their "political cultures." The resulting taxonomy would become a widely used product of the book, one with particular resonances for anyone concerned with the social roots of alternative party structures. It has the further advantage that all fifty states could be classified in this way, through their dominant cultures:

The *individualistic political culture* [*I*] emphasizes the conception of the democratic order as a marketplace. In its view, government is instituted for strictly utilitarian reasons, to handle those functions demanded by the people it is created to serve. . . .
    Since the *I* political culture eschews ideological concerns in its "business-like" conceptions of politics, both politicians and citizens look upon political activity as a specialized one, essentially the province of professionals, of minimum and passing concern to laymen, and no place for amateurs to play an active role.[27]
    The *moralistic political culture* [*M*] emphasizes the commonwealth conception as the basis for democratic government. Politics, to the *M* political culture, is considered one of the great activities of man in his search for the good society – a struggle for power, it is true, but also an effort to exercise power for the betterment of the commonwealth. . . .

[25] Mayhew, *Placing Parties in American Politics*, 21, 23.
[26] Daniel J. Elazar, *American Federalism; A View from the States* (New York: Thomas Y. Crowell, 1966).
[27] Elazar, *American Federalism*, 86, 88.

[I]t also embraces the notion that politics is ideally a matter of concern for every citizen, not just those who are professionally committed to political careers. Indeed, it is the duty of every citizen to participate in the political affairs of his commonwealth. ... Consequently, party regularity is not of prime importance.[28]

The *traditionalistic political culture* [T] is rooted in an ambivalent attitude toward the marketplace coupled with a paternalistic and elitist conception of the commonwealth. It reflects an older, pre-commercial attitude that accepts a substantially hierarchical society as part of the ordered nature of things, authorizing and expecting those at the top of the social structure to take a special and dominant role in government. ...

Political parties are of minimal importance in *T* political cultures, since they encourage a degree of openness that goes against the fundamental grain of an elite-oriented political order.[29]

A narrower but much more pointed application of the concept of party structure came from one of the two of us, in Byron E. Shafer, *Quiet Revolution: The Struggle for the Democratic Party and the Shaping of Post-Reform Politics.*[30] While the theoretical focus here was directly on the difference between organized and volunteer parties, its empirical scope was limited to their response to the sweeping reforms in the process of presidential nomination that characterized the late 1960s and early 1970s (and that receive some further attention later). Yet in the process, the staff of the key reform body, the Commission on Party Structure and Delegate Selection, collected detailed reports of party structure in the fifty states, reports that are easily recast into our terms:

This distinction is between volunteer and organized political state political parties. *Volunteer parties*, those which rely on independent activists to mount election campaigns, were much more likely to move early. *Organized parties*, those which can turn to the incumbents of a hierarchy of party offices when election time approaches, were much more likely to shy away from the entire reform process. ...

Volunteer parties are perhaps best classified through the activist character of their campaign workers. In general, those who do the work of the party are motivated by comparatively intangible, even transient considerations, like issues, personalities, or a sense of civic duty. ...

Organized parties, conversely, feature a continuing collection of party office-holders, who are reliably present in several campaigns at the same time, and in successive campaigns over a period of years. Ordinarily, a significant number of tangible, divisible rewards are necessary to guarantee this large aggregate of

---

[28] Ibid., 90–91.    [29] Ibid., 92–93.

[30] Byron E. Shafer, *Quiet Revolution: The Struggle for the Democratic Party and the Shaping of Post-Reform Politics* (New York: Russell Sage Foundation, 1983).

reliable party workers, and to guarantee that they will subordinate their personal preferences to a common, loosely connected ticket.[31]

The Shafer classification arrived in dichotomized form, effectively pre-packaged as organized versus volunteer. If those states with any remaining vestiges of traditional party organization in the Mayhew rankings are collapsed into the "organized category," the two categories (organized and volunteer) feature extremely high overlap with the Shafer classification. Elazar, whose political cultures underpin (but are not the same as) structural differences among political parties, presents the greatest surface deviance, since he believes in three, not two, cultural categories. Yet a parallel alignment for testing purposes is easily created by assigning his "Individualist" states to the organized category, his "Moralistic" states to the volunteer category, and his "Traditionalist" states to whichever category features in their secondary cultural layer, "Individualist" versus "Moralistic."[32]

When this is done, the three classifications show a powerful overlap, each to the others, with some specific state exceptions in each case. Only a handful of states are characterized differently by the three authors. Yet this overlap can be further checked (and further challenged) by conducting a factor analysis of all ten individual indicators *plus* these three classifications, an arrangement maximizing their chances to diverge from one another and cluster with other rankings. Table 1.1 does this, and an exploratory factor analysis shows the three impressionistic rankings generating a factor all their own, even in the presence of numerous additional measures. Despite being developed for quite separate purposes, then, and despite the presence of ten additional opportunities to muddy an underlying pattern, the three impressionistic rankings still prove to be highly correlated.

A further side benefit of this test is that all forty-eight states acquire scores on the common factor. There is a more or less natural break in the distributions of these scores, to the point of yielding the same number of organized and volunteer parties as a simple summation of the Elazar, Mayhew, and Shafer ratings individually. This makes it possible to go on and compare state parties as classified by their internal structures in this prior collection of what are effectively case studies with the state parties as classified by their internal structures when assessed through a scale constituted from ten theoretically derived indicators. This is done

---

[31] Shafer, *Quiet Revolution*, 281–282. The resulting state story is summarized most succinctly at fig. 10.1, 282.

[32] Elazar, *American Federalism*, does this most succinctly at figs. 3, 4, 97 & 108.

TABLE 1.1 *Associated Elements of State Party Structures:
A Common Factor from Previous Research*

| Variable | Factor 1 | Factor 2 | Factor 3 | Factor 4 | Factor 5 |
|---|---|---|---|---|---|
| Party Column vs. Office-Block Ballots | | .91 | | | |
| Straight Ticket Voting Facilitated | | .84 | | | |
| Referendum Available | | | | | −.52 |
| Filing Requirement for State Party Finance | | | | .81 | |
| Contribution from Organized Interests Permitted | | | | .86 | |
| Primary Used for Nomination | | | | −.35 | |
| Open vs. Closed Primary | | | .47 | | |
| Partisan Selection of Judges | | | .82 | | |
| Public Unionization | | | .78 | | |
| General Coverage of Merit System | | | | | .84 |
| Elazar | .86 | | | | |
| Mayhew | .84 | | | | |
| Shafer | .82 | | | | |

TABLE 1.2 *Impressions and Indicators:
States Classified by Party Structure*

| | | Ten-Item Scale | | | | | |
|---|---|---|---|---|---|---|---|
| | | <3 | 3 | 4 | 5 | 6 | >6 |
| E/M/S | Volunteer | 0 | 3 | 4 | 7 | 6 | 9 |
| | Organized | 4 | 3 | 6 | 4 | 1 | 1 |
| | | Rho = .66 | | | | | |

in Table 1.2. Rows are created by dichotomizing the forty-eight (and after 1959, fifty) states according to their scores on the combined factor from the Elazar/Mayhew/Shafer analyses. Columns are then the scores for the same states on the proposed aggregate measure.

The two arrays are unlikely to be identical. Indeed, one point of having a systematic index is its disregard for what an individual case analyst might believe, added to its ability to carry our central distinction forward, so that the impact of party structure can be observed beyond the dates of previous work. On the other hand, the two arrays ought to be clearly related – there should be a strong underlying consistency between the two rankings – else the argument that they are measuring different things cannot be dismissed. Individual case analysts might still believe that a particular state deviates from the score elicited by a new scale of indicators. Yet if any such idiosyncratic readings were actually closer to the truth, that fact should merely weaken the overall association between measures, while ultimately reducing the power of subsequent research using the new measure.

Fortunately and displayed this way, the two approaches to classifying state party structure, that is, melding composite portraits versus amassing specific indicators, prove highly related (Table 1.2). Volunteer parties are concentrated at the high end of the aggregate scale. Organized parties are concentrated at the low end, while being nearly absent at the high. Moreover, the correlation between a rank order based on cumulative scores on the new scale and a conceptual dichotomy drawn from a factor common to previous work is strong and in the appropriate direction, while not being so similar as to risk reflecting nothing more than the original impressionistic definitions, rather than a theoretically derived scale.

## THE GREAT TRANSITION

This method of classification provides an instrument for pursuing the impact of party structure on policy responsiveness and democratic representation, the point of all that follows. Before that, however, this aggregate instrument permits one other analysis, involving the fortunes of party structure itself. Ware and Mayhew argued directly that the year 1970 was a pivotal moment in the long war between organized and volunteer parties in American politics, perhaps the key turning point. Each in their different ways went in search of that change. Both believed that they had found it, though neither went on to write a "Volume II" surveying the distribution of party types *after* the purported change. Possessing an instrument calibrated in the generation after 1950 but continuing up to 2010, we are peculiarly able to do just that.

So the first task for this new measure is to confirm (or not) the perception by Ware and Mayhew of a major change in the balance between organized and volunteer political parties. The result might matter a great deal to the character of democratic politics. Or at least, the two models of party structure were entirely capable, in theoretical terms, of shaping partisan behavior. They could shape differences in this behavior in various geographic places. They could shape differences in this behavior in various substantive realms. They could shape both of those differences additionally at various points in time. They could go on to augment (or reduce) partisan alignment – and partisan polarization. In the process, they could strengthen (or weaken) the link between party activists and their rank and file.

If the behavioral difference between two alternative models of party structure accomplished any or all of these things – the central question for all the chapters to follow – then the reality and scope of an alleged "great break" in their comparative balance around 1970 was implicitly magnifying all such impacts.[33] Absent a measure of how much, where, and when this break occurred, however, scholars could not know how much magnification actually resided in the hypothesized shift among state political parties. So a new aggregate measure should be able to close this chapter by checking both the presence and the timing of this purported break, while estimating its size.

To cut again directly to the chase: this new measure tells essentially the same story of what was destined to be – in some but not all analytic hands – the last hurrah of an old order stretching well back into the nineteenth century.[34] In this narrative, a theoretical template for understanding party structure by way of the rise of organized parties, and then by way of the long war between these parties and voluntaristic reformers, was finally smashed around 1970, with the volunteer option broadly triumphant. In response, an organized party model that could be dated at least as far back as the 1880s, and perhaps as far as the 1820s, contracted sharply in the operational world of practical politics. That is a powerful initial finding – and stimulus – for work attempting to follow in these footsteps.

The headline story of partisan change at the time involved sweeping reform of the formal process of presidential nomination, so we shall begin there too. Though behind and beyond this headline event was a larger change in the internal structure of the political parties, within which delegate selection and presidential nomination were a single, serious, but

[33] Indeed, for Ware, the perceived magnitude of this breakdown provided not just the impetus for writing about its contours and causes but also the liberal title for the resulting book, *The Breakdown of Democratic Party Organization, 1940–1980*.

[34] In the Afterword, we return to the issue of whether the long war as a whole received a final resolution or only an impressive interregnum around 1970, the question raised by a new wave of research and writing on party structure.

TABLE 1.3 *The Headline Story of Institutional Reform:*
*A Changing Matrix for Delegate Selection*

| | A The Full Institutional Array | | | | |
| Year | Committee Selections | Traditional Caucuses | Delegate Primaries | Participatory Caucuses | Candidate Primary |
|---|---|---|---|---|---|
| 1976 | 1% | 2% | 10% | 24% | 63% |
| 1972 | 3% | 9% | 17% | 30% | 42% |
| 1968 | 9% | 24% | 21% | 25% | 22% |
| | | | | | |
| 1952 | 6% | 27% | 26% | 22% | 19% |

| | B Organized vs. Volunteer Institutions | |
| Year | Unreformed Institutions | Reformed Institutions |
|---|---|---|
| 1976 | 13% | 87% |
| 1972 | 29% | 71% |
| 1968 | 54% | 46% |
| | | |
| 1952 | 59% | 41% |

limited focus. It was this larger and encompassing change that carried broader implications for policy responsiveness and democratic representation. At the time, however, scholarly attention to what we can now recognize as a general phenomenon was focused more narrowly on an equally sweeping but more concentrated and highly symbolic incarnation in the realm of presidential nomination.[35]

At the core of this was a major institutional shift in the mechanics of delegate selection, one of the largest procedural shifts in all of American history yet one concentrated in a remarkably narrow temporal period, with a principal surge between 1968 and 1972 and a secondary echo between 1972 and 1976. To place this change in context, Table 1.3A records the shifting place of the five major institutions of delegate selection still in use in 1968, along with the delegate shares distributed by each:

---

[35] Shafer, *Quiet Revolution*, tells the story of the critical first round of this sweeping reform in detail.

- *Committee Selections:* In this oldest form of delegate selection to national party conventions, the sitting state committees of each major party convened at a date before the national convention and selected their state delegation to this national body.
- *Traditional Conventions:* More widely used during the nineteenth and well into the twentieth centuries was a system of nested party meetings in which officeholders in local party committees selected delegates to some higher gathering, which in turn selected the state delegation to the national party convention.
- *Delegate Primaries:* A curious product of an earlier round of the war between organized and volunteer party conceptions, these were state primary elections that featured the names of each aspiring delegate but not the names of the presidential candidates they supported.
- *Participatory Caucuses:* Structured like traditional conventions but beginning with an open public meeting at the grass roots available to anyone who turned out, these were the preferred reform device of those state parties that stayed with the convention system of delegate selection to their national convention.
- *Candidate Primaries:* In these public primary elections of the state delegation to the national convention, the names of presidential candidates rather than of delegate aspirants were featured, sometimes to the point where a vote for the presidential candidate was what elected the (unnamed) individual delegates.

In 1952, the first year of what would become the American National Election Study and thus a key cut-point in the chapters to follow, delegate primaries still dominated candidate primaries among primary states; traditional conventions still dominated participatory caucuses among convention states; and there was a non-negligible residuum of committee selections (Table 1.3A).[36] The addition of presidential primaries to this mix, whether of the delegate or candidate variety, had represented an extension of the reform drive in the long war over party structure at the turn of the twentieth century. Yet this particular victory had proved to be

---

[36] Because the initial impetus for this reform surge arose within the Democratic Party, Table 1.3A reports the distribution of Democratic institutions for delegate selection. A Republican version of the same story would feature slightly more prominence for reformed institutions initially, a slightly slower response to an increasingly generalized reform drive, but a parallel result in very short order. Byron E. Shafer, "Institutionalizing the Disappearance," chap. 2 in Shafer, *Bifurcated Politics: Evolution and Reform in the National Party Convention* (Cambridge, MA: Harvard University Press, 1988).

limited and tentative: the same institutional matrix was still essentially present in 1968, sixty years later, the year when the implosion of the Democratic National Convention set off what would become a reform surge with a very different outcome.

In that light, the focus by both Ware and Mayhew on the year 1970 as a rough pivot point seems fully consistent with the derivative realm of presidential nomination. In its specifics and within the first four years after 1968, candidate primaries replaced delegate primaries as the dominant form of primary election for convention delegates; participatory caucuses replaced traditional conventions as the dominant form of convention/caucus procedures; and committee selections headed for extinction.[37] Within one more iteration, four years later, candidate primaries had become the institutional device for selecting a majority of all delegates to national party conventions, a reform impact that was reinforced by the overwhelming dominance of participatory caucuses among states that retained the convention/caucus system. Delegate primaries retained a serious presence thanks only to the resistance by organized parties in the state of New York. Traditional state conventions and state committee selections had become museum pieces.[38]

Condensing the specifics of this institutional change further, into unreformed (organized) and reformed (volunteer) structures as in Table 1.3B, underlines the fact of only the slightest overall shift toward volunteer-type institutions during the long intervening period between 1952 and 1968, though really between, say, 1920 and 1968. By comparison and again, the change just between 1968 and 1976 merits all the attention it received. The institutional mix of 1968 was still an evolutionary descendant of the institutional matrix of the 1880s, when the long war was aggressively

---

[37] A sense of the aspirations of the reformers can be gleaned from Denis G. Sullivan, Jeffrey L. Pressman, & F. Christopher Arterton, *Explorations in Convention Decision Making: The Democratic Party in the 1970s* (San Francisco: W. A. H. Freeman, 1976), William J. Crotty, *Political Reform and the American Experiment* (New York: Thomas Y. Crowell, 1977), and Crotty, *Decision for the Democrats: Reforming the Party Structure* (Baltimore: Johns Hopkins University Press, 1978).

[38] Organized parties are not in the business of issuing structural manifestos, but a general dissenting view from the entire reform thrust can be found in the leading text on presidential selection of the time, Nelson W. Polsby & Aaron B. Wildavsky, *Presidential Elections: Strategies of American Electoral Politics* (New York: Charles Scribner's Sons, 1964). After the fact, Polsby would apply these doubts explicitly in Nelson W. Polsby, *Consequences of Party Reform* (New York: Oxford University Press, 1983), while an actual "counterprogram" was provided in James W. Ceaser, *Reforming the Reforms: A Critical Analysis of the Presidential Selection Process* (Cambridge, MA: Ballinger, 1982).

joined. The counterpart in 1976 bore nearly no resemblance to that far-off era. There was arguably no change of this scope in the mechanics of presidential nomination since the creation of the national party convention itself in the 1830s.

If that was the headline story of party reform around the year 1970, it was only the most widely recognized embodiment of a much larger shift from the organized to the volunteer model. This overall shift was much less widely recognized, even though it was connected to a broader and deeper change in the contours of a larger and longer war over party structure and its representational impacts. In principle, the shift from collected case studies to scaled indicators allows plenty of room to discover that the argument from Wilson, Ware, and Mayhew about this larger breakdown had been overstated, even to the point where the decline of organized parties and the associated shift toward the volunteer model did not really occur. Yet that is not at all what an aggregate translation shows.

Rather, what it suggests – formalizes and confirms – is that just such a transformation did indeed occur on a very substantial scale in the years around the hypothesized pivot point, a transformation perhaps even larger than those earlier observational accounts would suggest. Although if this larger story were deeper and more comprehensive in its practical implications, as indeed it was, its collective effect was also more dispersed, among and within the states. By comparison to reconstitution of the process of presidential nomination, this larger effect was more the result of cumulative but piecemeal reforms, making it harder to see (and catalog) as it occurred – which is one more way of saying that such a development more or less requires some sort of aggregate measure to tease it out of the political welter of its time.

To that end, Table 1.4 confirms the scope of this change around 1970 in two key regards. First, as registered in Table 1.4A, there had been a continuing shift toward the volunteer model during the previous generation. Indeed, as registered by our aggregate index of party structures, this broader thrust had reached into the vast majority of the American states. There were exceptions: seven of the now fifty states actually moved toward organized party structure rather than toward its volunteer opposite. Another eight essentially stayed where they had long been, though for most of these, this was because they could simply go no further in the volunteer direction. Yet the diagnostic point remains that thirty-five of the fifty states – now counting Alaska and Hawaii, which arrived with volunteer parties already in place – had moved in the direction of the volunteer model between 1950 and 1970.

TABLE 1.4 *Breakdown? The Reform Drift by the Early 1970s*

**A Movements toward – and Away from – Volunteer Party Structure, 1952–1972**

|  | Toward Organization | No Change | Toward Voluntarism |
|---|---|---|---|
| States | 7 | 8 | 35* |
| Population | 8% | 14% | 78% |

**B The Aggregate Fortunes of Organized and Volunteer Parties**

|  |  | 1952 | 1972 |
|---|---|---|---|
| States | Organized | 20 | 11 |
|  | Volunteer | 28 | 39* |
| Population | Organized | 53% | 23% |
|  | Volunteer | 47% | 77% |

* Alaska and Hawaii became states in 1959, both with clear-cut volunteer structures for internal party politics.

So the reform drift that finally triumphed around 1970 in impressionistic surveys from Ware and Mayhew remains very much in evidence in aggregate measures drawn from individual indicators. Few states managed to resist that drift categorically, though the result becomes even more striking if it is considered not just in raw tallies of the *direction* of the drift, but rather by way of critical cut points in those totals and the share of the American public that lived on one side or the other of this organized/ volunteer divide. Needless to say, one further virtue of having a scale of structural elements that continues across the entire postwar period is that it allows looking at these *same* cut points between organized and volunteer parties as time passes.

Table 1.4B tells this counterpart story, dichotomizing parties as organized or volunteer through a constant standard and producing some striking further implications. For analytic purposes in the investigation of structural impacts that follows, we have used Table 1.3 to demarcate the two party types. Scores of 4 and down are "organized"; scores of 5 and up are "volunteer." This permits our measure to conform as closely as it can with the Elazar/Mayhew/Shafer factor while insisting on objective indicators to produce the framework for overall analysis and limiting the analytic product to impacts that appear by way of this aggregate – and abstract – measure. It was already clear by the time Mayhew was survey-ing the fifty states with observational evidence that a solid majority of them had internal party structures that were volunteer rather than orga-nized in nature. Aggregated scale scores tell the same story. Yet those states that continued to hew to an older organizational model remained on average the larger states – California was the striking exception – with the result that the American public as a whole in 1950 had hardly lost the experience of doing practical politics through organized parties.

By 1970, however, and likewise very much in accord with the Ware and Mayhew projections, the roster of states with organized parties had been decimated, still by the same standards that would have been used in the previous twenty years. Now, only eleven of the fifty states retained the old structural pattern, where twenty of forty-eight had featured it in the predecessor period. But further – much further – to this distribu-tional point, fewer than one in four Americans still lived in states with organized party structures, where more than one in two previously did. An old organizational model for shaping practical politics appeared to be passing. With it, an old world whose demise had been so long anticipated but whose resilience constantly defied expectations appeared finally to be passing as well.

# Party Structure and Representational Impact

## Public Preferences on Social Welfare and Civil Rights

The more comprehensive but also more dispersed and more gradual triumph of the participatory model that was evident in state party politics along with the more focused triumph of the same thrust in the politics of presidential selection were inevitably intertwined. Established volunteer parties were much easier to reform at the presidential level. Successful reforms for presidential selection often spilled over into general reform efforts within organized parties. But in the end, the old world summarized in the overviews of Elazar and Mayhew, as reflected in the more systematic scale of structural indicators developed here, did indeed undergo the upheaval perceived by Mayhew and Ware around the pivotal year of 1970. Table 1.4 summarizes the distribution of party types that resulted.

But how does any such mix, especially in its diagnostic difference between organized and volunteer parties, affect policy responsiveness and democratic representation? That is, how do party types filter public wishes on their way into government? What is the nature of this filter? In what direction(s) does it operate? How large is it? And if there was a major change in the balance of organized versus volunteer parties around 1970, does the *collective* filtering character of this new balance look different from the old? As an intermediary variable, party structure can be neither the sum and substance of representational relationships nor their main driver. Still, a further contribution from this particular variable seems well worth pursuing, given its intervening and omnipresent character, along with its centrality to contested issues of democratic representation for so very long.

## MEASURING PARTY RESPONSIVENESS

In the abstract, the requirements for a preliminary answer to this linked set of analytic questions about the filtering effect of party structure are straightforward. It is necessary to have a measure of policy wishes within the general public on each of the major substantive conflicts of the period from 1952, when what became the American National Election Study (ANES) first appeared, until the current moment.[1] This measure must be capable of distinguishing party activists from their rank and file, just as it must be capable of distinguishing both populations within each of the two major parties, Democrats versus Republicans. And of course, the measure must make it possible to divide these elite-mass distinctions between residents of states with organized versus volunteer party structures.

A data set that will accommodate these needs comes from William J. M. Claggett and Byron E. Shafer, *The American Public Mind*.[2] Therein, long-running scales of policy preference are developed in what are commonly regarded as the four great realms of policy conflict across the postwar years, namely social welfare, civil rights, foreign affairs, and cultural values. Scores are standardized so that they range from −1.00 at the liberal end to +1.00 at the conservative end of the ideological continuum. Respondents are self-identified as Republican or Democratic according to the canonical seven-point scale,[3] in which "Republicans" are constituted from Strong Republicans, Weak Republicans, and Independent Republicans, and "Democrats" likewise from Strong, Weak, and Independent Democrats.

Inside these two parties, partisan *activists* are those who undertake specialized activities on behalf of a political party or its candidates, while

---

[1] For the creation of the NES, see Warren E. Miller, "An Organizational History of the Intellectual Origins of the National Election Studies," *European Journal of Political Research* 25(1994), 247–265. For crucial preliminaries, Herbert H. Hyman, *Taking Society's Measure: A Personal History of Survey Research* (New York: Russell Sage Foundation, 1991). For the same story in the long run, Jean M. Converse, *Survey Research in The United States: Roots and Emergence, 1890–1960* (Berkeley: University of California Press, 1987).

[2] William J. M. Claggett & Byron E. Shafer, *The American Public Mind: The Issue Structure of Mass Politics in the Postwar United States* (New York: Cambridge University Press, 2010).

[3] Angus Campbell, Philip E. Converse, Warren E. Miller, & Donald E. Stokes, "Perceptions of the Candidates and Parties," chap. 2 in Campbell, Converse, Miller, and Stokes, *The American Voter: An Abridgement* (New York: John Wiley & Sons, 1964). Warren E. Miller and J. Merrill Shanks, "Partisan Identification," Part III, in Miller and Shanks, *The New Americ An Voter* (Cambridge, MA: Harvard University Press, 1996).

the partisan *rank and file* does not undertake the earmarked activities but does still identify with a party and get to the polls in November of presidential years. The ANES has long carried a small battery of items that survey additionally specialized political activities, and in the mid-2000s, William Claggett and Philip Pollock submitted these activities to a comprehensive analysis of relationships among them. They concluded that the diagnostic behaviors for political activism were campaign participation and financial contribution, thus focusing on those two activities and implicitly dismissing a number of other, lesser possibilities.[4] Accordingly, our party activists are those who answered "yes" either to doing work for one of the parties or candidates or to giving money to a political party or individual candidate.[5]

Given a motivating concern with democratic representation and policy responsiveness, our focus is then on the presence and nature of partisan alignments within the four great policy domains. Three generic possibilities stand out. First, no issue needs to have any regularized connection to partisan politics. At the extreme, all four partisan populations – party activists and the rank and file, for both the Democratic and Republican parties – can be randomly attached to their parties in a given policy domain, and we shall see two such nonalignments (on foreign affairs and cultural values) for the early postwar years in Chapter 3. Second, if policy preferences *do* align with party attachments, this alignment has no automatic nature. We have come to expect a modern ideological array, running from Democratic activists on the left, to the Democratic rank and file, to the Republican rank and file, to Republican activists on the right, but there is no inherent need for this outcome, and we shall see some noteworthy alternatives, again especially in earlier periods. And third, levels of political activity can mottle the patterns of alignment that do appear. Activists may move into what will ultimately become a general alignment at an earlier time than their rank and files. Rank and files can actually flank their activists, to the left or the right. One or another of the

---

[4] William J. M. Claggett & Philip H. Pollock III, "The Modes of Participation Revisited, 1980–2004," *Political Research Quarterly* 59(2006), 593–600.
[5] The precise identity of "the activists" has long been a vexed aspect of political research. Some scholars are content with *any* activity beyond voting; others desire standards that can isolate some top, tiny percentage. Our adaptation of the Claggett and Pollock standard makes activists roughly the most active 10 percent of the voting population, relegating the other 90 percent to their rank and file. This allows a consistent comparison between the more participatory minority and its more passive (vast) majority counterpart, across both time and space. Anything narrower would quickly relegate the activists to statistical irrelevance, especially when we attend to regional distinctions among them, as we must.

four partisan populations can dissent from the general pattern. And of course, all three of these generic possibilities can differ by geographic region.

Among policy domains, social welfare and civil rights are particularly helpful in framing such an analysis, so they will be the focus of this chapter. As it develops, social welfare actually offered a fully developed partisan alignment by the time the National Election Study began its regular surveys. The early surfacing of such an alignment is testimony to the centrality of economic and welfare issues in the American politics of the time. The fact that we have continuing measures of this alignment makes them a kind of analytic bedrock for everything that follows. In contrast, civil rights showed only an incipient version of the same alignment in the immediate postwar years. Prospectively, this provided the opportunity to watch a second major policy domain emerge over time through the lens of party structure. In the perspective of its own time, however, there was no way of knowing where this domain was headed – if the result would be a lasting partisan alignment or how party structure would shape its evolution.

To pursue the impact of party structure within these (and other) policy domains, it is necessary to pool data across time, so that samples can be large enough for policy preferences to be examined simultaneously by party attachment, level of political activity, geographic region, and last but not least party structure. Fortunately, a simple generational cut is sufficient for these purposes. The National Election Study began in 1952, so the 1950 census can be our opening divide. The great shift in the balance of party structures came a generation later, around the structural pivot point of 1970, so the 1970 census can be our second divide. This means that our "old world" of American politics runs from 1950 through 1968, and the succeeding "reform era" goes from 1970 to 1988. By extension, the "modern world" begins with the 1990 census and runs from 1990 to 2008. This yields an aggregate survey N of about 5,000 per period, adequate for all but a few analyses in the earliest of these postwar periods.

## SOCIAL WELFARE

While all four grand policy domains become accessible through these measures, the almost-inescapable starting point for an examination of the link between party structure and the transmission of policy preferences is social welfare. Social welfare has long been thought of as the bedrock domain for policy preferences in the party system of the contemporary United States, a system commonly understood to begin with the Great Depression and the New Deal.[6] Indeed, issues of social welfare were the initial impetus for what came to be recognized as this "New Deal party system." Public preferences on social welfare are then available – and consequential – for all the years since. Partisan divisions on social welfare can still be argued to constitute the policy spine for that system a full eighty years later.[7]

So policy wishes for the critical opening investigation of party structure and policy responsiveness are taken from public preferences on social welfare. While items contributing to the social welfare index vary with the array of relevant questions that are asked in a changing ANES, they were selected to fall within a single explicit definition of this policy realm:

*Social Welfare* involves efforts to protect citizens against the randomness – that is, the harshness and individual inequities – of the economic marketplace. While there are myriad ways to accomplish this, direct personal benefits are the crucial touchstone, while *social insurance* provides the irreducible programmatic core.[8]

Within this array, certain "marker" items, widely accepted as belonging to the welfare domain, do recur, providing reasonable assurance that a slowly changing measure captures the same basic policy concerns over time. Among these markers for social welfare are the following:

Some people feel the government in Washington should see to it that every person has a job and a good standard of living. Others think the government should just let each person get ahead on his own.

---

[6] For social welfare within politics in the large, Michael Barone, *Our Country: The Shaping of America from Roosevelt to Reagan* (New York: Free Press, 1990), chaps. 6–14; for social welfare and the party system, Everett Carll Ladd Jr. with Charles D. Hadley, *Transformations of The American Party System* (New York: W. W. Norton, 1975), chaps. 1 and 2; and for social welfare and partisan attachments, Angus Campbell, Philip E. Converse, Warren E. Miller, and Donald E. Stokes, *The American Voter*, abr. ed. (New York: John Wiley, 1964), chaps. 2 and 7.

[7] For the evolution of social welfare as a policy domain, see James L. Sundquist, *POLITICS AND POLICY: The Eisenhower, Kennedy, and Johnson Years* (Washington, DC: Brookings, 1968); Robert X. Browning, *Politics And Social Welfare Policy In The United States* (Knoxville: University of Tennessee Press, 1986); Edward D. Berkowitz, *America's Welfare State: From Roosevelt to Reagan* (Baltimore: Johns Hopkins University Press, 1991); and James T. Patterson, *America's Struggle Against Poverty, 1900–1994* (Cambridge, MA: Harvard University Press, 1994).

[8] Claggett & Shafer, *The American Public Mind*, 5.

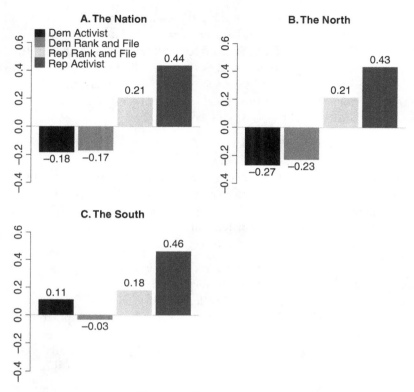

FIGURE 2.1 Partisan Populations and Issue Alignments: Social Welfare in the Old World, 1950–1968

Some feel there should be a government insurance plan which would cover all medical and hospital expenses for everyone. Others feel that medical expenses should be paid by individuals, and through private insurance like Blue Cross or other company paid plans.[9]

## The Old World: Partisan Alignments

Figure 2.1 begins the process of teasing out representational impacts from party structure by introducing the overall contours for partisan preferences on social welfare in our first postwar period, 1950 through 1968.

[9] Ibid., 21, which also catalogs lesser wording changes in the second marker item across time.

To that end, the figure offers graphic representations of the ideological location of our four key categories: Democratic activists, Democratic rank and file, Republican rank and file, and Republican activists. The resulting aggregate scores for the policy wishes of these four partisan populations in effect become part of the strategic landscape of American politics at particular points in time. Within them in the analysis that follows, critical further distinctions will most often involve

- the ideological distance between the preferences of active partisans, Democrats versus Republicans;
- the ideological distance between these activists and their own rank and files, hence Democrats versus Democrats and Republicans versus Republicans;
- both, of course, distinguished further by any differences between organized and volunteer political parties.

Within that framework, Figure 2.1A begins by offering a picture of the nation as a whole, one conforming very closely to the canonical version created by Herbert McClosky and colleagues in the 1950s.[10] While based on differing samples and differing items, both the McClosky portrait and this one make two basic points about partisan alignments in the early postwar years for the nation as a whole. First, there was already a clear ideological distance between rank and file Democrats and rank and file Republicans on social welfare, with Democrats to the left and Republicans to the right. Second, party activists held more clearly demarcated positions on these same concerns, though Democratic activists were just a hair off to the left of their rank and file while Republican activists were sharply off to the right of theirs. Both these activist preferences and those of their rank and file would change – evolve – over time.

To pursue the difference between organized and volunteer parties as intermediaries within this overall picture, it is essential to go on and stratify Figure 2.1 by party structure. But first, surely for this period but actually for both of its successors, it is necessary to stratify by political region as well, since the American South of the time had what was effectively a party system all its own.[11] Accordingly, even this opening

---

[10] Herbert McClosky, Paul Hoffman, & Rosemary O'Hara, "Issue Conflict and Consensus among Party Leaders and Followers," *American Political Science Review* 54(1960), 406–472.

[11] The story is a familiar one. See, for example, Nicol C. Rae, *Southern Democrats* (New York: Oxford University Press, 1994), and Stanley P. Berard, *Southern*

portrait of partisan relationships must look at North versus South before inquiring into our key structural divide, that is, organized versus volunteer. If this regional stratification had proved to be empirically unnecessary, it could have been dropped from the analysis. But as Figures 2.1B and 2.1C attest, further stratification was inescapable in this opening period, since the South was doing something very different from the rest of the nation when registered through the ideological alignment of partisan populations.

The result in fact makes the two political parties almost different *kinds* of ideological coalitions. If the focus were only on the Republican Party, this might not have been true: the three figures together – Figures 2.1A, 2.1B, and 2.1C – largely obviate the need for regional stratification. Which is to say: rank and file as well as activist Republicans were more or less ideologically interchangeable by region, at least when the focus was welfare preferences. The same situation would continue into the reform era, our second postwar period, finally changing a bit – Republican activists would actually evolve toward less regional homogeneity – when the modern era was reached.

Regardless, the same three early figures highlight a major regional divide inside the Democratic Party, and this distinction cannot be wished away. Within it, rank-and-file Democrats in the North appear as additionally left of the national mean (Figure 2.1B). As a result, mass Democrats and mass Republicans in the North were further apart than they appeared to be in the nation as a whole, courtesy of this Democratic repositioning. By extension, while Northern activist Republicans were no farther off to the right, Northern activist Democrats were now *half-again* as far away from the national average as they were in a picture of the composite nation, standing additionally left of their own rank and file while expanding the distance between active members of the two parties.

This suggests in passing that the original McClosky findings might have benefited from a further North/South division when creating a national portrait, given the clearly dissident alignment characterizing the American South at Figure 2.1C. Southern Republicans, whether activist or rank and file, were effectively a residual population (what is left of a once bigger one with little political impact) at this point in time, so that distinctions among Southern Democrats were the entire practical story. Yet those distinctions were empirically immense. Rank and file Democrats in the South, unlike

*Democrats in the U.S. House of Representatives* (Norman: University of Oklahoma Press, 2001).

their Northern counterpart, were only ever so slightly left of center on matters of social welfare. Among partisan categories, they were the truly centrist population for the nation as a whole. More strikingly, activist Southern Democrats were considerably to the *right* of their own rank and file. Indeed, they were considerably closer to rank and file Republicans than to rank and file Democrats, in the South and in the nation as a whole.

## The Old World: Party Structures

This graphic overview allows the analysis to move on to its central concern, the difference between organized and volunteer political parties. In the abstract, hypotheses could be generated in either direction for the impact of party structure on the representation of public preferences for the domain of welfare policy. Volunteer parties, being theoretically more responsive to their constituencies by way of greater input from a more fluid mix of issue activists, could have moved into alignment with the revised welfare preferences of the New Deal earlier than organized parties, with their stable personnel and resistant structures. This would imply that volunteer activists ought to be farther to the left of the national average among Democrats and farther to the right of that average among Republicans. Alternatively, organized parties, with the long and local service of party officeholders making them more focused on winning elections and delivering policy rewards, could have felt compelled to adopt the dominant ideology of the New Deal earlier than volunteer parties, composed of individuals with personalized careers and idiosyncratic issue bases. This would imply that organized activists should be farther to the left of the national average among Democrats but less far to the right of that average among Republicans.

Mayhew actually offers an empirically rooted hypothesis that goes directly to the choice between these two theoretical alternatives. Based on his structural survey of state parties in the immediate postwar years, he opts clearly for the second hypothesis. What he pictures is a grand deal between President Franklin Roosevelt and organized Democratic parties in the states, with welfare policy front and center.[12] By extension, it should be Democratic activists from organized parties who were more in

[12] Mayhew, *Placing Parties in American Politics*, 318, 321.

TABLE 2.1  *Party Structures and Issue Alignments:*
*Social Welfare, 1950–1968*

|                          | A. North | | B. South | |
| --- | --- | --- | --- | --- |
|                          | Org. | Vol. | Org. | Vol. |
| Democratic Activists     | −.31 | −.19 | +.06 | +.27 |
| Democratic Rank & File   | −.27 | −.20 | −.06 | +.03 |
| Republican Rank & File   | +.16 | +.27 | +.18 | * |
| Republican Activists     | +.37 | +.49 | * | * |

*Ns too small for reliable analysis.

line with the welfare program of the national Democratic Party, while Republican activists, albeit clearly to the right of their own rank and file, should be more moderate – closer to the national average – in organized parties, through the Republican version of the institutionalized ability to respond to a revised strategic environment

Explicit comparison of the role of party structures in filtering policy preferences is facilitated by converting Figure 2.1 and some successors to a more simplified and condensed form, using numerical scores in tabular form for the four key partisan populations. Table 2.1 does this. Hence, what appears as a bar of −.27 for Northern Democratic activists in Figure 2.1B is now divided into two numerical scores (of −.31 and −.19) in Table 2.1A. As earlier, scores remain standardized, ranging from a maximum of −1.00 at the liberal end to a maximum of +1.00 at the conservative end. It would be simple to add a column that stratified the nation as a whole by party structure in Table 2.1. Yet we have already seen that this would elide huge regional differences during the immediate postwar years, where such a "national average" would reflect no underlying regional reality.

That fact alone argues not just for attending to geographic regions within the nation but also for presenting the impacts of party structure by region, which Table 2.1 actually does. So will the fact that different regions come into alignment with a common pattern at different points in time: we shall see this happen inside social welfare during the reform era that follows this opening period. A final argument for regional presentation comes from the fact that party structures can in principle work differently within regions that have superficially similar aggregate profiles. This will prove to be the structural story of the modern world. Once again, in those rare residual cases where presentation of the evidence by region is not empirically necessary, the fact of parallel regional impacts will be readily apparent.

With that as prologue, Table 2.1 offers a Northern structural story (Table 2.1A), a Southern structural story (Table 2.1B), and some powerful similarities between these stories, similarities masked by ideological differences in two great political regions and genuinely invisible if the analysis were concentrated on a national picture. Two central points can be teased out of these structural portraits, though the first is straightforwardly evident, while the second becomes clear only in light of the first.

First and most dramatically, it was organized parties in the North that directly reflected what would come to be recognized as the generic national alignment on social welfare. Volunteer parties in the same region were still out of alignment, especially within the Democratic Party, which was the driving vehicle for welfare initiatives. This result is consistent with hypothesis #2, in which active Democrats in organized parties should be more extreme (and thus more liberal) than counterparts in volunteer parties, while active Republicans in organized parties should be more moderate (and thus less conservative) than counterparts in volunteer states, who remained more steadfast in their opposition.

Yet second and more subtly, once this difference in the impact of party types has been isolated, it proves possible to find *the same* relationships in the South and not just the North. Southern parallels are limited to the Democratic side of the aisle, given the exigent state of the Southern Republican Party. But once the analyst takes account of the sharply different ideological points at which two regional alignments are anchored, it is possible to see organized and volunteer parties doing essentially the same thing, Southern as well as Northern – though it does require exposition of the Northern story first to see this Southern echo. A verbal walk through the two regional pictures, as captured in Table 2.1, should make both points clear.

An evident structural difference stands out in our opening analysis of the North (Table 2.1A). Here, organized parties show a fully realized and substantially polarized version of what would come to be recognized as the generic alignment on social welfare across all the postwar years. Yet this stands out as distinctive because volunteer parties in effect dissented from this alignment. Stratified this way, it becomes clear that it was Northern *organized* parties that were underpinning the alignment characterizing the nation as a whole, an alignment that would come to characterize both geographic regions and both party types during the successor period. In the old world of American politics, however, volunteer parties did not yet display this generic alignment, even in the North. Instead, among Northern volunteer parties, the Democratic rank and file contributed the ideological left, and partisan alignment ran from them at one extreme to Republican activists at the other.

Moreover, within organized parties in the North, Democratic and Republican activists had actually come into a kind of ideological symmetry, with Democrats clearly to the left at −.31 and Republicans clearly to the right at +.37. This previously hidden symmetry was principally a contribution of the revised leftward placement now evident among Democratic activists in organized parties, though the comparative moderation of Republican activists also contributed. For the nation as a whole, Democratic activists stood at −.18 on social welfare. Northern Democratic activists in volunteer parties stood essentially at the same moderately liberal position, at −.19. Yet Northern Democratic activists in organized parties had moved solidly left of that − being more than half-again as liberal at −.31.

A counterpart focus on the South must perforce be a focus on structural impacts inside the Democratic Party, for what was still essentially a one-party region (Table 2.1B). Within the Southern Democratic Party, however, there was much to see, including most especially the same contribution from the difference between organized and volunteer parties. In the South, both party types did feature Democratic activists comfortably to the right of their rank and file and actually to the right of the national average. But now, stratified by party structure, Democratic activists within organized parties could be seen to be considerably closer to their rank and file than were Democratic activists within volunteer parties. Moreover, while this hardly made organized-party activists into ideological liberals (at +.06), it did sharply distinguish them from volunteer-party activists (at +.27), who were strikingly conservative, farther to the right than the national *Republican* rank and file (at +.21 in Figure 2.1A).[13]

Implicit in this regional comparison, now as stratified by party structure, was one other background fact. To wit: a national picture at this point in time did not come close to applying nationwide. This was true of

[13] Key, *Southern Politics in State and Nation,* showed the Southern Republican parties as skeletal in most places, and the Ns for Southern Republican activists are derisory in the Claggett and Shafer data during these years. When they are further subdivided into organized versus volunteer, the numbers simply become too small for any ideological ratings to be stable and robust, so small that measures based upon them should rightfully be ignored, as Table 2.1B indeed does.

overall partisan alignments by region, North versus South, which were different in kind (Figures 2.1B and 2.1C). Everyone knew that. But it was also true of overall alignments by party type, with their tendency for organized parties to pull toward an emerging policy consensus, while volunteer parties appeared immune to that pull in the North and pulled actively against it in the South (Tables 2.1A and 2.1B). In that sense and seen in context, the representational difference between organized and volunteer parties operated in the *same* fashion, North and South.

Said the other way around, what is underlined is just how much the partisan alignment on social welfare for the nation as a whole depended centrally on the surviving organized parties. These were the parties that were in sync with the new national alignment, even if that was evident in the North and obscured by ideological placement in the South. Left to their own devices, volunteer parties had not yet arrived at this resolution, even among Democrats, while among Republicans, volunteer parties continued to offer an aggressive ideological resistance to an emerging policy world.

### The Reform Era: Partisan Alignments

That was an older world of party structure, the one addressed by Ware and Mayhew in their accounts of the staying power of organized parties but one destined to shift precipitously around 1970. Much else was shifting in the issue alignment of American politics at that point, so larger changes were hardly driven by shifting party structures alone.[14] Yet a shifting balance between organized and volunteer parties did represent the long-delayed triumph of a reform model first articulated in the late nineteenth century, the great era of organized parties in American politics. So it would have been surprising if structural change of this magnitude, on the part of what were after all the main political intermediaries of their time, did not make contributions of its own to the changing nature of American politics. As indeed it did.

Once again, it is necessary to begin with the overall contours to partisan preference in this successor period, before looking for differences between

---

[14] Particularly rich reminders of the larger context could include: Iwan W. Morgan, *Beyond The Liberal Consensus: A Political History of the United States since 1965* (London: Hurst, 1994); Edward D. Berkowitz, *Something Happened: A Political and Cultural Overview of the Seventies* (New York: Columbia University Press, 2006); and John Ehrman, *The Eighties: America in the Age of Reagan* (New Haven: Yale University Press, 2005).

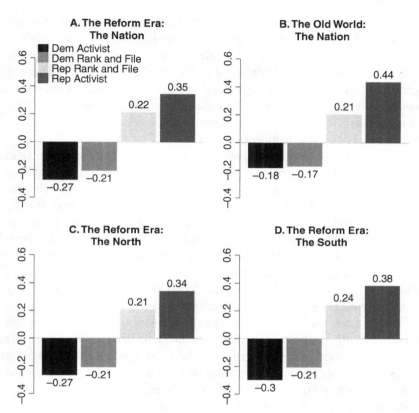

FIGURE 2.2 Partisan Populations and Issue Alignments: Social Welfare in the Reform Era, 1970–1988

organized and volunteer parties within those contours. For the nation as a whole, the situation in this new world is easily summarized. From 1970 to 1988 as opposed to 1950 to 1968, the national picture had acquired an increasingly symmetric alignment (Figures 2.2A and 2.2B). The two rank and file populations moved only slightly farther apart but became essentially equidistant from the national mean. Their activist counterparts diverged even less while likewise becoming more symmetrically aligned. Though of course for this activist symmetry to surface, Democratic activists had to move farther to the left of the national average, while Republican activists had to pull back toward it, as both did.

What was additionally different in this reform era – an effect truly striking in its scale – was that contemporary adjustments to a previous national picture resulted largely from the *demise* of an old (and variously hallowed or maligned) regional distinction, North versus South, the one still so central to the preceding period. The two great regional subdivisions not only came into parallel partisan alignment on issues of social welfare, a big enough change in its own right (Figures 2.2C and 2.2D). The two great regions actually came into nearly identical alignment, a change of remarkable scale. Absent a look at the differences contributed by organized versus volunteer parties, it might have seemed that all of American politics had become one uniform piece.

Even then, however, for the two regions to come into a common (and hence national) alignment, they obviously had to do very different things. For its part, the North looked almost identical in both old and new eras (Figures 2.2C and 2.1B). Its Republican activists moderated slightly between periods, such that the national movement back toward the center among Republican activists was largely fueled by activist Republicans from the North. Otherwise, the three remaining partisan categories stayed essentially as they had been in the preceding period, a stability only underlined by the fact that partisan and ideological change in the American South was convulsive on the ground and far-reaching in its implications.

For its part, the South was politically transformed, coming into full alignment with a national picture from which it had dissented aggressively in the immediate past. This required the same moderating move back toward the middle on the part of Southern Republican activists, and that move was accomplished (Figures 2.2D and 2.1C). The Republican rank and file did move opposite to its own activists, becoming more conservative, but this too was a moderate change. So the real differences – what explained the overall Southern convergence – were inside the Southern Democratic Party.

There, the rank and file moved clearly leftward, to the point of converging on the same ideological terrain as its Northern counterpart (again Figures 2.2D and 2.1C). This was an aggregate shift of impressive scope (from −.03 to −.21), though as we shall see, even among the rank and file, this shift was comprised of two very different pieces. Simultaneously, Southern Democratic activists moved even more sharply leftward (from +.11 to −.30), traveling all the way across the middle of American society until they came to rest not just to the left of the national average but slightly to the left of their Northern colleagues. Put together – activists plus their rank and file – this was a convulsive transformation of the Southern Democracy.

At the time, scholars disputed the impact on this overall picture of the general move toward volunteer parties driven by issue activists, a debate fuelled initially (but also partially obfuscated) by a more explicit conflict over proper institutions for delegate selection and presidential nomination. By hindsight, however, many of these scholars moved ultimately into a conditional consensus about the propensity – and power – of newly consequential activists to drive toward the ideological extremes. It was just that some analysts applauded this result, while others judged it to be harmful to democratic representation.[15] Either way, as scholars came generally to refocus on the ideological polarization that increasingly characterized American national politics, an underlying activist dynamic was more and more explicitly recognized and elevated in its importance. We too shall pay particular attention to the evolving preferences of these party activists in all the analysis that follows.[16]

## A New South?

Before any effort to tease out the impact of organized versus volunteer parties in this reformed world, with its greater ideological symmetry and its shrinking regional differences, it is necessary to add a fresh control to the analytic mix. For in fact, there is every reason to expect that a major aspect of Southern change was not shifting party structures, nor even shifting policy preferences, but rather a shifting *social composition* to the participants in Southern politics. In fact, it will be easy to demonstrate that the largest single force bringing the region into national alignment during this new period was the enfranchisement of black Southerners, producing a one-way flow – really a one-way flood – of new Southern Democrats. So this enfranchisement must be added to the mix before analysis can proceed.[17]

---

[15] See Morris P. Fiorina & Samuel J. Abrams, *Disconnect: The Breakdown of Representation in American Politics* (Norman: University of Oklahoma Press, 2009) versus Alan Abramowitz, *The Disappearing Center: Engaged Citizens, Polarization, and American Democracy* (New Haven: Yale University Press, 2010).

[16] Geoffrey C. Layman, Thomas M. Carsey, John C. Green, Richard Herrara, & Rosalyn Cooperman, "Activists and Conflict Extension in American Party Politics," *American Political Science Review* 104(2010), 324–346. Consequential precedents for this argument include Thomas M. Carsey & Geoffrey Layman, "Changing Sides or Changing Minds? Party Identification and Policy Preferences in the American Electorate," *American Journal of Political Science* 50(2006), 464–477, and Delia Baldassarri & Andrew Gelman, "Partisans without Constraint: Political Polarization and Trends in American Public Opinion," *American Journal of Sociology* 114(2008), 408–446.

[17] For the old world, Everett Carll Ladd Jr., *Negropolitical Leadership in The South* (New York: Atheneum, 1969); for two case studies in enfranchisement, William R. Keech, *The Impact Of Negro Voting: The Role of the Vote in the Quest for Equality*

By far the most dramatic change in partisan alignments between time periods for either major geographic region in the entire postwar era arrived between our first and second periods in the American South. On the one hand, this change does not appear to have been driven by the great shift in the balance of party structures nationwide, since there is no counterpart change to partisan alignments outside the South, where the bulk of that structural shift actually occurred. On the other hand, the two party types remained fully capable of working differently within this larger change, giving it further shape. This is, after all, their crucial intermediary role, even when they do not drive the initial change itself.

So the immediate question is *what else* would have been changing the nature of Southern politics between these two periods, and the leading answer is inescapable. This was the period of black enfranchisement in the American South, and the social composition of the Southern electorate changed greatly as a result. In substantive terms, this change is tied most directly to civil rights as a policy domain. We shall turn to that domain, and return to this change, in the back half of the chapter. But the shift of Southern preference alignments was large with regard to social welfare too, so attention to the changing social composition of key partisan populations cannot be deferred.

To that end, Table 2.2 begins the search for the impact of a changing social composition by comparing three pictures of partisan alignment in the old versus the new South.[18] Table 2.2A1 shows partisan preferences on social welfare in the old world, here limited to non-blacks only, though this was very close to the total (enfranchised) South in that period. Table 2.2A2 then shows partisan preferences on social welfare in the successor period, the reform era, still for non-blacks only. And Table 2.2A3 puts the whole South, both black and non-black, back into the picture. Three things stand out.

First, the two parties differed greatly in the ideological impact of black enfranchisement. Ideologically, the Democratic Party was a fundamentally different institution with and without its new black identifiers (Tables 2.2A2 and 2.2A3). By contrast, the Republican Party was

(Chicago: Rand McNally, 1968); for a comprehensive overview after enfranchisement, Katherine Tate, *From Protest To Politics: The New Black Voters in American Elections* (New York: Russell Sage Foundation, 1993).

[18] The roots of this changing social composition are themselves a contested topic, with a voluminous literature. For our purposes, the resulting change in partisan alignments for the black South, the non-black South, and the South as a composite region is what is essential to set out here.

TABLE 2.2 *Sources of Change in the South:*
*Social Welfare Impacts and a Changing Social Composition*

| A. Ideological Impacts of a Changing Social Composition | | |
|---|---|---|
| | 1. Non-Blacks Only | 2. Non-Blacks Only | 3. All South |
| | 1950–1968 | 1970–1988 | 1970–1988 |
| Democratic Activists | +.14 | –.06 | –.30 |
| Democratic Rank & File | +.02 | +.01 | –.21 |
| Republican Rank & File | +.24 | +.27 | +.24 |
| Republican Activists | +.59 | +.39 | +.38 |

| B. Aggregate Shares of a Changing Social Composition | | |
|---|---|---|
| | 1. Non-Blacks Only | 2. Non-Blacks Only | 3. All South |
| | 1950–1968 | 1970–1988 | 1970–1988 |
| Democratic Activists | 9% | 8% | 9% |
| Democratic Rank & File | 67% | 49% | 55% |
| Republican Rank & File | 18% | 35% | 29% |
| Republican Activists | 6% | 9% | 7% |

essentially unchanged in ideological terms, though as we shall see later, its social composition was changing too.

In these terms, there was little further to see within the Republican Party, much more to see among the Democrats, where the two levels of political activity developed very differently. Among Southern Democratic activists, both ideological and social changes were at work in roughly equal measure. Non-black Democratic activists as a social aggregate did move all the way across the ideological center of American society, from clearly conservative (+.14) to modestly liberal (–.06). Yet the total activist population owed its ultimate landing place (at –.30 rather than –.06) to the inflow and addition of black Democratic activists.

The Democratic rank and file as a social aggregate also changed between periods, likewise moving leftward. But this time, the entirety of that change was contributed by the new black rank and file (Tables 2.2A2 and 2.2A3). By contrast, the non-black rank and file simply did not move (Tables 2.2A1 and 2.2A2). Sitting effectively on the national average in the old world (at +.02), they continued to sit almost exactly on the national average in the reform era (at +.01).

Summarized in policy terms, this changing social composition of the two Southern parties had major representational impacts within the Democratic Party, nearly none within its Republican counterpart. Table 2.2B is an immediate reminder, however, of what this did *not* imply. Most definitely, it did not imply that stable policy preferences were accompanied by a stable social composition for the Republican Party. Even in the face of a huge new increment of Democratic identifiers, the Republican Party was growing as a share of the whole South, while the Democratic Party was already in modest decline (Tables 2.2B1 and 2.2B3).[19]

Seen the other way around, with a focus on the non-black South only, the share of Southern identifiers in the Republican rank and file effectively doubled between the old world and the reform period (Tables 2.2B2 and 2.2B3). It was just that this had no further impact on the policy preferences of the two Republican populations, old or new. Said one way, those non-blacks who were newly Republican obviously shared the welfare preferences of previous Republican identifiers. Said the other way, partisan growth in the Southern Republican Party was constituted from those who shared the social welfare orientation of the national Republican Party.

### The Reform Era: Party Structures

With those further adjustments in place, it becomes possible to return to the story of organized versus volunteer parties within a changing picture of overall partisan alignment. Here, however, despite the developing regional convergence, the role of party structures in filtering policy preferences continued to feature a clear regional disjunction. In the North, the story of changing influences from party structure was one of decline to the point of disappearance, a disappearance of the distinction between organized and volunteer parties that had characterized the old world. But in the South, the story was the opposite: the appearance, perhaps for the first time ever, of a version of the distinction between party types that had characterized the North in the previous period.

In the North, where the two party types had differed fundamentally in the composite alignments associated with them (Table 2.1A), a common

[19] For an earlier tour of the changing partisan situation in the South, see Louis M. Seagull, *Southern Republicanism* (Cambridge, MA: Schenkman, 1975); for a later tour, Earl Black & Merle Black, *The Rise of Southern Republicanism* (Cambridge, MA: Harvard University Press, 2002).

TABLE 2.3 *Party Structures and Issue Alignments: Social Welfare, 1970–1998*

| | A. North | | B. South | |
| --- | --- | --- | --- | --- |
| | Org. | Vol. | Org. | Vol. |
| Democratic Activists | −.27 | −.27 | −.30 | −.24 |
| Democratic Rank & File | −.17 | −.21 | −.23 | −.18 |
| Republican Rank & File | +.32 | +.20 | +.26 | +.21 |
| Republican Activists | +.44 | +.33 | +.35 | +.43 |

alignment now characterized both organized and volunteer parties (Table 2.3A). To create this common alignment, Northern volunteer parties, which had previously lagged their organized counterparts in accepting the overall national alignment, had moved into conformity with it. Moreover, volunteer parties had managed this in a world where organized Democratic parties were moving left and organized Republican parties were moving right. If this shift among volunteer parties was temporally lagged, then, arriving a generation later than the counterpart alignment among organized parties, it had to be (and was) a much bigger shift to eradicate the old structural gap.

Table 2.3A confirms that it was. The key point here is that in the old world, Democratic activists in organized parties were already left of the Democratic rank and file, while Democratic activists in volunteer parties were actually if modestly to its right (Table 2.1A). In the reform era, Democratic activists were to the left of their rank and file in both party types, and an old ideological disjunction had disappeared. Yet at the same time, temporal change was producing a very different structural story in the other great geographic region of American politics.

In this, the South now featured the same overall partisan alignment as the North for the policy domain of social welfare. That basic alignment was no longer different, and this was a momentous change (Figures 2.2C and 2.2D). For the South now featured organized parties whose Democratic activists were further left of the national average than their volunteer counterparts, but whose Republican activists were more moderate than their volunteer opposite numbers (Table 2.3B). But beneath this radically new alignment for the South, the two party types were pulling in directions closer to the old, and not the new, Northern pattern. In effect, the reform era had eliminated an old structural difference in the North, but realized it – embodied it – in the South.

Inside the North, then, the old difference between organized and volunteer parties in their filtering effect on policy preferences had disappeared, courtesy of the acceptance by volunteer parties of the national alignment that previously characterized only organized parties. Yet inside the South, a new Southern incarnation of the old Northern difference was now going hand in glove with an overall regional convergence. The South was joining the nation in its partisan alignment on welfare preferences, but not by adopting the pattern of alignment characterizing organized versus volunteer parties in the North during the reform era. Instead, it was joining the nation as a whole by adopting the pattern that had characterized the North when it first accepted the national alignment in the previous period.

When the South came into alignment with national patterns, the region itself was transformed by definition. Moreover, when the South as a region came into national alignment, the politics of social welfare were simultaneously, finally, and fully nationalized. Yet in the process of joining the nation and coming to rest on a parallel partisan alignment, the South actually resurrected the structural distinction that had previously characterized welfare alignments in the North. Accordingly, in this transformed South, organized parties were more liberal on social welfare within the active Democratic Party and more moderate within the active Republican Party. Conversely, volunteer parties were more moderate among Democratic activists than in their organized counterparts and more conservative among Republican activists – the very pattern that had characterized the North in the old world, but which it abandoned in the reform era.

So state parties still evidently needed to be broken out both by structure and by region to understand the change in partisan alignments. Though even when this was done, there remained a further structural effect on policy filtering and partisan alignment for the reform era, an effect that was always at risk of being overlooked – by being implicitly masked. For the ideological positioning of the four major partisan populations in the old and the new eras was itself being applied to a changing *balance* of organized versus volunteer parties, a balance moving in favor of the latter and against the former. Within the active Democratic Parties in both regions, where the comparison can reasonably be made, the larger ideological moves between eras were among Democratic activists in volunteer states, and this shift was even larger as a share of the national aggregate than changing raw scores would suggest, precisely because there were now considerably more volunteer parties than there had been in the preceding era.

## The Modern World: Preferences and Structures

In any case, a successor to the reform era was inevitable too. This is the world in which we all currently live, the modern world, captured here through the years from 1990 to 2008.[20] Once again, analysis must begin with the overall contours of partisan politics, as a critical preliminary to looking for the role of organized versus volunteer parties within those contours. On the one hand, these background contours remained nationalized, continuing to rub out the old regional background differences. On the other hand, that fact hardly implied that converging contours had eliminated the prospects for policy impact from party structure, much less that the contours themselves were simple extrapolations from any earlier period.

Figure 2.3 begins the analytic process. In the modern portrait of partisan alignment for the nation as a whole, ideological polarization had become the dominant theme. Even the two rank and files were noticeably more polarized than in the reform era, though almost all of this increase was due to a substantial shift among Republican identifiers (Figures 2.3A and 2.3B). As usual, there was an even larger increase in ideological polarization among activists, though this too received the lion's share of its impetus from the Republicans. It was not that Democratic activists did not shift additionally leftward; it was just that Republican activists shifted much further in the opposite direction.

Two further changes were then embedded within these first two. As between the two major parties, the ideological symmetry that had been on the rise between the old world and the reform era fell back toward an older pattern, whereby both Republican populations were further from the national average than their Democratic counterparts. (Compare Figures 2.1A, 2.2A, and 2.3A.) Inside the two major parties, both sets of activists moved away from their respective rank and files, though this disjunction too became even more noticeable among Republicans than among Democrats this time.

The biggest change within the two great regions that once belied this national picture had actually occurred in the previous period, at the point

[20] A rich overview running into this period is James T. Patterson, *Restless Giant: The United States from Watergate to Bush v. Gore* (New York: Oxford University Press, 2005). One stylized effort to encompass the whole period is Byron E. Shafer, "A Political Structure for the Modern World: The Era of Partisan Volatility, 1992–2016," chap. 4 in Shafer, *The American Political Pattern: Stability and Change, 1932–2016* (Lawrence: University Press of Kansas, 2016).

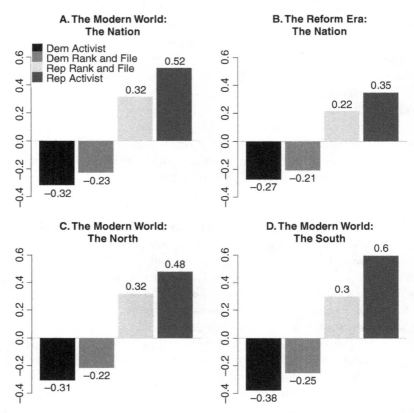

FIGURE 2.3 Partisan Populations and Issue Alignments: Social Welfare in the Modern World, 1990–2008

when the South joined the national pattern – joined it so thoroughly, in fact, that both its rank and file and its party activists were slightly more polarized in the South than in the North (Figures 2.2C and 2.2D). Nothing anywhere near as consequential characterized regional change into the modern world. Rather, the same story – parallel alignments in two major regions, slightly augmented in the South – was sustained and extended more or less directly, with one noteworthy exception: Southern Republican activists (though not their rank and file) made an augmented shift to the right on social welfare, even by comparison to their Northern compatriots (Figures 2.3C and 2.3D).

Once more, that sets up the possibility of analyzing differences between organized and volunteer parties within the larger picture. Abstractly, the

TABLE 2.4 *Party Structures and Issue Alignments:*
*Social Welfare, 1990–2008*

| | A. Nation | | B. North | | C. South | |
|---|---|---|---|---|---|---|
| | Org. | Vol. | Org. | Vol. | Org. | Vol. |
| Democratic Activists | −.34 | −.31 | −.31 | −.30 | −.42 | −.38 |
| Democratic Rank & File | −.27 | −.20 | −.26 | −.20 | −.28 | −.21 |
| Republican Rank & File | +.32 | +.31 | +.30 | +.32 | +.32 | +.28 |
| Republican Activists | +.47 | +.54 | +.36 | +.51 | +.57 | +.62 |

power of contemporary polarization might suggest that room for further impact from party structures had been constricted. Concretely, however, the opposite was true. While the impact of party structure within these increasingly national contours may have grown more subtle, this impact simultaneously became more regular and omnipresent, while actually retaining some regional nuances. Though with social welfare in the modern era, the convergence between two grand geographic regions was sufficient – essentially the same overall alignment within both – to make this one of those cases where it is worth showing the national picture as stratified by party structure before delving into the regional situation.

Seen this way, the nation as a whole now featured two neatly consistent relationships between party structure and policy preferences (Table 2.4A). In the weaker of the two relationships, activists in volunteer parties were more polarized than those in organized parties. Either volunteer activists were pulling away from the national average or organized activists were pulling toward it or, of course, both – and this effect will be only stronger in a moment, when we reintroduce stratification by geographic region. In the much stronger of the two relationships nationwide, Democratic activists were further from their rank and file – and the representational gap was thus larger – in volunteer rather than in organized parties, and the same was true of Republican activists with regard to their rank and file (Tables 2.4A Org. and 2.4A Vol.). Not surprisingly, overall regional convergence meant that the same two relationships could be teased out in both the North and the South (Tables 2.4B and 2.4C). The first of these, the one involving greater ideological polarization among activists by volunteer parties, remained consistent but quite modest in both regional theaters. Yet the second, involving a greater representational gap by volunteer parties, looked even more impressive when state parties were stratified by geographic region. So this is probably the place to jump ahead of the story and note that both relationships are nevertheless at their weakest in the policy domain of social welfare. Both will apply, and both will be larger, in all three of the other great domains for policy conflict in the postwar years.[21]

Inside these larger relationships, some further nuances, both regional and structural, did remain. As between the two geographic regions, the active party was more extreme in the South than in the North in every category: organized and volunteer, Democratic and Republican (Tables 2.4B and 2.4C). As between the two party types, the left wing on social welfare was always held by Democratic activists from organized parties, while the right wing was held by Republican activists from volunteer parties. Still, the main findings that surface with party structure as a filtering influence on social welfare in the modern world were the two that would look only larger in the other policy domains: more polarized among volunteer than among organized parties, with a considerably greater representational gap inside volunteer as opposed to organized parties, now in all three theaters – nation, North, and South.

These effects could never be as striking as those from the old world, where organized parties had been pulling, even in the South, toward what would over time become the uniform national alignment, while volunteer parties were doing something different and idiosyncratic. Over time, organized parties had continued to polarize, while volunteer parties had not only come into a parallel alignment but had made this ideological move on the scale necessary to catch up to their organized counterparts. Both effects were simply invisible – gone – by the modern era.

Yet the structural effects surfacing (and visible) in this modern world retained a power and gained a uniformity that made them well worth serious attention. Said differently, these effects were now sufficiently strong that they no longer required regional controls to isolate their impact. In that sense, party structure had very much remained at the center of partisan intermediation in the modern world, just in a different, updated fashion.

What should the analyst make of these comparisons in their totality? On the one hand, the power of partisan polarization across time has meant that the difference between organized and volunteer parties can no longer sustains partisan alignments that are different in kind. On the other hand, reliable structural distinctions, involving contributions to ideological polarization between the parties and to the representational

---

[21] Chapter 4, most especially at Table 4.7, will array the specific coefficients for interparty polarization and intraparty representation in full and comparative detail.

gaps within them, continued into the modern world and has remained straightforwardly visible. One further inescapable implication – probably the best one to emphasize at this point in the analysis – is that what the analyst can make of comparisons limited entirely to the policy domain of social welfare, as central as these have been to modern American politics, should remain conditional until other major policy domains have also been considered.

## CIVIL RIGHTS

Among the four major domains for policy conflict in American politics during the postwar years, social welfare stands out for having produced a partisan alignment by the time scholars had continuing measures with which to track the evolution of any such alignments. Some work suggests that what became recognized as the associated "New Deal party system" did not really arrive in anything like a lasting form until the first postwar presidential election in 1948.[22] Yet it was evidently in place by the point at which we have continuing data to track its evolution, as a hunt for differences in the way organized and volunteer parties filter public wishes certainly confirms. Moreover, an effort to track the specifics of this filtering effect suggests that this particular policy domain, rather than *de*-aligning as other domains gained prominence, actually generalized its national reach across time even as it was simultaneously polarizing.

That said, our first period for analyzing the impact of party structure on policy responsiveness and democratic representation, 1950–1968, would also be demarcated in important ways by the addition of a newly consequential – and newly demanding – policy realm, namely civil rights.[23] The 1950s was the decade of an emergent protest movement in this policy domain. It was the decade of the greatest Supreme Court decision on civil rights in modern American history, in *Brown* v. *Board*. And it was marked by the first major legislation on civil rights since Reconstruction.[24]

[22] Helmut Norpoth, Andrew H. Sidman, & Clara H. Suong, "Polls and Elections: The New Deal Realignment in Real Time," *Presidential Studies Quarterly* 43(2013), 146–160; Eric Schickler & Devin Caughey, "Public Opinion, Organized Labor, and the Limits of New Deal Liberalism, 1930–1945," *Studies In American Political Development* 25(2011), 162–189.

[23] The other newly emergent and electorally powerful issue was foreign affairs, courtesy of the Cold War and the centrality of American political institutions within it, about which, much more in Chapter 4.

[24] C. Vann Woodward, *The Strange Career of Jim Crow* (New York: Oxford University Press, 1955); James T. Patterson, *Brown v. Board of Education: A Civil Rights*

The 1960s would then see civil rights protest explode. It would see Court decisions ramify. And it would produce the truly landmark legislation in this domain, most especially the Civil Rights Act and the Voting Rights Act, altering the American political landscape in key regards.[25]

In some ways, the partisan alignment on civil rights in the American politics of the time would prove initially to be just a weaker – a lagged – version of the counterpart alignment on social welfare. Yet in other important ways, civil rights bring a fresh analytic element to the hunt for differential impacts from party structure. The existing alignment on social welfare was sufficiently established by the opening years of our survey to generate clear expectations about the differential impact of organized versus volunteer political parties, while an emerging alignment on civil rights was sufficiently muddled to allow contending expectations about future developments, and the structural contributions to go with them. But even when the first option proved to be the shape of the future – partisan alignments on social welfare would indeed be a harbinger of many characteristics of partisan alignments on civil rights – the latter still brought the first good opportunity to compare the role of party structures in filtering public preferences on an emergent as opposed to an established policy domain.

Items contributing to the civil rights index again vary with the array of substantively relevant questions that were asked in a gradually changing ANES. Yet they were selected to fall within a single explicit definition of the policy realm, and refining this is even easier for civil rights than for social welfare:

*Civil rights* could be given an abstract formulation, making it in effect a sub-domain of civil liberties. Yet civil rights in the postwar period has been most centrally a matter of race policy for black Americans, so that in the search for an issue structure, it seemed essential to retain *racial concerns* as the essence of a policy definition.[26]

---

*Milestone and Its Troubled Legacy* (New York: Oxford University Press, 2001); Richard M. Valelly, *The Two Reconstructions: The Struggle for Black Enfranchisement* (Chicago: University of Chicago Press, 2004).

[25] Jeffrey A. Jenkins & Justin Peck, "Building toward Major Policy Change: Congressional Action on Civil Rights, 1941–1950," *Law and History Review* 31(2013), 139–198; Hugh Davis Graham, *The Civil Rights Era: Origins and Development of National Policy, 1960–1972* (New York: Oxford University Press, 1990); Michael J. Klarman. *From Jim Crow to Civil Rights: The Supreme Court in the Struggle for Racial Equality* (New York: Oxford University Press, 2004).

[26] Claggett & Shafer, *The American Public Mind*, 5.

Within the resulting array, certain marker items, even more generally accepted as belonging to the rights domain, provide the same sort of assurance as their counterparts did with welfare policy, assurance that a slowly changing measure still captures the same basic policy focus. Among these markers from the civil rights measure are the following:

> Some people feel that if black people are not getting fair treatment in jobs, the government in Washington ought to see to it that they do. Others feel that this is not the federal government's business.
>
> Some people say that the government in Washington should see to it that white and black children are allowed to go to the same schools. Others claim that this is not the government's business.[27]

## The Old World: Partisan Alignments

It should probably not seem surprising that the overall partisan alignment within the general public was considerably weaker for civil rights as opposed to social welfare in the immediate postwar years (Figure 2.4). While both policy domains were in some sense perennials in American politics, rising and falling in the public's attention with events of the day, voters had been moved centrally by welfare concerns since at least 1930, while the driving concerns for civil rights were only gaining traction as the postwar world unfolded. More to the practical point, the *parties*, and most especially their active members, had assumed clear positions on social welfare, ideologically distinct if still moderate by the standards of what was to come. Those positions were not just less clear on civil rights; they were actually mottled and confusing.[28]

That said, a picture of the policy preferences of partisan populations in the nation as a whole did show the same general alignment for the two policy domains – left to right from Democratic activists to the Democratic rank and file to the Republican rank and file to Republican activists (Figures 2.4A and 2.4B). So civil rights certainly did not cross-cut social welfare as a policy domain. What it did do was to offer a considerably weaker version of the shared pattern, along with tweaks distinctive to each party. For the nation as a whole, literally every one of the four great

[27] Ibid., 81.
[28] Edward G. Carmines & James L. Stimson, *Issue Evolution: Race and the Transformation of American Politics* (Princeton: Princeton University Press, 1989), especially chap. 6, "Modeling Change in Mass Identification," most especially at fig. 6.4, p. 150.

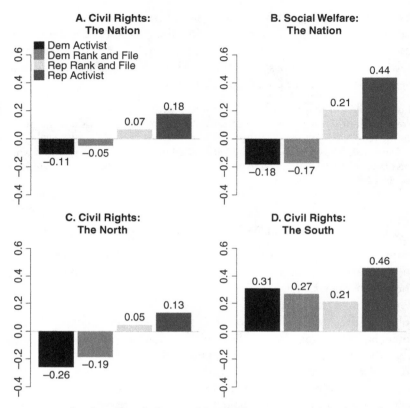

FIGURE 2.4 Partisan Populations and Issue Alignments: Civil Rights and Social Welfare in the Old World, 1950–1968

partisan populations was more moderate in its policy preferences on civil rights than on social welfare. Though because regional differences could still be sharp, as could the impact of organized versus volunteer parties, individual partisan populations within geographic regions or party types could nevertheless be more extreme on civil rights than on social welfare.

Within this overall alignment, the two parties went on to tweak their welfare stories in recognizable ways on civil rights. In the North, both Democratic populations were again clearly to the left of national party preferences, even more so with civil rights than with social welfare (Figures 2.1B and 2.4C) Both Republican populations actually stood to the left of their national party preferences as well – that was quite different from the story on social welfare – with the result that rank and file Republicans in the North emerged as the truly moderate population on civil rights for the nation as a whole. On the other hand and especially in these early postwar years, this Northern story was, arithmetically and by definition, at least partially a product of subtracting the South from the national picture. And in the case of civil rights, this was truer than with any other major policy domain.

The South was strikingly out of line with the national picture on civil rights, more so even than in the domain of social welfare (Figures 2.4D and 2.1C). In this contrary regional alignment, every one of its four partisan populations was clearly conservative. Rank and file Democrats had been ever so weakly liberal on social welfare; no Southern population was anywhere close to that on civil rights. Rank and file Republicans were as close to moderate as the region could provide, though that still landed them well to the right of their Northern co-partisans. Yet in an effectively one-party region, the North-South contrast within the Democratic Party was inevitably the main story. And there, the gap between the two rank and files, North versus South, was huge, the gap between the two activist populations even greater (Figures 2.4C and 2.4D).

One further result of the difference in these regional alignments was that the battle over civil rights inside the active parties was led by Northern Democrats from the left but Southern Democrats from the right. The Southern Republican leadership, still numerically derisory, was of little relevance. So it became Northern Republicans, both activists and their rank and file, who emerged as the key swing populations for policy conflicts in the civil rights domain. A further way to see the difference between the two domains, along with the exaggerated impact of region on civil rights, was to say that every partisan population in the North was further from the national average on social welfare as opposed to civil rights. In the South, three of the four populations were instead further from the center on civil rights; while those nearly exigent Republican activists were equally far away in both policy domains, their preferences qualified as the extreme right on civil rights, too.

### The Old World: Party Structures

Those are the crucial background contours for an attempt to unpack the role of organized versus volunteer parties in the domain of civil rights. With rights politics, however, this effort requires a quick detour through the political history of the policy domain, precisely because the two parties had played such historically different roles from those on social welfare *by party*. Since the Civil War, it was the Republicans who had been the party pursuing civil rights, though priority for the issue had been declining in party circles while the priority of social welfare had risen sharply. Since the Civil War and conversely, it was the Democrats who had been the party of inaction on civil rights – they might have called it "nonintervention" – even as they were bringing the welfare state to the center of American politics.[29] Accordingly, the filtering effect of any operative distinctions between organized and volunteer parties had to be exercised not just through a substantively different policy domain, but through one that featured more extreme regional differences and one that placed the two parties in very different starting places when the postwar period began.

Still, with all of that as context, there was an evident and immediate difference, even in the North, between the two party types in the domain of civil rights (Table 2.5A) It was just that this was simultaneously different from the same general effect in social welfare. With civil rights in the nation as a whole, Democratic and Republican activists from volunteer parties pulled their adherents toward alignment on what was becoming the great rising issue of American politics, even though it was not yet fully institutionalized. Hence, there were volunteer Democrats pulling to the left and volunteer Republicans pulling to the right (Table 2.5A1). By contrast, Democratic and Republican activists from organized parties were simply less engaged, resting a hair to the right of their rank and file among Democrats, only modestly to the right of the national average among Republicans.

Recall that on social welfare in the same region at the same time, both Democratic and Republican activists in organized parties were pulling their adherents toward an established national program (Table 2.5A2). There were Democrats pulling to the left and Republicans leaning toward the center. Activists in volunteer parties were then the opposite, with Democrats much more disengaged from the same programs and Republicans much more obviously resisting them: Democrats leaning

---

[29] Franklin Roosevelt had accepted the need to sway liberal preferences on civil rights to secure liberal preferences on social welfare, most poignantly with anti-lynching legislation: Alonzo L. Hamby, *For The Survival of Democracy: Franklin Roosevelt and the World Crisis of the 1930s* (New York: Free Press, 2004), 344–346. When he subsequently decided to confront the Southern Democrats directly, he was ineffective. James T. Patterson, "The Failure of Party Realignment in the South, 1937–1939," *Journal of Politics* 27(1965), 602–617. For the party system that lived into the reform era, see Ladd with Hadley, *Transformations Of The American Party System*, Part I, "Intertwining."

TABLE 2.5 *Party Structures and Issue Alignments:*
*Civil Rights and Social Welfare, 1950–1968*

| A. The North | | | | |
| --- | --- | --- | --- | --- |
| | 1. Civil Rights | | 2. Social Welfare | |
| | Org. | Vol. | Org. | Vol. |
| Democratic Activists | −.22 | −.27 | −.31 | −.19 |
| Democratic Rank & File | −.23 | −.16 | −.27 | −.20 |
| Republican Rank & File | +.02 | +.07 | +.16 | +.27 |
| Republican Activists | +.10 | +.17 | +.37 | +.49 |

| B. The South | | | | |
| --- | --- | --- | --- | --- |
| | 1. Civil Rights | | 2. Social Welfare | |
| | Org. | Vol. | Org. | Vol. |
| Democratic Activists | +.18 | +.69 | +.06 | +.27 |
| Democratic Rank & File | +.22 | +.37 | −.06 | +.03 |
| Republican Rank & File | +.21 | * | +.18 | * |
| Republican Activists | * | * | * | * |

* Ns too small for reliable analysis.

toward the center and Republicans pulling to the right. Both were already filtering impacts from party structures, just not the *same* impact by policy domain. One further result of this differential impact was that for the North as a political region, it was Democratic activists from organized parties who were the left on social welfare, but Democratic activists from volunteer parties who were the left on civil rights. In contrast, every one of the Northern Republican populations – activist or rank and file, organized or volunteer – was far more conservative on social welfare and genuinely moderate on civil rights.

None of that could serve as a summary portrait of the South in the same period, though, once again, some of the same relationships could be teased out of a set of regional policy preferences anchored in far different ideological territory (Table 2.5B). The Republican side of this story could still be dispatched quickly. Activist Republicans were too rare to support a further division by party type, and even rank and file Republicans were scarce in volunteer states. But where they could plausibly be measured, in the handful of largely Appalachian strongholds that featured organized parties, there was little difference among rank and file Republicans in their conservative preferences for both social welfare and civil rights (Tables 2.5B1 and 2.5B2).

All of which meant, as ever, that the Southern story at this point remained overwhelmingly a Democratic one. Recall that on social welfare, Southern Democratic activists from organized parties had been modestly more conservative than their own rank and file, while Southern Democratic activists from volunteer parties had been much more conservative than theirs (Table 2.5B2). On civil rights, the same general outline was present but grossly exaggerated (Table 2.5B1). Southern Democratic activists in organized parties were nearly in line with their rank and files, while Southern Democratic activists in volunteer parties were strikingly off to the right of theirs. Indeed, at +.69, these Southern Democratic volunteer activists were the most conservative population in either party type in either geographic region in either policy realm – and indeed *in either party* – on this issue.

Said differently, on civil rights in both the North and the South, activists from organized parties essentially reflected the policy preferences of their rank and files, while activists from volunteer parties pulled strongly toward the ideological extremes. With social welfare, activists from organized parties in both regions instead pulled toward an established national position, albeit starting from very different ideological points, while activists from volunteer parties resisted that pull. For social welfare, this meant that activists in organized parties were pulling leftward in their regions while activists in volunteer parties were pulling rightward. But with civil rights, activists from organized parties were pulling toward the dominant position in their *regional* party, while volunteer parties pulled toward the ideological extremes – which meant that this activist pull was leftward in the North but rightward in the South.

One other way to say the same thing – a way peeking through all of this – is that organized parties remained more attached to the existing national program, the one that was already aligned when the postwar world arrived, while volunteer parties were more responsive to a newly emergent issue, again inside both parties. Activists in organized parties in effect inherited their position on the established concern of social welfare. Activists in volunteer parties, relying on policy issues for motivation, were more responsive to the intense new concern of civil rights. Yet regionalism retained an important mediating effect on this otherwise common behavior, an influence affecting ideological positions and policy responsiveness.

Organized parties among the Democrats were contributing an actively liberalizing influence on social welfare in both the North and the South, though they were pulling left from very different starting points. Yet volunteer parties among these Democrats were pulling to the left on civil rights in the North – another actively liberalizing influence – but to the right, an actively conservatizing influence, in the South. Meanwhile, Republican parties were showing much less impact from civil rights at all, as a growing conservatism on social welfare was paired with an older but increasingly tepid support for civil rights.

### The Reform Era: Partisan Alignments

The defining characteristic of our middle period, 1970–1988, was the triumph of the reforms associated with the volunteer side in the long war over party structure and democratic representation. Yet concurrent with that change, partially shaped by it but largely autonomous, was the further evolution of partisan alignments in the policy domain of civil rights.[30] In the immediate postwar years, civil rights could be described as manifesting a weak overall version of the clearer alignment on social welfare. Informed by hindsight, later analysts would slip easily into that comparison. Yet in its time, the parallels were weak enough that a reasonable analyst would have considered the possibility that a connection this modest had no inescapable implications for the future. The arrival of the reform era should then have strengthened the first interpretive position and weakened the second, though enough divergence remained between the two domains to prevent awarding the argument definitively to one side or the other.

Be that as it may, the two partisan rank and files in the reform era were considerably further apart in their policy preferences, Democrats to the left and Republicans to the right, now with a range of .32 rather than .12 (Figures 2.5A and 2.5B). So there could no longer be any doubt that civil rights had acquired a partisan alignment at least crudely parallel to the one found originally on social welfare, an alignment strong enough to put not just activists but also the rank and file in their "appropriate" ideological order. At the same time, however, Democratic activists had plunged off to the left, while Republican activists had hardly moved. So polarization

---

[30] Many elements of the evolving context for civil rights politics in this period are gathered in Hanes Walton Jr., *African American Power and Politics: The Political Context Variable* (New York: Columbia University Press, 1997).

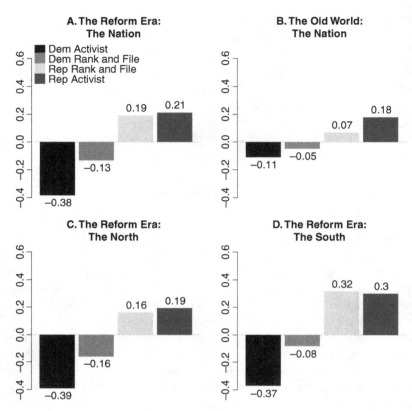

FIGURE 2.5 Partisan Populations and Issue Alignments: Civil Rights in the Reform Era, 1970–1988

between the active parties was entirely a Democratic phenomenon, highlighting a major difference between civil rights and social welfare while leaving open the prospect that other partisan populations might do equally idiosyncratic things in some subsequent period.

When the two policy domains were compared in detail, further distinctions appeared, both within and between the two major parties (Figures 2.5A and 2.2A). Among the individual partisan populations, activist Democrats were now further from the national average on civil rights, while the other three populations remained more moderate in this domain and further from the center on social welfare. Between the two parties, Democratic activists were closer to their own rank and file than Republican activists to theirs on social welfare, while on civil rights the situation was reversed: Republican activists were nearly on top of their rank and file, while Democratic activists were impressively distant from theirs. This suggested a different policy focus between the two active parties, featuring civil rights for the Democrats and social welfare for the Republicans.

Yet beneath this national narrative, the regional stories constituting the national picture on civil rights had changed in nearly every detail (Figures 2.5C and 2.5D versus 2.2C and 2.2D). First and most consequential, the partisan alignment of the South had been transformed on civil rights as it had been on social welfare, in fact even more so. This proved to be the biggest such realignment in any period for any region in any policy domain across all the postwar years. Though close behind was a different kind of change in the overall nature of partisan politics, with the appearance of an incipient but serious Republican Party in the South, one that now required analytic attention in its own right. One consequence was that new regional differences inside the national parties were now greater for the Republicans than for the Democrats on civil rights.

For their part, the Democrats had reached a roughly parallel alignment on civil rights as between the two great regions (Figures 2.5C and 2.5D). As with social welfare, this required monumental movement in the South, most especially among Southern Democrats. That movement did occur. For the Republicans, by contrast, the old regional difference on civil rights continued to shine through – and mattered more than before, courtesy of that newly invigorated Southern Republican Party. So while Democratic populations in the North and South now looked roughly similar in their policy preferences, Northern Republicans remained more moderate and Southern Republicans more conservative on civil rights, and this was true both of activists and their rank and files, though it is important to keep in mind that this ideological difference by region inside the national Republican Party characterized civil rights but not social welfare. And just to cap off all this regional change, the South was now modestly more polarized than the North on civil rights as on social welfare, again between both its active parties and their respective rank and files.

By comparison to the old world, then, the main change in the North was the clear move leftward on civil rights among Northern Democratic activists (Figures 2.5C and 2.4C). Yet when this was echoed in the South, the resulting regional change was far more dramatic (Figures 2.5D and 2.4D). Southern Democratic activists moved phenomenally leftward, from clearly conservative at +.31 to clearly liberal at −.37. No other partisan population would approach that shift, in any region at any time for any other issue domain. Still, there was change everywhere in the

South. The Democratic rank and file had also moved all the way across the ideological center, from +.27 to –.08, while Republican activists had actually moderated on civil rights, from +.46 to +.30. Only the Republican rank and file went against the trend, moving from +.21 to +.32.

## The New South Revisited

The lead question for this entire project always comes back to some variant of "How does party structure shape the partisan alignment of policy preferences, and hence ultimately of democratic responsiveness?" For most purposes, the answer is by itself an important element of the intermediary character of American politics, whatever this alignment is and wherever it comes from. That is, after all, the main reason scholars attend to political intermediaries in the first place. Even more than with social welfare, however, interpreting the Southern shift that was so critical to partisan realignments on civil rights during the reform era requires further consideration not just of the change in policy preferences within the four partisan populations of a previously one-party region – Democratic and Republican, activist and rank and file – but also of the shift in the social composition of all four.

Again, change in this partisan alignment can come from at least two major sources. First, people can change their preferences. This may be because experience teaches them something different about a stable issue in the course of time, or it may be because previously secondary issues become highly salient in a different period. Chapter 3 will present two different examples of this process, in the domains of cultural values and foreign affairs. But second, people can maintain their preferences but change the associated partisan attachments. Here, individuals can shift allegiances from one party to the other or, less sweepingly, they can shift to a more or a less active role within the same party. This chapter has already attended to this for social welfare and its changing alignments within the American South, a side trip that is even more necessary for civil rights.

These considerations about alternatives roots of political change led to an inquiry into the changing social composition of partisan populations in the American South for the domain of social welfare shown in Table 2.2. The fact of an even larger change in partisan alignments in the domain of civil rights suggests a return to this particular side trip, and Table 2.6 provides it. Table 2.6A brings back partisan alignments in the old South, now for non-blacks only. Table 2.6B updates that picture for the reform

TABLE 2.6 *Sources of Change in the South:*
*Civil Rights Impacts from a Changing Social Composition*

| | A. Non-Blacks Only 1950–1968 | B. Non-Blacks Only 1970–1988 | C. All South 1970–1988 |
|---|---|---|---|
| Democratic Activists | +.39 | −.08 | −.37 |
| Democratic Rank & File | +.37 | +.23 | −.08 |
| Republican Rank & File | +.28 | +.36 | +.32 |
| Republican Activists | +.61 | +.32 | +.29 |

era, still for non-blacks only, in effect asking where partisan alignments would have stood in the reformed South if there had not simultaneously been a major enfranchisement of Southern blacks. Finally, Table 2.6C adds black Southerners back into the picture, showing partisan alignments as they actually existed for the whole South.[31]

This setup makes it possible to ask the following questions: "Which elements of the single greatest change in partisan alignments in the entire postwar period could be found within the previously existing Southern electorate, that is, in changed *preferences* for the established partisan populations, and which elements were instead due to a change in the social composition of this electorate itself, that is, changed preferences courtesy of major additions to the old populations?"

For an answer, we can dispense quickly with Southern Republicans: there was little to distinguish policy preferences for Republican activists or the Republican rank and file as between the non-black South and the whole South in the reform period, 1970–1988 (Tables 2.6B and 2.6C). Removing black Republicans from the sample makes both aggregate populations slightly more conservative, but the difference is minor. For civil rights as for social welfare, then, a rapidly growing Southern Republican Party did not demand a change in the preferences of either its activists or its rank and file in the course of that growth. Said the other way around, new members shared the preferences of old members, on civil rights as on social welfare.

[31] For black enfranchisement as a central focus in its own right, Valelly, *The Two Reconstructions*.

The Southern Democratic story, however, was different in kind, with major elements of changing social composition joined by major elements of changing policy preference. Though to isolate these two influences, it is necessary to carve Southern Democrats not just by racial background, a fundamental demographic, but also by level of political activity, a structural characteristic. When this is done, three aspects of Southern Democratic change stand out. One of these is social composition in its purest form. Black Democrats pulled both the activists and their rank and file strongly leftward on civil rights, in almost identical proportions (again Tables 2.6B and 2.6C). Activists were .29 further leftward when black Democrats were added to the picture, going from −.08 to −.37. And the rank and file was .31 further leftward, going from +.23 to −.08.

The remainder of Southern Democratic change was then a mix of social composition and attitudinal change among non-black Southerners. Yet this divides further into a very different mix as between activists and the rank and file. Within the Democratic rank and file, change in aggregate policy preferences on civil rights was overwhelmingly a matter of social composition. There was a modest shift leftward among non-black Democrats between periods, from a very conservative +.37 to the still-conservative +.23 (Tables 2.6A and 2.6B). So the major overall change among rank and file Democrats was rooted in the simple addition of black Democrats to their ranks, moving aggregate policy preference for the rank and file population as a whole all the way across the center of American society, from solidly conservative at +.23 to modestly liberal at −.08.

Among Democratic activists, however, the shift in aggregate policy preferences was actually more a matter of ideological change among those who remained active Democrats than of some simple change in their social composition, though both contributions were clearly present (Tables 2.6A, 2.6B, and 2.6C). The addition of black activists did pull this population leftward by itself, from −.08 to −.37. But an even larger change occurred within the aggregate population of *non-black* activists, who shifted from +.39 to −.08 – half again the size of the change directly rooted in social composition.

On the one hand, what shines through here are the liberal policy preferences of new black participants wherever they appear, to an even greater degree than was true with social welfare. If ideological position tapped policy priority, then these newly enfranchised black voters cared (even) more about civil rights than social welfare. On the other hand, the larger moves within the activist stratum stemmed from actual changes in the aggregate preferences of an established population, while larger moves in their rank and file resulted instead from changes in its social composition.

To repeat: there was no need to be concerned with changing social composition per se between temporal periods inside the Southern Republican Party. Partisan populations in both party types were ideologically consistent over time, with or without the small corpus of black Republicans. The party was growing; its black identifiers were not. For the Southern Democratic Party on the other hand, major contributions came both from a policy sift within previously enfranchised populations and from a changing social base to those populations, courtesy of the newly enfranchised. For the Democratic rank and file, the major effect came from adding new black Southern voters; the non-black rank and file moved very little between periods. But for Democratic activists, the larger effect came instead from change inside the non-black population. Activists in the aggregate moved additionally left when newly enfranchised blacks were added to these totals, but an even larger part of this shift was within those populations as they had been previously defined in the old world.

### The Reform Era: Party Structures

That was a greatly changed world for party structures to mediate, so perhaps it should not be surprising that their mediating role shifted in the context of a new era (Table 2.7). This time, the story of regional evolution in policy alignments on civil rights crossed with the remaining distinctions between organized and volunteer parties in a major – but different – way. Recall that in the North, the old world had featured organized parties whose Democratic activists were essentially in sync with their rank and file on civil rights, while volunteer parties featured Democratic activists pulling aggressively away from theirs, to the left. And

TABLE 2.7 *Party Structures and Issue Alignments: Civil Rights, 1970–1988*

|  | A. North | | B. South | |
| --- | --- | --- | --- | --- |
|  | Org. | Vol. | Org. | Vol. |
| Democratic Activists | −.23 | −.42 | −.54 | −.24 |
| Democratic Rank & File | −.10 | −.17 | −.06 | −.10 |
| Republican Rank & File | +.23 | +.15 | +.36 | +.30 |
| Republican Activists | +.38 | +.18 | +.29 | +.28 |

all the while, the Republican story had been one of comparatively undif-
ferentiated moderation within both party types (Table 2.5A1).

In the North of a reformed world, this picture had become additionally
complex (Table 2.7A). Both organized and volunteer parties had come
into full alignment with the national pattern, running from Democratic
activists on the left to Republican activists on the right, with appropriate
stops in-between. For organized parties, however, the big move was
among active Republicans, who abandoned their old (and presumably
longtime) moderation on civil rights and came into stereotypical alignment with the new pattern, shifting from +.10 in the old world to +.38 in
the reform era. For volunteer parties, the major action instead remained
among active Democrats, who had pioneered the overall party drive to the
left on civil rights and continued that move in the reform era, shifting from
−.27 in the old world to −.42 in the new.

So the Northern story was one of organized parties accepting a familiar
alignment on the new issue, while volunteer parties continued the push
toward this alignment that they had pioneered. In the South, however, the
internal story was not just different but actually opposite. Recall that in
the South, the previous one-party world had featured Democratic activists
in organized-party states essentially in sync with their rank and files, while
Democratic activists in volunteer-party states pulled wildly off to the right
of theirs (Table 2.5B1). In that peculiar sense, both regions had been doing
the same thing: Democratic activists in organized parties marking time
on civil rights while Democratic activists in volunteer parties plunged
ahead. It was just that they had been plunging leftward in the North,
rightward in the South.

Yet in the South of a reformed world, this picture had been transformed
(Table 2.7B). All four Democratic populations − organized and volunteer,
activist and rank and file − had moved solidly leftward, amazingly so in
the case of Southern Democratic activists, still impressively so for the
Democratic rank and file. Comparisons with the old world of Southern
Republican politics are statistically risky, but two things were clear.
In one, both Republican populations were solidly conservative in both
party types in the reform era. And in the other, the newly invigorated
(and newly measurable) Southern Republican activists were nevertheless
slightly *less* conservative on civil rights than their own rank and file.

Still, the larger story lived inside the Southern Democratic Party, and
this internal story remained heavily colored by the difference between
organized and volunteer parties. In a world where racial liberalism had
become a national Democratic position, even the volunteer parties − the

old militant resisters – were now pulling left of their rank and file, though organized parties were doing so with remarkable abandon. Within this reform world, Democratic activists ended up much further left of their rank and file in organized parties (at -.54 versus -.06) than in volunteer counterparts (at -.24 versus -.10). Though by comparison to the old world, volunteer activists had actually moved further compared to their organized counterparts, even though this still left organized parties more in sync with the national pattern.

In some key regards, then, the overall regional picture no longer bespoke two different political worlds. Where the full partisan alignments on civil rights for the North versus the South in the old world had been essentially different in kind, they had now come into parallel alignment (Figures 2.5C and 2.5D). In that sense, regional differences were confined to the ideological placement of these parallel alignments. On the other hand, the difference in this ideological placement, still essentially regional, remained substantial. With civil rights as with social welfare, the regional story could rightfully be summarized as one of the South (re)joining the nation, rather than one of compromise, much less one of the North moving in a southerly direction. Yet within this summary, the two *party types* were still doing something fundamentally different in regional terms.

In the North, every partisan population, now stratified by party structure, remained more ideologically extreme on social welfare as opposed to civil rights – with the striking exception of Democratic activists in volunteer parties, who had pioneered the Democratic leap leftward on civil rights and who now still appeared to prioritize it over social welfare (Tables 2.7A and 2.3A). But in the South, while organized parties were leading the parade on both social welfare and civil rights, it was these organized parties, rather than their volunteer counterparts, that strongly prioritized civil rights among Democratic activists (Tables 2.7B and 2.3B). Though on the Republican side of the aisle, there was a further twist: the only rank and file population to be more ideologically extreme on civil rights than on social welfare – North or South, organized or volunteer – was the Southern Republican rank and file.

### The Modern World: Partisan Alignments and Party Structures

To begin with, the coming of the modern era put paid to any lingering arguments about the parallelism of partisan alignments between civil rights and social welfare. The two domains had already offered the same general *ordering* of the four main partisan populations in the first postwar period: left to right from Democratic activists to the Democratic rank and file to the Republican rank and file to Republican activists (Figures 2.4A and 2.4B). So the argument of the time had been over whether the much weaker version of this alignment in civil rights was an emerging parallel or just an accidental approximation.

This argument had then tilted substantially in the direction of a common alignment in the reform era, as all four populations moved further from the national average on civil rights (Figures 2.5A and 2.2A). What kept that shift from being decisive was that Democratic activists leapt so far left of the rest of the American public as to be off in their own ideological world, while Republican activists became nearly indistinguishable from their rank and file. Any argument for contrary alignments simply died with the coming of the modern world.

A quick visual scan of the two alignments suggests the obvious complementarity (Figures 2.6A and 2.6B). So do the relevant measures. Activists were genuinely equidistant as between the two policy domains: .85 on civil rights and .84 on social welfare. Their rank and files were equidistant as well: .55 on civil rights and .54 on social welfare. On the other hand, parallelism was not identity. Especially in the case of the active parties, civil rights offered a kind of partisan symmetry between Democratic and Republican activists, while social welfare returned to the asymmetry of the immediate postwar years, with active Republicans once more sharply off to the right while active Democrats shifted only much more modestly to the left.

In turn, if the modern world reduced overall differences between civil rights and social welfare, it went even further in reducing differences between political regions inside the rights domain. In the earliest period, these had been genuinely fundamental, that is, different in kind (Figures 2.4C and 2.4D). The North had anchored a version of the national alignment in slightly more liberal territory for all four partisan populations, while the South simply manifested a blanketing conservatism. This difference in kind was then converted into a simple difference of degree in the reform period (Figures 2.5C and 2.5D). Both regions accepted the national alignment, though the South anchored it in more conservative territory, especially among Republicans. A major autonomous move leftward by Democratic activists was also reflected in both regions.

What the modern world did was to come close to eliminating these remaining distinctions, that is, before party structure is put back into the picture. Both the North and the South moved into an alignment that was

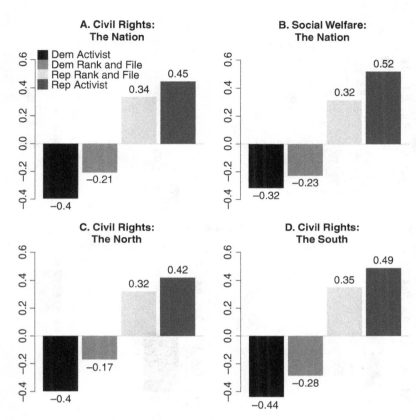

FIGURE 2.6 Partisan Populations and Issue Alignments: Civil Rights in the Modern World, 1990–2008

seriously polarized and roughly symmetric (Figures 2.6C and 2.6D). Within this shared alignment, the South, once comprehensively dissident from national patterns, was now *more* polarized than the North: .93 versus .84 among party activists and .63 versus .49 among their rank and file. Moreover, while further distinctions were truly modest, every Southern Democratic population was now left of its Northern counterpart on civil rights, while every Southern Republican population was now right of its Northern opposite number. This had been true for Republicans but not Democrats in the reform era. It was true for both parties in the modern world.

The modern world did go a long way toward reducing previous differences by party type as well. Organized and volunteer parties had

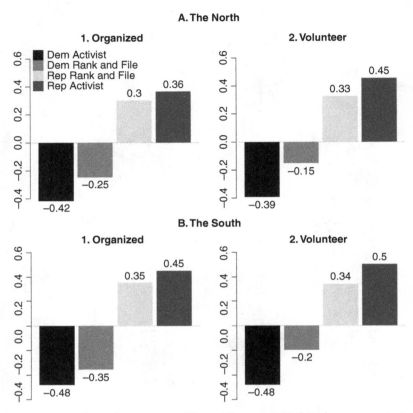

FIGURE 2.7  Party Structures and Issue Alignment: Civil Rights, 1990–2008

still been doing quite different things in the rights domain during the reform era (Tables 2.7A and 2.7B). Most strikingly within both parties, volunteer parties in the North but organized parties in the South had driven a leftward push on civil rights. In its time, this appeared to reflect a kind of time lag, in which the South, coming into alignment later than the North, came into that alignment with the old and not the new relationship to party structure as it did so. What strikes the eye first in Figure 2.7 is instead their generalized conformity to a single template in the modern world. Apparently, the previous differences by party structure that had characterized the regional response to what was then a rising new issue, first in the North and then in the South, had evanesced now that civil rights was an established (and institutionalized) concern for all.

On the other hand, with actual measures rather than just an ocular test, what had emerged to characterize the modern world was a structural difference between party types that we have already seen in social welfare and will see much more forcefully with cultural values and national security in the next chapter. If this emergent distinction is less striking than the original difference in kind, it is even more impressive in being regular, generalized, and most especially tied directly to notions of policy responsiveness and democratic representation. So in closing the story of civil rights, it is necessary to do two things: first, look back at the evolutionary cycle of this policy domain as influenced by structural distinctions between organized and volunteer parties and, subsequently, highlight the modern version of a generalized effect by these same party structures.

For the first of these closing concerns, the one centered on policy evolution, the three periods did indeed capture changing roles for structural differences:

- As the postwar period began, this policy domain had underpinned the great regional difference in American party politics, such that organized and volunteer parties could be expected to – and did – drive in opposite ideological directions by region: leftward among volunteer parties in the North but rightward among volunteer parties in the South, with organized parties resisting the pull in both regions.
- As the great rising issue of the successor period, civil rights then came second only to social welfare as a defining component of national party policy. Yet in its time, the reform era, this meant that organized parties in the North stayed with social welfare while volunteer parties picked up on civil rights. Just as it meant the opposite in the South, where organized parties, as part of their move into alignment with the national party, picked up civil rights in a manner that volunteer parties did not.
- A further generation later, much had again changed. The once-great political regions had continued to converge, such that interacting them with structural distinctions was no longer central to the character of American politics beneath its national picture. Simultaneously, in the modern period, the civil rights domain had become so thoroughly integral to national party programs that it no longer left much space for either of the older impacts from differing party structures.

What this implied was not the end of a structural story but rather a shift, a refocus, on fresh impacts, impacts increasingly generalized not just across geographic regions but also across policy domains. These impacts were now registered through two main indicators of structural influence for the modern era: (a) the degree of partisan polarization – the raw ideological distance – between Democratic and Republican activists in the two parties for both great geographic regions, and (b) the representational gap – the comparative ideological distance – between activists and their rank and file within each of the major parties, again for both regions.

With partisan polarization, measured through the ideological distance between Democratic and Republican activists, this distance was greater for volunteer than for organized parties in all four available categories: organized versus volunteer parties in the North (Figures 2.7A1 and 2.7A2) and in the South (Figures 2.7B1 and 2.7B2). With a representational gap, measured through the ideological distance between party activists and their own rank and files, this measure was likewise larger in volunteer than in organized parties in all four categories. Again, Chapter 4 will provide and pursue the specifics of both of these measures for all four policy domains, most especially at Table 4.7.

What appeared to be happening, though this can only be confirmed by data from a generation yet to come, was that as policy issues came into parallel with an established national alignment and as regional differences inside this alignment dissipated, all the major policy domains became subject to the diagnostic impacts of party structures in the modern world. While that can be argued to follow logically from shared partisan alignments and shared party structures, this logic cannot be tested empirically without the appearance of that further generation. What can be done is to add the two other key policy domains of the postwar years, namely cultural values and national security, to this picture of social welfare and civil rights. Chapter 3 will do exactly that.

# 3

## Party Structure and Representational Impact

### *Cultural Values, Comprehensive Ideologies, and National Security*

Social welfare is almost universally taken to be the spine of the New Deal party system. So if scholars argue about its role in modern times, this is usually just an argument over the degree to which it still plays that role or, alternatively, the degree to which the role is in decline. While the consensus is not as neat on the main policy *competitor* in this successor world, the leading alternative is ordinarily some variant of cultural values. Accordingly, we open Chapter 3 by giving cultural values the same compare-and-contrast treatment given to social welfare and civil rights in Chapter 2. In the process, cultural values serves simultaneously as the leading example of the way in which a major policy domain can lack any partisan alignment and as a testimonial to the power of differential party structures when the domain finally comes to share an alignment common to other major realms.

Yet a cultural analysis of partisan alignments and party structures more or less automatically raises the possibility that economics and culture, together, could provide an even richer substantive context for American politics during the postwar years, within which party structure must inevitably operate and to which it might make further contributions. This follows from the fact that these two policy realms can jointly be used as dimensions to classify the comprehensive ideologies of American politics, namely liberalism, conservatism, populism, and libertarianism. So once policy preferences in these two domains are arrayed – mapped – in this joint and mutual fashion, it becomes possible to ask about the filtering effect of party structures on these larger programmatic combinations and thus to seek the contributions of structural change to the main comprehensive ideologies of postwar politics. We shall attend to that possibility in the second part of Chapter 2.

The chapter then closes with foreign affairs, another realm with some theoretical challenges on the front end, but also one that can portray both a world where partisan alignments are largely missing, except for some provocative twists, along with one where the move to an ultimately common alignment showcases the effects on that alignment of different party types. So after making some initial choices about how to handle the domain as a whole – opting for a focus on national security, where our demand for the ability to track policy preferences across time is most easily met – we close by subjecting national security to the same general analysis as the previous three domains. Among other things, this high-lights the way that both cultural values and national security achieved partisan alignment later than social welfare and civil rights but showed an even stronger impact from party structure when they finally did so.

## CULTURAL VALUES

As a policy domain, cultural values differs at the start from both social welfare and civil rights by featuring a much greater scholarly dissensus on how to translate the substantive essence of the domain into specific items capable of measuring public opinion on it. Thus scholars argue over the proper way to conceptualize culture. They argue over how to measure whatever their conceptualization implies. They argue about the timing of the empirical product revealed by any appropriate measure. And they argue, last but crucially for our purposes, about the degree to which this rise has muscled into territory that was once dominated by social welfare.[1]

Still, if economic policy is hard to avoid in a study of the representa-tional impacts from party structure, cultural policy is next hardest to ignore. Moreover, despite the scholarly dissensus, this is hardly a neglected candidate for analysis in the American context. Students of American politics in fact recognize in cultural values a set of policy

---

[1] Efforts to establish order in this theoretical and methodological thicket while giving the domain its proper analytic place would include Kara Lindeman and Donald R. Haider-Markel, "Issue Evolution, Political Parties, and the Culture Wars," *Political Research Quarterly* 55(2002), 91–110, and Emily Wurgler and Clem Brooks, "Out of Step? Voters and Social Issues in U.S. Presidential Elections," *The Sociological Quarterly* 55(2014), 683–704. Even grander frameworks for the enterprise might include David C. Leege, Kenneth D. Wald, Brian S. Kreuger, and Paul D. Mueller, *The Politics of Cultural Differences: Social Change and Voter Mobilization Strategies in the Post–New Deal Period* (Princeton: Princeton University Press, 2002), and Ronald Inglehart, *The Silent Revolution: Changing Values and Political Styles among Western Publics* (Princeton: Princeton University Press, 1977).

concerns that have risen and fallen across all of American history. In the most common narrative, these concerns – about appropriate norms to govern social life – were at a high point in the late nineteenth century.[2] They declined to a low point during the Great Depression, in the middle third of the twentieth century. And they began to rise at some point thereafter, though the specific point is contentious.

There are scholars who like the late 1960s and early 1970s as this new turning point, perhaps with the presidential candidacy of George McGovern as the symbolic beacon. There are scholars who prefer the 1980s as the turning point, often with the presidency of Ronald Reagan as the operational catalyst. And there are scholars who tie this cultural rise to the early 1990s, where the congressional elections of 1994 serve for its practical crystallization.[3] Regardless, those historic waves and subsequent declensions suggest a world in which economic policy is still rarely absent as a central focus of politics for any extended period of time, but in which it can be joined – even intermittently displaced – by cultural policy as a central concern.

Perhaps unsurprisingly, everything about concrete measurements for public preferences on cultural values is more challenging than parallel efforts for social welfare or civil rights. If the theoretical contents of the domain are initially less consensual among professional students of public opinion, the available items to embody them go on to vary widely in their substantive focus, potentially frustrating even theoretical agreements. And just to make matters worse, the items themselves change more rapidly, so fewer individual markers continue in a stable form than in any other policy domain.[4] Still, the domain is generally understood to be a major realm of

---

[2] For rich examples, Paul Kleppner, *The Cross of Culture: A Social Analysis of Midwestern Politics, 1850–1900* (New York: Free Press, 1970), and Kleppner, *The Third Electoral System, 1853–1892* (Chapel Hill: University of North Carolina Press, 1979).

[3] The book that brought the domain back to self-conscious scholarly investigation was Richard M. Scammon and Ben J. Wattenberg, *The Real Majority: An Extraordinary Examination of the American Electorate* (New York: Coward-McCann, 1970); a systematic effort to embed it in American politics thereafter is Geoffrey Layman, *The Great Divide: Religious and Cultural Conflict in American Party Politics* (New York: Columbia University Press, 2001); and the argument for the domain at its greatest modern extension is James Davison Hunter, *Culture Wars: The Struggle to Define America* (New York: Basic Books, 1991).

[4] A sense of what is available within the domain can be gained from three works, all appearing at the point when the rise of cultural issues in the modern era of American politics was generally acknowledged: Benjamin L. Page and Robert Y. Shapiro, *The Rational Public: Fifty Years of Trends in American Policy Preferences* (Chicago:

postwar policy conflict, and it is certainly possible to offer an abstract definition of the realm, one capable of isolating items with a common surface content. This definition centers on behavioral norms:

*Cultural Values* involves the norms within which social life should proceed, and cultural policy involves the governmental role in supporting those norms. The flash-points for conflict over cultural policy in the postwar period were heterogeneous in the extreme; that is the great challenge of the realm. Yet *the character of social life* is in some sense the focus of them all.[5]

Moreover, some marker items within the available array do feature recurrent concerns widely agreed to belong to the domain, including the public role of religion, abortion policy, sex roles, and homosexual rights. While even repeat concerns acquire noticeably different wording over time in this domain, continuing substantive references are not hard to follow. Accordingly, marker items for the four substantive concerns cited earlier would include the following:

Some people think it is all right for the public schools to start each day with a prayer. Others feel that religion does not belong in the public schools but should be taken care of by the family and the church.

Abortion should never be permitted; abortion should be permitted only if the life and health of the woman is in danger; abortion should be permitted if, due to personal reasons, the woman would have difficulty in caring for the child; abortion should never be forbidden, since one should not require a woman to have a child she does not want.

Some people feel that women should have an equal role with men in running business, industry, and government. Other people feel that women's place is in the home.

Do you favor of oppose laws to protect homosexuals against job discrimination?[6]

### The Old World: Partisan Alignments and Party Structures

In the absence of an available comparison to partisan alignments in the key domain of social welfare, partisan alignments in the domain of

University of Chicago Press, 1991); Samuel L. Popkin, *The Reasoning Voter: Communication and Persuasion in Presidential Campaigns* (Chicago: University of Chicago Press, 1991); William G. Mayer, *The Changing American Mind: How and Why American Public Opinion Changed between 1960 and 1988* (Ann Arbor: University of Michigan Press, 1992).

[5] Claggett and Shafer, *The American Public Mind*, 5, as slightly edited here.

[6] Chap. 4 in Claggett and Shafer, *The American Public Mind*, "The New Issues: Cultural Values" isolates these markers and traces at least some of their textual evolution.

cultural values would have rated little more than a shrug in the years following World War II (Figure 3.1A). All four populations – Democratic and Republican, activists and their rank and file – were very close to the national average in these immediate postwar years. So there was little to say about the partisan structuring of a nearly invariant issue on its own terms. Said differently, as framed by social welfare and even civil rights, cultural values appeared distinctive not through its partisan pattern but rather for its very lack of alignment. In that far-off time, social welfare had already arrived as the central substantive domain for postwar politics, neatly divided even at the rank-and -file level between Democrats and Republicans (Figure 3.1B). Activists then flanked their rank and files, though the truly distinguishing characteristic of the active parties was the strong additional conservatism of Republican activists. Civil rights then showed what might be an incipient version of the same alignment (Figure 3.1C). Though without prescient knowledge of subsequent eras, the analyst would have had to be cautious in asserting any such parallels, especially since Republican activists were different – comparatively much more moderate – on civil rights as opposed to social welfare.

Possessing just such subsequent knowledge, we know that civil rights would indeed travel down the same road as social welfare. Still, an analyst of the time would have had to ignore the contemporary situation – and hence the real data – to foresee any such development for cultural values. The two rank and files were ever so modestly distant from each other in a direction parallel to the two other great policy domains, Democrats to the left (at −.03) and Republicans to the right (at +.05). But the two sets of activists (at .00 for the Democrats and +.01 for the Republicans) were essentially at the same position, dead on the national average and in-between those two rank and files.

So there was just no obvious overall alignment, certainly not one that paralleled social welfare or civil rights. As with both social welfare and civil rights on the other hand, this national (non)alignment on cultural values did not eliminate the need to check for regional differences. And here, there was a modest but perceptible regional divide: the South was more conservative than the North among all four major partisan popula- tions (Figures 3.1D and 3.1E). As a result, all four populations in the North appeared as ever so slightly more liberal than their ideological positions in the nation as a whole would have suggested, by virtue of subtracting Southern conservatives from national averages. Yet this time and very unlike either social welfare or civil rights, a uniformly conserva- tive South *was* aligned in the national pattern incipiently characterizing

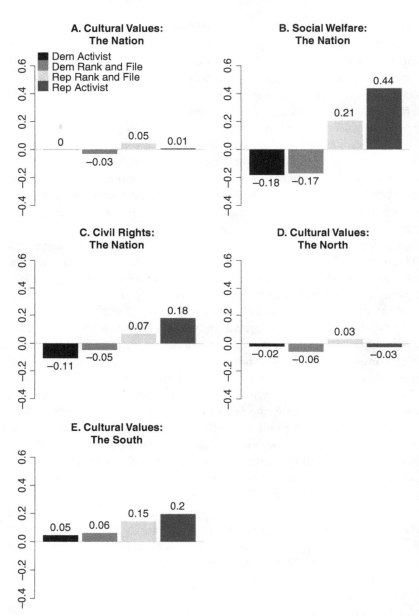

FIGURE 3.1 Partisan Populations and Issue Alignments: Cultural Values in the Old World, 1950-1968

TABLE 3.1 *Party Structures and Issue Alignments:*
*Cultural Values, 1950–1968*

|  | A. Nation | | B. North | | C. South | |
|---|---|---|---|---|---|---|
|  | Org. | Vol. | Org. | Vol. | Org. | Vol. |
| Democratic Activists | +.03 | −.04 | −.01 | −.05 | +.05 | +.05 |
| Democratic Rank & File | +.03 | −.10 | .00 | −.11 | +.08 | +.10 |
| Republican Rank & File | +.11 | −.03 | +.11 | −.04 | +.16 | * |
| Republican Activists | +.05 | −.02 | +.01 | −.03 | * | * |

\* Ns too small for reliable analysis.

both those domains, running left to right from Democratic activists to rank and file Democrats to rank and file Republicans to Republican activists, while the North did not offer so much as a hint of a similar internal patterning. In that light, if the Northern alignment on cultural values in the immediate postwar years was to become the national pattern over time, then cultural values would *never* acquire the orthodox partisan pattern.

Unsurprisingly, given the general lack of ideological variance by partisan population for the nation as whole, on top of a regional difference characterized mainly by a blanketing Southern conservatism, there was little further distinction to be uncovered through stratification by party structure (Table 3.1A). Effectively unaligned populations on cultural values in the North produced only idiosyncratic variation among those populations when they were further distinguished through organized versus volunteer parties (Table 3.1B). The Southern counterpart in these immediate postwar years again had to be almost purely a *Democratic* story, but within the dominant Democratic party, a blanketing conservatism was still all that there was to see, even when stratified by party type (Table 3.1C).[7]

### The Reform Era: Partisan Alignments

For professional analysts, and indeed for the viewing public, the evening news at the opening of the reform era might have suggested a period of

---

[7] The apparently greater conservatism of rank and file Republicans in the domain of cultural values may have owed much to the fact that the old patrician elite of Southern society – a reliably more educated population – was at this point still Democratic, but the data are too thin to take that argument further.

resurgence for cultural issues in modern American politics.[8] Or at least, war protest, racial rioting, and rising crime coincided with the shift from an old world to the reform era. Major social movements that bespoke cultural values rather than social welfare likewise appeared: the environmental movement, the women's movement, even a self-described "countercultural" movement. Moreover, these essentially cultural eruptions attracted national candidacies to give them a voice: the McGovern presidential nomination from one side in 1972, an actual Reagan presidency from the other side in 1980. These were arguably the most dramatic aspects of the issue context surrounding the simultaneous triumph of volunteer over organized party structures around 1970.

On the other hand, this overall context proved to be especially confounding in the domain of cultural values. For the reform era, the story of social welfare in the nation as a whole was one of roughly stable overall alignment, coupled with augmented partisan polarization and increasing ideological symmetry (Figure 3.2B). For civil rights, the story was instead one of increasing alignment, albeit coupled with a striking *asymmetry*, Republican activists hewing closely to their rank and file but Democratic activists plunging off to the left of theirs (Figure 3.2C). Yet the story of cultural values, finally, featured nothing that could safely be treated as partisan alignment, much less serious polarization, for the four partisan populations as a collectivity – with the evident exception of the same leftward leap among Democratic activists as was found with civil rights (Figure 3.2A).

Otherwise, rank and file Democrats and rank and file Republicans showed an ever-so-modest ideological distinction similar to the one they had evinced in the first postwar period (at –08 and +.06 respectively). Only time would tell if this was anything more than random perturbation. Its ideological direction might be consistent with that of other policy realms, yet its scale was small enough that it could be altered by a serious shift in either rank and file population. Moreover, Republican activists, by remaining where they had been in earlier days, not only continued to sit right on the national average (at .00) but were now much closer to both the Republican *and* the Democratic rank and files than were Democratic activists, which could have been a very different harbinger.

---

[8] For a comprehensive sense of flux, see Gareth Davies, *From Opportunity to Entitlement: The Transformation and Decline of Great Society Liberalism* (Lawrence: University Press of Kansas, 1996). For the period itself, Morgan, *Beyond The Liberal Consensus;* Berkowitz, *Something Happened;* Ehrman, *The Eighties;* and Patterson, *Restless Giant.*

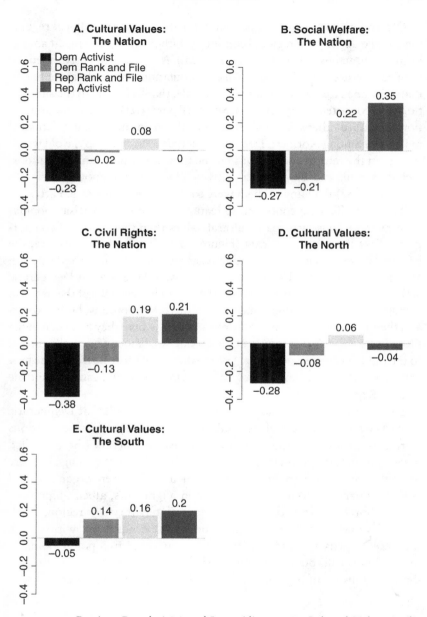

FIGURE 3.2 Partisan Populations and Issue Alignments: Cultural Values in the Reform Era, 1970–1988

Old and new ideological positioning for the two great political regions then mixed an ongoing regional continuity with that one major shift among Democratic activists (Figures 3.2D and 3.2E). As before, the North aped the national picture, with all four partisan populations modestly more liberal than they appeared for the nation as a whole, thanks largely to the subtraction of a consistently conservative South (Figure 3.2D). Yet these populations remained otherwise unaligned, while the major increment of leftward movement among Northern Democratic activists (from .00 in the old world to -.28 in the reform era) meant that the three other partisan populations, including rank and file Democrats, were closer to one another (at -.08, +.06, and -.04) than any of them were to the active Democratic Party.

The South likewise continued to feature all four of its partisan populations as more conservative on cultural values than their national counterparts. That much was not new (Figure 3.2E). Yet in the reform era, the leftward jump among Democratic activists on cultural values for the nation as a whole now extended to the South as well. So Southern Democratic activists (at an otherwise modest -.05) were no longer right of the national average. Yet the newly consequential Southern Republicans, both activists and their rank and file, remained almost exactly where they had been in the preceding period, while rank and file Southern Democrats actually moved to the right. The latter were more *conservative*, not more liberal, in the new era, effectively closing any ideological gap with the Republican rank and file or even Republican activists.

So it could be said of the South as well as the North that Democratic activists were off by themselves, while the other three partisan populations were closer to one another than to the active Democrats who propelled what was putatively their own party. Which leads the analysis more or less naturally on to the difference, if any, between organized and volunteer parties within roughly common alignments, albeit alignments still anchored in very different ideological territory by region. With cultural values, however, this question must be answered within such a different partisan context than that for the other two policy domains that it almost calls out for an analytic detour of its own, before addressing the contributions of organized versus volunteer political parties.

## No New South?

Recall that with social welfare and civil rights, it was necessary to move on analytically, not just from the remaining North-South distinctions but also especially from the transformative changes characterizing the South

TABLE 3.2 *Sources of Change in the South:*
*Cultural Values Impacts from a Changing Social Composition*

|  | A. Non-Black Only | B. Non-Black Only | C. All South |
|---|---|---|---|
|  | 1950–1968 | 1970–1988 | 1970–1988 |
| Democratic Activists | +.06 | –.04 | –.05 |
| Democratic R & F | +.06 | +.14 | +.14 |
| Republican R & F | +.14 | +.16 | +.16 |
| Republican Activists | +.18 | +.19 | +.20 |

in the reform era. The question for the analytic detour in those policy domains was whether a reconfigured Southern story was the product of changing policy preferences, a changing social composition, or some specifiable combination of the two. Unlike the situation with social welfare and civil rights, however, this prior story of regional transformation simply did not surface in the domain of cultural values. The South of course possessed the same (transformed) social base for this policy realm as for all others. Yet it evinced essentially no policy change in the realm of cultural values, with the exception of its Democratic activists – and their changes were the same, North and South.

On the other hand, while no transformation of the partisan alignment on cultural values rivaled the one characterizing social welfare and civil rights, it is not difficult to repeat the analysis comparing our four key partisan populations as they had been defined in the old South and as they now were in the reform era. So Table 3.2 brings back the analytic framework used in Chapter 2 for social welfare and civil rights. From one side, what stands out is the complete absence of any impact from a massively changed social composition for the partisan alignment of public preferences on cultural policy. From the other side, what matters in the absence of any serious impact from demographic change is just the question of whether the inhabitants of any given partisan population – Democratic or Republican, activist or rank and file – actually changed their minds. Only those Democratic activists ultimately did. What stands out most strikingly in Table 3.2, especially in light of counterpart analyses for social welfare and civil rights (Tables 2.2 and 2.6), is the near-perfect identity between preferences on cultural values for each of the partisan populations in the American South, whether they are reconfigured as they had been in the old world or whether they are instead presented as they actually were in the reform era (Tables 3.2B and 3.2C). Different populations did end up in ever so slightly different ideological positions. But the presence or absence of large numbers of black Southerners had no effect at all on this tiny shift (–.04 versus –.05, +.14 versus +.14, +.16 versus +.16, and +.19 versus +.20).

As a result, any change in partisan alignments on cultural values for the reform era in the South is the result of changes in aggregate preferences for particular partisan populations, and these ranged from exiguous to modest. In the case of the two Republican populations, there was effectively no change. Non-black Republicans in the reform era, both activists and their rank and file, stood essentially where they stood in the old world (Tables 3.2A and 3.2B), and the presence or absence of the few black Republicans did not amend this picture of stable preferences in any way (Tables 3.2B and 3.2C). More strikingly, for the two Democratic populations, where the presence or absence of black Democrats is of huge statistical importance, that presence remained irrelevant to aggregate policy preferences on cultural values (Tables 3.2A and 3.2B). Both activist Democrats and their rank and file likewise stood in the same position when analyzed for the whole South or for non-blacks only.

Yet for the Democrats, and very unlike the situation within the Republican Party, these two partisan populations were otherwise doing something very different. The Democratic rank and file now looked indistinguishable from the Republican rank and file, or for that matter, Republican activists. Yet to get to that result for the reform era, rank and file Southern Democrats actually had to move to the right on cultural values – again, non-black and black alike – which in fact they did (Tables 3.2A, 3.2B, and 3.2C ). By contrast, Southern Democratic activists shifted modestly but crucially leftward, abandoning a modest conservatism on cultural values and adopting a modest liberalism instead (Tables 3.2A and 3.2B). Yet this change in aggregate policy preferences, albeit opposite to the one made by rank and file Democrats, was once more unaffected by the presence or absence of black Democrats in these policy figures (Tables 3.2B and 3.2C).

Summarized differently, new black voters, rather than altering an old partisan alignment as they had on both social welfare and civil rights, helped to cement the previous alignment on cultural values. Even new black Democratic activists, who contributed so strongly to energizing the liberal position on social welfare and civil rights, did not play that role on cultural values. So an identical change in social composition proved to have major effects in the realms of social welfare and civil rights but no serious effect in the realm of cultural values. Said the other way around,

TABLE 3.3 *Party Structures and Issue Alignments:*
*Cultural Values, 1970–1988*

| | A. North | | B. South | |
| --- | --- | --- | --- | --- |
| | Org. | Vol. | Org. | Vol. |
| Democratic Activists | −.15 | −.30 | −.06 | −.02 |
| Democratic Rank & File | +.03 | −.10 | +.15 | +.13 |
| Republican Rank & File | +.10 | +.06 | +.19 | +.14 |
| Republican Activists | +.10 | −.05 | +.17 | +.25 |

newly enfranchised Southern voters brought fresh policy preferences to social welfare and civil rights, where these preferences had a significant impact on the Southern Democratic Party as a whole. Yet sharing policy preferences with previously enfranchised populations on cultural values, these new Southern voters brought no counterpart change there. Cultural values thus interacted with social backgrounds in a manner very different from that same interaction on social welfare or civil rights.

## The Reform Era: Party Structures

Table 3.3 sets out the basics for an analysis of the impacts from party structure in the domain of cultural values, comparing the old world and the reform era; the North and the South; and now, within them, our two party types. Perhaps surprisingly, for a policy realm that featured little overall alignment anywhere, apart from that idiosyncratic plunge to the left among Democratic activists, two developments that characterized civil rights as it was acquiring an alignment nationwide can already be teased out within cultural values as well, even in the absence of any such overall alignment.

In both the North and the South, as for the nation as a whole, major changes were in fact concentrated among Democratic activists. For the North, volunteer parties were making larger moves between eras than were organized parties, among both Democrats and Republicans. So a rising issue was again more attractive to the active members of volunteer rather than organized parties, as it had been with civil rights. In the South, however, the relationship between party types was reversed, likewise as it had been on civil rights. Here, organized Democratic acti-vists adhered much more to their national pattern than volunteer counter-parts did with theirs.

For the North among Democrats, volunteer activists ended up twice as far left as organized Democratic activists, -30 versus -.15 (Table 3.3A). Moreover, a comparison with Table 3.1B confirms that in an era where the main policy change was among these activists, volunteer parties had moved considerably further between eras (to the left) than had their organized counterparts, -.25 versus -.14. This would have been the Northern story on civil rights in both regards.

Conversely, for the South among Democrats, it was organized activists who ended up to the left of their volunteer counterparts, albeit modestly so, -.06 versus -.02 (Table 3.3A). This was also a modestly larger change between eras, -.11 for organized and -.07 for volunteer activists (Tables 3.1B and 3.3A). Modest changes looked a bit more impressive than their absolute numbers would suggest, in that the Southern Democratic rank and file had actually moved *rightward* in both periods, but more so in organized party states.

On the one hand, then, partisan alignments in the reform era showed some incipient changes in the cultural domain only within the active Democratic Party. So there was little overall evidence of any serious impact from the cultural conflicts that made frequent appearances on the evening news. On the other hand, two structural developments were associated with cultural values in the reform era that were noteworthy, and the fact that they differed by region was additionally noteworthy in its own regard. In the North, volunteer parties were more responsive to – and more moved by – the emergent domain of cultural values, as they had been on civil rights, while organized parties remained more responsive to the established domain of social welfare and hence more resistant to cultural values, as they too had been with civil rights.

Yet beyond this first evolutionary effect, party structure interacted with continuing regional differences to underpin a second ideological impact, and this one was the same for cultural values as for social welfare and civil rights. To wit: as a region came into alignment with an established order, it came into alignment with the structural dif-ferences that had characterized this policy domain when that align-ment initially appeared. So the South in the reform era did not come into alignment with the structural differences that characterized the North in this same period, the ones that would continue to character-ize it going forward. Instead, the South came into alignment with the structural differences that had characterized the North when *it* first came into alignment with the national pattern, in the immediate postwar years.

## The Modern World: Partisan Alignments

In any case, it all changed with the arrival of the modern world, 1990–2008. After forty years in the postwar partisan wilderness, cultural values came into alignment with the overall template that had already characterized social welfare in the old world and that came to characterize civil rights during the reform era (Figures 3.3A, 3.3B, and 3.3C). By itself and on its own terms, this was a huge change for the realm of cultural values. Seen in a wider context, in the process of coming into alignment, cultural values also contributed to – and confirmed – the power of a common ordering, one that was drawing more and more policy conflicts into its (increasingly shared) framework.

The new partisan alignment for cultural values did lag both social welfare and civil rights in its degree of polarization. Thus the ideological distance between Democratic and Republican activists in the nation as a whole was .84 for social welfare, .85 for civil rights, and .61 for cultural values – less than those two other domains with their earlier alignments but still a large ideological distance. And the same could be said of partisan rank and files in these three policy domains: an ideological distance of .55 on social welfare, .55 on civil rights, and .33 on cultural values. Yet if the force of this common alignment continued to lag those other two domains, it was also true that culture had produced the biggest *change* in the modern era: .21 for social welfare, .26 for civil rights, and .38 for cultural values.

Each of the three domains did retain some individually distinguishing characteristics. Thus social welfare featured a growing polarization between the two active parties, within which active Republicans were the ideologically extreme population (Figure 3.3A). Civil rights instead featured a rough symmetry between Democratic and Republican activists, with Republicans only slightly more distant from the national average (Figure 3.3B). And cultural values featured a gathering polarization within which active Democrats were the slightly more distant population (Figure 3.3C).

Beyond all that was a further sense in which cultural values was now more like civil rights than either of the two was like social welfare. In the modern world, social welfare continued to feature a smaller representational gap between activists and their rank and file among Democrats as opposed to Republicans. Yet for both civil rights and cultural values, the situation was reversed. During the reform era, Democratic activists had already moved further from their rank and file than Republican activists in

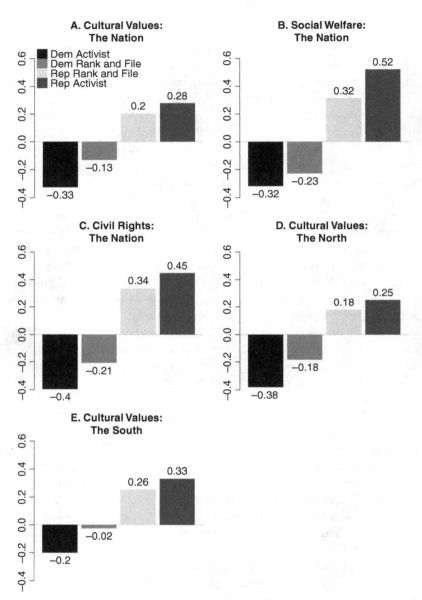

FIGURE 3.3 Partisan Populations and Issue Alignments: Cultural Values in the Modern Era, 1990–2008

the domain of civil rights. This pattern continued into the modern world, joined now by the same pattern in cultural values, that is, Democratic activists even further from their rank and file than Republican activists were from theirs.

Still, the change between periods in the overall alignment of cultural values was what deserved the most notice. What had been essentially a flat ideological line in the immediate postwar years and remained a non-alignment during the reform period, distinguished only by that leftward plunge among activist Democrats, was now a full-blown alignment in the conventional form: left to right once more from Democratic activists to the Democratic rank and file to the Republican rank and file to Republican activists. Though to realize this alignment, it was activist *Republicans* who had to make the biggest ideological shift this time, which in fact they did. Sitting right on the national average in the reform period at .00, they moved to anchoring the ideological right in the modern era at +.28. If this was still their most moderate position among the three policy domains, it was simultaneously a sharp – indeed, the biggest – ideological shift in the modern world.

It is probably also worth noting that this evidence-based picture of the partisan evolution of cultural issues fits uneasily with many anecdotal narratives. The coming of cultural issues to the center of partisan politics is frequently dated to the McGovern campaign of 1972.[9] Systematic evidence suggests that the change from an old world to the reform era does indeed roughly coincide with the changed preferences of Democratic *activists*, though they appear largely to have moved on their own: all other partisan populations, including Republican activists, were largely immune.

The coming of cultural issues to the center of partisan politics is also frequently dated to the Reagan presidency of 1980.[10] Unlike McGovern, Reagan was an actual objective winner. Yet systematic evidence is even

---

[9] For the self-conscious counterculture, Todd Gitlin, *The Sixties: Years of Hope, Days of Rage* (New York: Bantam, 1993); for the McGovern adventure, Bruce Miroff, *The Liberals' Moment: The McGovern Insurgency and the Identity Crisis of the Democratic Party* (Lawrence: University Press of Kansas, 2007); for the long battle to rein in these effects, Kenneth S. Baer, *Reinventing Democrats: The Politics of Liberalism from Clinton to Reagan* (Lawrence: University Press of Kansas, 2000).

[10] There were certainly acolytes who were willing to assert – and carry – this cultural banner, as with Richard A. Viguerie, *The New Right: We're Ready to Lead* (Falls Church, VA: The Viguerie Company, 1981). Yet most students of the Reagan presidency view it as much less narrowly focused on cultural issues, as with W. Elliott Brownlee and Hugh Davis Graham, eds., *The Reagan Presidency: Pragmatic Conservatism & Its Legacies* (Lawrence: University Press of Kansas, 2003).

more unkind to this perception. Both Republican populations, that is, Republican activists and their rank and file, showed little change during the reform era, a summary statement that can be extended to the Democratic rank and file.

Lastly, the other anecdotal candidate for a turning point in the partisan career of cultural values is the congressional elections of 1994, the ones restoring Republicans to control of the House of Representatives for the first time in fifty years.[11] This was an indisputable change in the generalized partisan character of national politics, and it did coincide with the modern world when examined through survey evidence, though that same evidence is a reminder that other things – that is, things other than cultural issues – were also changing at the same time.

Be that as it may, the scope of the newly realized alignment for cultural values was even more impressive than these national figures would suggest, since the national alignment now characterized both the North and the South, penetrating both regions in the same way at the same time (Figures 3.3D and 3.3E). So a common alignment had arrived not just as an overall summary but also as a further measure of convergence within the two major parties by geographic region. Otherwise, within both regions, Republican activists were only modestly off to the right of their rank and file, while Democratic activists were roughly three times as far off to the left of theirs. So cultural values as a policy domain stressed the Democratic coalition considerably more than its Republican counterpart.

## The Modern World: Party Structures

When the structural difference between organized and volunteer parties is (re)introduced into this modern partisan matrix, a further mix of evolutionary developments stands out. There is no point in asking what had happened to the impact of party structure on the *original* partisan alignment for the policy domain of cultural values. There was nothing resembling an alignment in the old world, where all four partisan populations had clustered around the national average. A differentiated answer to the same question – the impact of party structure on partisan alignment – remained limited to Democratic activists in the successor period, the reform era, since they were the only ones showing serious change.

---

[11] This time, there was an explicit agenda, though it too mixed cultural values with other policy domains. Ed Gillespie and Bob Schellas, eds., *Contract With America* (New York: Times Books, 1994). This had its true believers.

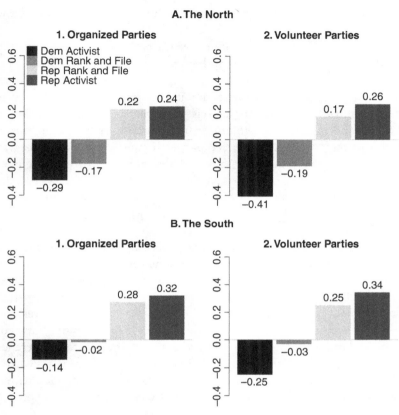

FIGURE 3.4 Party Structures and Issue Alignments: Cultural Values in the Modern World, 1990–2008

Democratic activists in volunteer parties did jump further off to the left in the North, Democratic activists in organized parties only further to the left in the South, but outside of these activist populations in one party, there remained little evidence of structural impact.

That summary judgment too changed in a major way in the modern era (Figure 3.4). Indeed, our main structural distinction became instrumental in isolating and comparing a raft of associated shifts: between the two major parties themselves, between the great political regions within those parties, inside the modern incarnation of the organized versus volunteer divide, and ultimately in the interactions of party structure with all of these concerns. Pictured this way – two major parties, two political regions, four partisan populations, and two structural types – there were now four noteworthy impacts on policy responsiveness and democratic representation.

First, it becomes possible to compare the two Democratic versus the two Republican populations in both great regions for both party types. In effect, this is the difference in the way the two political parties put their policy coalitions together, and it is a striking one. There was relatively little variety among activist Republican populations, North to South and organized to volunteer, ranging only .10 from organized parties in the North to volunteer parties in the South. And this was equally true of the Republican rank and file, ranging .09 from volunteer parties in the North to organized parties in the South. In other words, the Republican Party was largely put together in the same way on cultural values wherever one looked in the modern world; it had a shared ideological core.

By contrast, Democratic populations were far more heterogeneous. On cultural values, their activist populations ranged an impressive .27, from –.14 among organized parties in the South to –.41 among volunteer parties in the North. Rank and file Democrats range from truly centrist, at –.02 within organized parties in the South, to clearly (but not extremely) liberal, at –.19 among volunteer parties in the North. The total range of .39 is as large a gap within the *same* party as the greatest difference between rank and file Democrats and rank and file Republicans anywhere. Said the other way around, the Democratic Party was as divided within itself as it was from opposition Republicans when the focus was cultural values.

This should not, however, be allowed to obscure the combination of a rough regional convergence with some familiar and ongoing, if lesser, regional divides (Figure 4.4A versus Figure 4.4B). On cultural values, all four partisan populations – North and South, organized and volunteer – once looked similar by default, thanks to a uniform lack of partisan alignment, though that contrasted sharply with the situation on social welfare and civil rights, where what would become the conventional alignment had already begun to arrive. There was still a certain rough similarity in the modern world, thanks to common but polarized differences among all four partisan populations. Yet this should not be taken to mean that regional differences had evaporated: every partisan population in the North remained more liberal than every counterpart population in the South, and of course vice versa.

That said, neither the fundamentally different ways in which the two parties put their pieces together nor the continuingly different ways in which the two great regions colored these coalitions went nearly far enough to abolish – even to blur – the distinction between organized and volunteer parties (Figures 4.4A1 and 4.4B1 versus 4.4A2 and 4.4B2). Between the active parties, volunteer activists were always more extreme than organized activists, for both major parties and in both political regions. Inside these parties, the distance between active partisans and their rank and files was always greater for volunteer as opposed to organized parties. So both of those key democratic measures, together – greater activist polarization and a greater representational gap – likewise characterized both major parties in both geographic regions.

Lastly, the difference between organized and volunteer parties, when imposed on four partisan populations stratified by region, created some distinctions of consequence for individual populations. On cultural values, the population furthest from the national average to the left was Democratic activists from volunteer parties in the North, while the population furthest from the national average to the right was Republican activists from volunteer parties in the South. Not surprisingly given the preceding paragraphs, both of those were activist (and not rank and file) populations, and both were from volunteer (and not organized) parties. Conversely, the most moderate activist population among Democrats – the one closest to the national average – was Democratic activists from organized parties in the South, while the most moderate activist population among Republicans was Republican activists from organized parties in the North. So examined either way – most extreme or most moderate – party structure had a greater relationship to policy preferences than political region in the modern world.

## COMPREHENSIVE IDEOLOGIES

In principle, possessing a portrait of policy responsiveness on both social welfare and cultural values allows the investigation of an even larger role for organized versus volunteer parties in the representation of public wishes. Social welfare and cultural values are leading candidates to play this role because they are generally perceived to follow from key social cleavages, pitting divisions on material distributions against divisions on behavioral norms. One early effort to think about politics in this sense, as a two-dimensional phenomenon with these two underlying dimensions, came from Seymour Martin Lipset and Stein Rokkan in "Cleavage

Structures, Party Systems, and Voter Alignments."[12] Writing about the attitudinal and policy nature of politics in the first postwar generation for a variety of developed nations, they homed in on two widely shared institutional revolutions, one national (and hence cultural) and one industrial (and hence economic), as providing the essential dimensionality for postwar politics.

In this light but seen the other way around, policy preferences on these two major conflicts in postwar American politics represent responses to the main underlying cleavages shaping politics in the large. Nations, like individuals, may emphasize one cleavage (and attitudinal alignment) at one point in time, another cleavage (and hence the other alignment) at some other point. Yet both cleavages are sufficiently fundamental as to be unlikely to be absent for very long, so public opinion can usually be analyzed as a two-dimensional distribution, most commonly combining public preferences on economics (social welfare) and culture (cultural values). The resulting portraits are still contingent, in that the applied impact of each grand cleavage is likely to be colored by (changing) positions and preferences on the other. But the point here is that in the world of preference measurement, social welfare and cultural values provide the obvious stand-ins for two critical underlying dimensions.[13]

There are, in turn, two distinct ways to put these grand policy domains to work. The first considers the two key realms at the same time but still individually, on the theory that the simple *combination* of partisan alignments might be revealing. Unsurprisingly, particular respondents – not to mention entire partisan populations – can and do mix the ideological locations of individual or aggregate preferences from the two domains in varying ways. Yet it is also possible to put social welfare and cultural values together jointly, using the two domains not as separate measures but as *axes* delineating the space occupied by more comprehensive ideologies. Individuals can thus locate themselves in different ways within this two-dimensional space. As it turns out, so can the four partisan populations.

Once the situation is mapped, then, it becomes possible to ask about the effect of structural change on the fortunes of comprehensive ideologies

---

[12] This is the introduction to Lipset and Rokkan, eds., *Party Systems and Voter Alignments: Cross-National Perspectives* (New York: Free Press, 1967).

[13] For a rich embodiment and vigorous defense of this approach, see Edward G. Carmines, Michael J. Ensley, and Michael W. Wagner, *Beyond The Left-Right Divide: Conditional Mass Polarization and the Future of American Politics* (in manuscript and forthcoming).

TABLE 3.4 *Partisan Populations and Issue Alignments:*
*Social Welfare and Cultural Values Jointly*

| | Democratic Activists | | Democratic Rank & File | | Republican Rank & File | | Republican Activists | |
|---|---|---|---|---|---|---|---|---|
| | SW | CV | SW | CV | SW | CV | SW | CV |
| 1950–1968 | −.18 | 0 | −.17 | −.03 | +21 | +.05 | . +.44 | +.01 |
| 1970–1988 | −.27 | −.23 | −.21 | −.02 | +.21 | +.08 | . +.34 | 0 |
| 1990–2008 | −.32 | −.33 | −.23 | −.13 | +.32 | +.20 | +.52 | +.28 |

and not just major policies. The four great ideological families present in American society – liberals, conservatives, populists, and libertarians – all appear in this framework, and all evolve across the postwar years. So if party structures are helping to shape the alignment and evolution of individual policy domains, they are presumably doing the same with this two-dimensional world, where organized and volunteer parties should be either facilitating or retarding one or another of these comprehensive ideologies. As it turns out, the fortunes of one of these great ideological families, the populists, prove to be especially influenced by the triumph of volunteer over organized party structures.

### The Partisan Evolution of Economics and Culture in Tandem

Table 3.4 begins a simultaneous investigation of social welfare and cultural values in the simplest way possible, bringing back the scores by era of the four partisan populations on these two policy domains and arraying those scores side by side.[14] Much of the resulting picture summarizes familiar developments, while teasing out some further implications that are not so easily perceived when proceeding one domain at a time. Familiar developments include the propensity of the old world of partisan politics, 1950–1968, to center on social welfare, which it more or less had to, since cultural values had as yet no partisan implications. The same could be said of the reform era, 1970–1988, except for those

---

[14] For a rich and suggestive application of this same theoretical approach, see Mark D. Brewer and Jeffrey M. Stonecash, *SPLIT: Class and Cultural Divides in American Politics* (Washington, DC: CQ Press, 2006). For an earlier exercise within the same general framework, Byron E. Shafer and William J. M. Claggett, *The Two Majorities: The Issue Context of Modern American Politics* (Baltimore: Johns Hopkins University Press, 1995).

leftward-plunging Democratic activists, who laid the implicit ground-work for attracting some individuals and repelling others on cultural and not just economic grounds. It was only the successor period, however, the modern world, 1990–2008, that brought both policy domains into full alignment; while a common alignment hardly meant that the two domains would be equally influential at any single point in time, it did strongly increase strategic options for the two major parties, as well as alternative possibilities for their outcome.

Table 3.5 goes in search of the structural distinctions within these period portraits, stratifying by geographic region as well as party type. The result is a picture of organized versus volunteer parties, in the North and in the South, now for social welfare and cultural values on the same page. Much of this result remains familiar from individual pictures of the two domains. Thus for the immediate postwar years, this fourfold array underlines the extent to which the national alignment on social welfare was almost entirely a product of a stronger version of this alignment within organized parties in the North (Table 3.5A). These parties were clearly the standard-bearers for a New Deal party system, to which even volunteer parties of the North had not yet adapted (Table 3.5B). Yet for none of the four categories, organized or volunteer in the North or the South, was there any counterpart alignment on cultural values. So the national picture of a politics centered on social welfare was not belied by any party type in any major region.

The greater symmetry of partisan alignments on social welfare in the successor (reform) period thus had to come from somewhere other than Northern organized parties. The smaller of the two main contributions to this generalized alignment came from volunteer parties in the North, which moved into parallel with their organized counterparts. The larger of these two contributions was the transformative change on social wel-fare in the South. Simultaneously, cultural values showed the first stirrings of what would become a parallel alignment for the cultural domain in the period to follow, though for the reform era, this stirring was still limited to Democratic activists.

On the one hand, even this activist movement begins to register some less familiar developments that emerge when two domains are considered jointly. For there was now a partisan population more extreme on culture than on economics, namely Democratic activists from volunteer parties in the North (Table 3.5B1). On the other hand, there was little further to be squeezed from a presentation of this period, as those newly aligned Southern parties, organized and volunteer, were just uniformly more

TABLE 3.5 *Party Structures and Geographic Regions:
Social Welfare and Cultural Values Jointly*

### A. The North, Organized Parties

| | 1. Democratic Activists | | 2. Democratic Rank & File | | 3. Republican Rank & File | | 4. Republican Activists | |
|---|---|---|---|---|---|---|---|---|
| | SW | CV | SW | CV | SW | CV | SW | CV |
| 1950–1968 | −.31 | .01 | −.27 | .00 | +.16 | +.11 | +.37 | +.01 |
| 1970–1988 | −.27 | −.15 | −.17 | +.03 | +.32 | +.10 | +.44 | +.10 |
| 1990–2008 | −.31 | −.29 | −.26 | −.17 | +.30 | +.22 | +.36 | +.24 |

### B. The North, Volunteer Parties

| | 1. Democratic Activists | | 2. Democratic Rank & File | | 3. Republican Rank & File | | 4. Republican Activists | |
|---|---|---|---|---|---|---|---|---|
| | SW | CV | SW | CV | SW | CV | SW | CV |
| 1950–1968 | −.19 | −.05 | −.20 | −.11 | +.27 | −.04 | +.49 | −.03 |
| 1970–1988 | −.27 | −.30 | −.21 | −.10 | +.20 | +.06 | +.33 | −.05 |
| 1990–2008 | −.30 | −.41 | −.20 | −.19 | +.32 | +.17 | +.51 | +.26 |

### C. The South, Organized Parties

| | 1. Democratic Activists | | 2. Democratic Rank & File | | 3. Republican Rank & File | | 4. Republican Activists | |
|---|---|---|---|---|---|---|---|---|
| | SW | CV | SW | CV | SW | CV | SW | CV |
| 1950–1968 | +.06 | +.05 | −.06 | +.08 | * | * | * | * |
| 1970–1988 | −.30 | −.06 | −.23 | +.15 | +.26 | +.19 | +.21 | +.17 |
| 1990–2008 | −.42 | −.14 | −.28 | −.02 | +.32 | +.28 | +.57 | +.32 |

### D. The South, Volunteer Parties

| | 1. Democratic Activists | | 2. Democratic Rank & File | | 3. Republican Rank & File | | 4. Republican Activists | |
|---|---|---|---|---|---|---|---|---|
| | SW | CV | SW | CV | SW | CV | SW | CV |
| 1950–1968 | +.27 | +.05 | +.03 | +.10 | * | * | * | * |
| 1970–1988 | −.24 | −.02 | −.18 | +.13 | +.26 | +.14 | +.21 | +.25 |
| 1990–2008 | −.38 | −.25 | −.21 | −.02 | +.28 | +.25 | +.62 | +.34 |

attuned to social welfare, where they had actually come into national alignment, than to cultural values, where they still rested close to the national average (Tables 3.5C and 3.5D).

The outstanding characteristic of the modern period, when viewed through the lens of partisan alignment, was that the overall alignment pioneered by social welfare in the old world had finally arrived in the realm of cultural values as well, colonizing it in fact within both geographic regions and both party structures. Seen now through the lens of social welfare and cultural values in tandem, it was clear that almost every partisan combination – four partisan populations in two policy domains crossed by two geographic regions and two party structures – had polarized between the reform era and the modern world. Indeed, only one of these thirty-two combinations moved seriously in a moderating direction.[15]

Now, however, within those general alignments, the combination of social welfare and cultural values went on to highlight some further developments. Thus Democratic activists in organized parties in the South held the ideological extremes on social welfare (Table 3.5C1) and by Republican activists in volunteer parties in the same region (Table 3.5D1), continuing the trend of greater Southern polarization. Conversely, Democratic activists in volunteer parties in the North held the ideological extremes on cultural values (Table 3.5B1) and by those same Republican activists from volunteer parties in the South (Table 3.5D1).

For Republicans, this joint ideological leadership highlighted the emergent policy extremism of Southern activists from volunteer parties, more numerically important and more consistently extreme than they had ever been. For Democrats, what stood out instead was the continuing cultural extremism of Northern activists from volunteer parties, an extremism unlike any other in that they had managed to be the leading cultural outlier in two successive periods. So activists had extended the tendency for volunteer parties to pull additionally toward the extremes on cultural values, along with the tendency for organized parties to lean back toward a concern with social welfare, a tendency by party structure that was then duplicated in both the North and the South.[16]

---

[15] This was Republican activists in organized parties in the North on social welfare (Table 3.5A4).

[16] And just to extend this individualized tour of activist populations, the Democratic population closest to an ideological balance between the two domains was Democratic activists from organized parties in the North (Table 3.5A1), while the Republican population closet to ideological balance was Republican activists from organized parties in the North (again Table 3.5A1).

Those are some products from searching for the impact of party structure on the transmission of policy preferences when social welfare and
cultural values are considered in tandem, rather than one at a time.
The results are mostly additive in a straightforward fashion. Knowing
each story individually, the analyst knows their collective story as well.
Yet there are additional aspects of the impact of party structure that are
difficult to perceive when proceeding domain by domain. The more
numerous examples involve individual partisan populations that put
these domains together in a distinctive – and deviant – fashion. The
more consequential examples involve larger social processes, affecting
entire policy domains, that are furthered or constrained by one or the
other party type.

At a minimum, the peculiar roles of certain individual populations
are far easier to perceive when presented this way. Realm by realm, it
would be very difficult to appreciate the distinctive place of Northern
Democratic activists from volunteer parties on cultural values, Southern
Democratic activists from organized parties on social welfare, or
Southern Republican activists from volunteer parties in both domains
simultaneously. Beyond that, consideration of the two domains jointly is
essential to perceiving the different developmental roles that organized
versus volunteer parties play in established versus emergent realms of
policy conflict. Presented this way, organized parties now show up as
more focused on the older issue of social welfare, while volunteer parties
are more focused on the newer issue of cultural values, where "old" and
"new" refer to the time when comprehensive partisan alignments were
achieved.

### The Partisan Evolution of Comprehensive Ideologies

There is another, wholly different means of mobilizing two major policy
domains to examine the representational impact of party structures. This
approach turns the preceding on its head, using those two domains not
to produce individual scores for simultaneous comparison but rather
to generate *axes* that situate individuals respondents within a two-
dimensional policy space. Because the quadrants of this space correspond
rather neatly with the comprehensive ideologies common to American
politics across the postwar years, the analysis can move on to consider the
changing fortunes of these ideologies themselves. And the relationship
between organized versus volunteer parties within these larger ideologies
can then move to the center of the analysis.

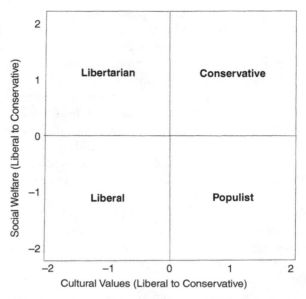

FIGURE 3.5 Ideologies in Two Dimensions: Social Welfare and Cultural Values

In principle, there are many ways to do this. In practice, one simple approach can instantiate those major ideologies while guaranteeing that the analysis of their evolution remains explicit, transparent, and data driven. To repeat: this involves deriving the requisite two-dimensional framework by using social welfare and cultural values as axes that scale the *joint* preferences of survey respondents. Those left of the zero point on each dimension are coded as liberal; those right of the zero point are coded as conservative. Those favoring expansion of the welfare state are the liberals on social welfare, while those favoring individual responsibility are the conservatives. Those favoring individual autonomy are the liberals on cultural values, while those favoring collective norms are the conservatives. Figure 5 sets out the underlying template for this kind of analysis.[17] Ideological designations are then formalistic and

[17] Two previous incarnations are Edward G. Carmines, Michael J. Ensley, and Michael W. Wagner, "Political Ideology in American Politics: One, Two, or None?" *The Forum* 10(2012), Issue 3, Article 4, and William J. M. Claggett, Pär Jason Engle, and Byron E. Shafer, "The Evolution of Mass Ideologies in Modern American Politics," *The Forum* 12(2014), Issue 2, Article 2.

straightforward.[18] Within this framework, those who are left of the national average on both dimensions are *Liberals*. Those who are right of the national average on both dimensions are *Conservatives*. Those who are left of the national average on social welfare but right of it on cultural values are *Populists*. And those who are right of the national average on social welfare but left of it on cultural values are *Libertarians*. Sophisticated students of these ideologies could no doubt add further twists to their definition, but this stripped-out approach does guarantee that all individuals can in effect self-locate in ideological space, while the analyst can both track the evolution of these larger ideologies and, most crucially, go on to ask about the contribution of party structure to that evolution.

What emerges first is a picture of the overall context contributed by comprehensive ideologies to postwar politics. In the immediate postwar years, the ideological struggle at the mass level pitted Populists against Conservatives (Figure 3.6A). There was, however, a substantial leaven of Libertarians within this general public, with Liberals, though hardly absent, clearly bringing up the rear. Such a picture would come to seem anomalous when viewed through the ideological lens of party positions in the modern era. Yet in the immediate postwar years, it looked like nothing so much as a world in which the class-based divisions crystalized by the New Deal were alive and well.[19] Thus many cultural liberals were found among the economically better off – and therefore among economic conservatives – while many cultural conservatives were found among their opposite numbers, the economic liberals. A politics of Conservatism versus Populism, with a healthy leaven of Libertarianism, seems fully appropriate to such a world.

Within a further generation, however, the popularity of those ideological combinations had begun to shift (Figure 3.6B). In truth, Conservatives

---

[18] Comprehensive investigations within this approach would include Byron E. Shafer and Richard H. Spady, *The American Political Landscape* (Cambridge, MA: Harvard University Press, 2014), and Carmines, Ensley, and Wagner, *Beyond The Left-Right Divide*.

[19] These are helpfully gathered in relevant chapters in Michael Barone, *OUR COUNTRY: The Shaping of America from Roosevelt to Reagan* (New York: Free Press, 1990). For a detailed portrait at one point in time, Alonzo L. Hamby, *Man Of The People: The Life of Harry S. Truman* (New York: Oxford University Press, 1995). The great student of ideology in American party politics is John Gerring, in *Party Ideologies In America, 1828–1996* (New York: Cambridge University Press, 1998), here most directly in his chapters on "The Neoliberal Epoch" among Republicans and "The Populist Epoch" among Democrats.

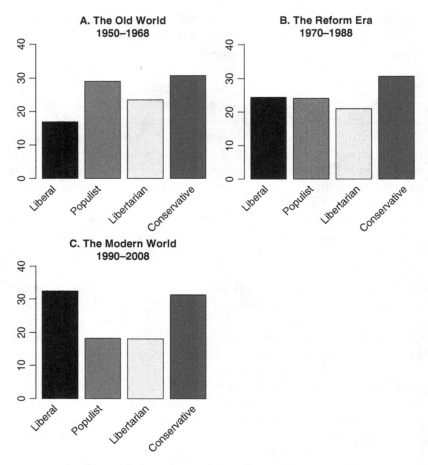

FIGURE 3.6  Ideologies across Time: Shares of American Society

and Libertarians still looked much as they had in the old world. But Populists were evidently in decline while Liberals were on the rise. When the analytic focus was still on the combination of social welfare and cultural values as individual scales (as in the preceding section), the most striking characteristic of this reform period was a plunge to the left on culture by Democratic activists. Now considered through a distribution of comprehensive ideologies instead, a growth in the number of true Liberals should not be surprising: those Democratic activists, already liberal on economics, were becoming much more liberal on culture as well. At the same time, the shift back toward the center by Republican activists on social welfare had apparently stabilized the distribution of Conservatives and Libertarians.[20] As a result, Figure 3.6B strongly suggests that the growth in Liberals during the reform period was largely at the expense of previous Populists.

Figure 3.6C then brings a sharply different modern world into focus. Now, the two dominant ideological groupings are not Conservatives and Populists, but rather Conservatives and *Liberals*. In that sense, the growth ideology across all the postwar years was clearly Liberalism, while the great decline occurred within Populism. Though in fact, the modern era was actually hard on both off-diagonal blocs, the Populists and the Libertarians.[21] It was just that never having achieved the predominance of the Populists, the Libertarians did not suffer the same diminishment. Some of them must have prioritized culture over economics sufficiently to migrate to the Liberal cluster; they would have been joined there by a much larger body of former Populists who prioritized economics over culture enough to move to the Liberal bloc.

Once more, however, this national picture masked some very different developments in the great political regions. With the focus as the four main ideological clusters, the old world was distinguished – perhaps the only time in these early years when this was true – by the fact that the North and the South were *not* powerfully different (Figures 7.A1 and 7.A2). Moreover, as if to emphasize the analytical distinctiveness of this focus on comprehensive ideology, it was the *South* that stereotypically exemplified the national pattern. There, Populism truly faced off against Conservatism, with the other ideologies relegated to a back seat.

[20] The Democratic part of this story has attracted more scholarly attention, as with Jeffrey Berry, *The New Liberalism: The Rising Power of Citizen Groups* (Washington, DC: Brookings Institution, 1999). Gerring, *Party Ideologies in America*, pulls important parts of the story together in his chapter on "The Universalist Epoch." For the other side of the partisan aisle, Charles O. Jones, *The Republican Party in American Politics* (New York: Macmillan, 1965), and Robert Mason, *The Republican Party And American Politics From Hoover To Reagan* (Cambridge: Cambridge University Press, 2012).

[21] Comprehensive histories with temporal detachment are inevitably in short supply, but many aspects of the modern background story can be gleaned from comprehensive studies of presidential campaigns, as with Richard Johnston, Michael G. Hagen, and Kathleen Hall Jamieson, *The 2000 Presidential Election And The Foundations Of Party Politics* (New York: Cambridge University Press, 2004); John Sides and Lynn Vavreck, *THE GAMBLE: Choice and Chance in the 2012 Presidential Election* (Princeton: Princeton University Press, 2013); and James W. Ceaser, Andrew E. Busch, and John J. Pitney Jr., *Defying The Odds: The 2016 Election and American Politics* (Lanham, MD: Rowman & Littlefield, 2017).

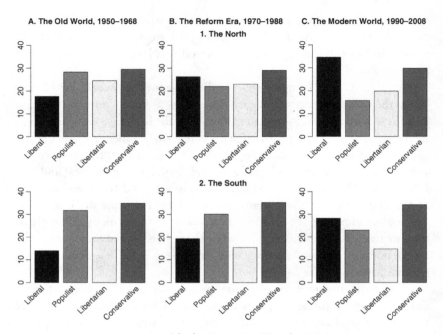

FIGURE 3.7  Ideologies across Time by Region

By comparison, the North was kinder to these residual ideologies, Libertarianism and Liberalism, though its ideological politics too remained anchored by Populists and Conservatives.

The two regions then parted company in the middle period, our reform era. Yet once again, where the leading change in this era in so many other regards was the transformation of the South, it was instead the South that remained closer to the old order when the focus was mass ideologies (Figures 7.B1 and 7.B2). So, the South still embodied the national picture from the old world, with Populism and Conservatism continuing to anchor ideological conflict. In sharp contrast, the North was previewing what would come to be recognized as the modern pattern. In this, Liberalism was already challenging Conservatism as dominant ideologies, though the North also featured the closest balance among the four ideological families of any region at any time.

In any case, it was the North that proved ultimately to be a harbinger for the modern world. In this world, the two regions moved back toward each other, and thus back toward the regional convergence that characterized their positions on individual policy domains in the modern era

(Figures 7.C1 and 7.C2). Although in common with regional portraits in those individual domains, the two regions did sustain residual but obvious differences in their ideological balance. Liberalism and Conservatism were now the dominant ideologies in both regions, with Populism and Libertarianism clearly secondary. That much was no longer different. The two regions went on to balance these developments in opposite fashions. So Liberalism fared even better in the North and Conservatism in the South, just as Libertarianism survived more vitally in the North, while Populism retained its strongest remaining hold in the South.

## The Plight of the Populists

Those pictures present the context – they set the stage – for an investigation of the impact of party structure, this time on the democratic representation of comprehensive ideologies. And the analytic crux of this investigation is immediately and painfully clear. Where Populism was one of two ideologies contending for national dominance in mass politics during the immediate postwar years, it had been reduced in the modern era to the status of even a serious secondary presence in only one region, the American South. So the question immediately becomes: did structural differences between the two major parties, along with the changing mix of organized and volunteer parties for the nation as a whole, make a contribution to this ideological evolution, most pointedly as embodied in the diminishment of Populism?

As with the analysis of policy domains, there was no reason to believe that party structure dominated the felt needs of major social groups or that it could consistently cancel the influence of major issues of the day. Instead and once again, the question is whether structural impacts can be teased out from within these other, often prior, influences on American politics. Though in the case of comprehensive ideologies and especially with a focus on the great change in the fortunes of Populism, the specific measure of concern is the share of Populists found in various populations inside both major parties. Unlike the situation for social welfare or cultural values individually, however, an attempt to address this question requires initial attention to a different aspect of party structure, namely, the simple generic difference – and here, tension – between activists and their own rank and file. Table 3.6 turns first to this opening structural question.

In fact, the larger structural impact on the representation of Populists resides fundamentally in this elite-mass disjunction, one remarkably

TABLE 3.6 *The Plight of the Populists*

**A. Party Structure and Populist Fortunes in the Full Partisan Array**

|  | Democratic Activists | Democratic Rank & File | Republican Rank & File | Republican Activists |
|---|---|---|---|---|
| Populists, 1950–1968 | .34 | .35 | .22 | .15 |
| Populists, 1970–1988 | .21 | .31 | .20 | .11 |
| Populists, 1990–2008 | .14 | .22 | .15 | .07 |

**B. Party Structure and Populist Fortunes among Partisan Activists**

|  | 1. The North | | | | 2. The South | | | |
|---|---|---|---|---|---|---|---|---|
|  | Democratic Activists | | Republican Activists | | Democratic Activists | | Republican Activists | |
|  | Org. | Vol. | Org. | Vol. | Org. | Vol. | Org. | Vol. |
| Populists, 1950–1968 | .37 | .33 | .19 | .10 | .35 | .24 | * | * |
| Populists, 1970–1988 | .21 | .19 | .13 | .10 | .30 | .27 | .13 | .12 |
| Populists, 1990–2008 | .14 | .09 | .12 | .06 | .25 | .19 | .06 | .06 |

deleterious to Populism (Table 3.6A). The Democratic Party actually did a reasonably good job of reflecting the views and preferences of its Populist adherents in the immediate postwar years, 1950–1968. This was never true among Republicans, and the bottom was to fall out among Democrats too after this initial period. By the reform era, 1970–1988, Populists were strikingly underrepresented among Democrats and miserably underrepresented among Republicans. In the modern period, 1990–2008, things only got worse.

Among Democrats, party activists managed to deny rank and file Populists a major share of their numerical entitlement in both the reform era and the modern world. Among Republicans, the counterpart damage was even greater. Both active parties shared an activist hostility toward an ideology that was nevertheless serious within their respective rank and files. To say the same thing differently, among Democrats, the rank and file lost a third of its Populists over time (from .35 to .22) but 60 percent of their representation within the active party (from .34 to .14). Republicans had fewer Populists among their adherents to begin with, but while the Republican rank and file lost a third even of these over time (from .22 to .15), it lost fully half of their (always lesser) representatives within the active party (from .15 to .07).

But did continuing structural differences between organized and volunteer parties have a further impact on the ideological proclivities of these activists? Table 3.6B turns to this question; despite the superficial intricacy of the setup, the further story of Populist fortunes is simple and brutal. In both geographic regions for both Democrats and Republicans in every political era, Populists fared better in the active parties of organized as opposed to volunteer states. Or, said the other way around, volunteer parties were consistently and continually more unkind to their indigenous Populists when it came to representing the partisan rank and file at the activist level. When applied to both parties in the nation as a whole across the postwar years, then, this key structural distinction brought only more bad news for Populism as an ideology, though the two parties did process this impact in somewhat different fashions.

In both geographic regions, the natural home of these Populists was the Democratic Party, though their presence was not negligible among Republicans. Regardless, the evolving situation by party structure is easily summarized. Among Democrats in the North, volunteer parties contributed an additional increment to the decline of Populism in every period (Table 3.6B1). This effect was modest but consistent across periods, actually growing in the modern era. Among Republicans in the North, the same effect was more brutal (Table 3.6B1). In two of our three eras, the Populist presence among active Republicans in the North was literally halved within volunteer parties.

Among Democrats in the South, where Populism had its deepest roots, this same structural effect surfaced in a similar fashion, in what should have been happier territory (Table 3.6A2). As in the North, organized parties were more responsive and volunteer parties less so at the activist level. Only among Southern Republicans was this structural effect missing, yet the main point here is that its absence hardly mattered. In the old world, Republican activism as a whole had been derisory. By the time there was an active Republican Party, in the reform period, classic Populism had become irrelevant to its fortunes. And back behind all those direct impacts was the growth of volunteer parties and the shrinkage of their organized counterparts, inflicting a further major, but largely hidden damage on the prospects of the surviving Populists.

## NATIONAL SECURITY

When it came to the policy domain of cultural values, scholarly analysts differed over the diagnostic substance from which to derive appropriate measures of an underlying dimension of policy preferences. When it comes to our last major domain of policy conflict during the postwar years, foreign affairs, analysts differed instead over whether to treat it as possessing an ongoing dimension of policy preferences at all.[22] Few analysts of postwar American political history would have regarded foreign affairs as inconsequential. Yet there were serious scholars who treated public preferences on foreign policy as inherently episodic, being triggered by extra-national crises and limited intrinsically by the nature and duration of these. Just as there were other scholars who regarded foreign affairs as a home ground for what are known as "valence issues," where public opinion centers not so much on policy preferences as on judgments about performance, that is, simple success or failure.

There were also scholars, among whom we obviously number, who regarded foreign affairs as a separate realm for policy conflict, one where the public might reasonably have continuing preferences that members could in turn apply to subsequent events and which might (or might not) be drawn into any particular partisan alignment, thereby becoming subject to the filtering impact of party structure. In this view, conflicts over issues of international relations had been regularly present in postwar American politics, so that they certainly had the *potential* to generate or reflect a pattern of continuing preferences within the general public.[23] That would make foreign affairs little different from our other great policy realms – social welfare, civil rights, and cultural values – which can likewise be conceptualized as ongoing dimensions of public

[22] Substantial efforts to organize this conceptual minefield include Jon Hurwitz and Mark Peffley, "How Are Foreign Policy Attitudes Structured: A Hierarchical Model," *American Political Science Review* 81(1987), 1099–1120; Barbara A. Bardes and Robert W. Oldendick, "Public Opinion and Foreign Policy: A Field in Search of Theory," *Research In Micropolitics* 3(1990), 227–247; Ronald H. Hinckley, *People, Polls, And Policymakers: American Public Opinion and National Security* (New York: Lexington, 1992); Ole R. Holsti, *Public Opinion And American Foreign Policy* (Ann Arbor: University of Michigan Press, 1996); and Bruce W. Jentleson, *American Foreign Policy: Dynamics of Choice in the 21st Century* (New York: W. W. Norton, 2000).

[23] That the policy domain itself was perennial and intrusive across all the postwar years was rarely at issue. Among many: John Lewis Gaddis, *The United States and The Origins Of The Cold War, 1941–1947* (New York: Columbia University Press, 1972); Alonzo L. Hamby, *The Imperial Years: The United States since 1939* (New York: Weybright & Talley, 1976); Robert A. Pastor, *Congress and the Politics of U.S. Foreign Economic Policy, 1929–1976* (Berkeley: University of California Press, 1980); Gaddis, *Surprise, Security, And The American Experience* (Cambridge, MA: Harvard University, 2004).

opinion crystalized by specific incidents and embodied in concrete policies.

As with our other major domains, then, proceedings begin with a formal definition of the realm of international relations and foreign policy:

*International Relations* involves connections between the United States and the non-American world. Foreign policy thus reflects efforts to manage the interaction of the United States – its government, its citizens, and their organizations – with the same elements of other nations.[24]

Approached this way, public preferences in international relations do have a less simple dimensionality than that in any of the three other main policy realms.[25] Yet the Claggett and Shafer analyses from which we derive our measures do highlight policy issues of *national security* as the leading dimension within the domain, that is, the cluster of opinions most often central to preferences on foreign policy and a substantive cluster that continues (and can be measured) across all the postwar years. This allows us to proceed with the current inquiry into national patterns of opinion, regional distinctions within the nation, partisan differences within the regions, and most consequentially the cut between – the filtering effect of – alternative models of party structure.

Moreover, the available measure of policy preferences on national security is straightforward and easily recognized, running across all the postwar years in a substantively consistent form. Early marker items were focused on the Cold War, itself impressively long running, while later markers were focused on defense preparedness and a willingness to use the resulting instruments of force. Cold War items did vary in terms of their foreign referents – Russia, Korea, Cuba, Vietnam, Afghanistan – as well as their focus – trade, negotiation, containment, threat, but all correlated and all aligned. The defense marker most commonly used after the Cold War is even more straightforward, involving generic national defense. Fortunately, because the key item entered ANES surveys before the Cold War ended, correlation and alignment with those earlier items can be guaranteed:

Some people believe that we should spend much less money for defense. Others feel that defense spending should be greatly increased.[26]

---

[24] Claggett and Shafer, *The American Public Mind,* 5, as slightly edited here.
[25] Ibid., chap. 2.
[26] Wording did wobble a bit in the earliest years, before settling down in 1980 into its continuing format. Permutations are covered in ibid., 50.

## The Old World: Partisan Alignments and Party Structures

When the postwar period began, issues of social welfare already offered a strong partisan alignment for the nation as a whole. Democratic and Republican rank and files leaned clearly if modestly left and right, while Democratic and Republican activists flanked them in the same fashion, though it was Republican activists who contributed most of this further polarization in these early years. At the time, civil rights offered only a pale copy of the same pattern, probably strong enough to be considered by contemporaries, certainly strong enough to be recognized by analysts looking backward. And our third domain, cultural values, was simply unaligned. All four of its partisan populations sat close to the national average, no reasonable patterning could be imputed to the tiny residual differences, and even hindsight would not change this perception.

In this initial sense, national security looked most like cultural values when the focus was the nation as a whole (Figures 3.8A and 3.8B). Indeed, its four partisan populations managed to be even closer to the national average, such that imputing a consistent pattern to them would have seemed truly fanciful. Seen from a modern world in which national security too is fully aligned and seriously polarized in partisan terms, this lack of overall differentiation might appear anomalous; we know that foreign policy can be infused by as much partisan bite as any other policy realm. Yet the context of that time was very different. Most Americans had just endured – and few families had been untouched by – a worldwide international conflict, and many had lived through a Great Depression before that. So a sense of commonality with regard to the outside world should at the very least not seem strange.[27]

On the other hand and very unlike cultural values, this initial picture of nonalignment disappeared when the nation was divided back into its two main geographic regions. With cultural values, a lack of national alignment reflected nonalignments in both major regions. With national security, national nonalignment instead reflected *opposite* patterns by region: left to right in the North but right to left in the South (Figures 3.8C and

---

[27] David M. Kennedy, *Freedom From Fear: The American People in Depression and War* (New York: Oxford University Press, 1999), is a rich introduction to the context of the time. Moreover, there remained some genuine deference to the old adage of that day that "Politics stops at the water's edge." Senator Arthur H. Vandenberg, R-MI, uttered that specific language in his introduction on May 11, 1948, to what became known as the Vandenberg Resolution (S. Res. 23) to the Senate Foreign Relations Committee, a keystone in the creation of major international security institutions for the postwar world.

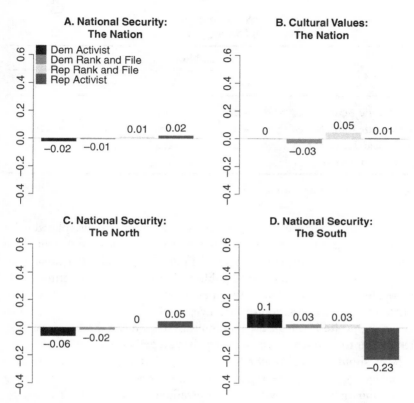

FIGURE 3.8 Partisan Populations and Issue Alignments: National Security in the Old World, 1950–1968

3.8D). The general public, that is, the two partisan rank and files, still alignment in all three places – the nation, the North, and the South. So it was partisan activists who created opposing regional pictures, and while these pictures remained a pale version of what would characterize the domain subsequently, they were indeed opposite. In the North, active Democrats were modestly dovish, being less enthusiastic about a strong defense, while active Republicans were modestly hawkish, being clearly if still modestly more enthusiastic (Figure 3.8C). In the South, active Democrats were the ones who were clearly hawkish, while active Republicans were even more strongly dovish (Figure 3.8D).

In the abstract and in isolation, this regional disjunction could be treated as a surprise and an anomaly. Yet in the context of its time, this difference too followed more or less naturally from diverse regional histories and

TABLE 3.7 *Party Structures and Issue Alignments:*
*National Security, 1950–1968*

| | A. North | | B. South | |
|---|---|---|---|---|
| | Org. | Vol. | Org. | Vol. |
| Democratic Activists | –.08 | –.02 | +.10 | +.17 |
| Democratic Rank & File | –.03 | .00 | .00 | +.10 |
| Republican Rank & File | +.05 | –.04 | +.02 | * |
| Republican Activists | +.10 | .00 | * | * |

* Ns too small for reliable analysis.

mixed regional alliances that were not yet dominated – disciplined – by a nationwide partisan alignment. To wit: in the practical politics of these early postwar years, the main support for pursuit of a Cold War came from the Democratic South and the Republican Northeast, two longtime internationalist areas, while the main opposition came from their respective hinterlands, where isolationism had deep roots.[28] What they added up to was an opposite ideological positioning by region for the active parties, netting out to zero when they were put back together nationally.

So it should probably not be surprising that a further division into organized versus volunteer parties did not impose any comprehensive patterning on a realm of weak and contradictory alignments (Table 3.7). Even in these early days and in such an unpromising context, some structural effects appeared. Once again, the most substantial involved organized parties in the North, where a modest version of the overall alignment on social welfare was already in evidence, if anyone had had the prescience to perceive it (Table 3.7A). It was nowhere near as strong as the counterpart alignment among Northern organized parties on social welfare, where these parties really *constituted* the national alignment. But it was actually stronger than the Northern counterpart on civil rights. So once again, the harbinger of modern national alignments was already

[28] These divisions could already be perceived in the prewar battles over neutrality versus rearmament: Robert A. Divine, *The Illusion Of Neutrality* (Chicago: University of Chicago Press, 1962). For the South in foreign affairs during the immediate postwar period, Ira Katznelson, *Fear Itself: The New Deal and the Origins of Our Time* (New York: W. W. Norton, 2013); for the North, Lawrence S. Kaplan, *The Conversion of Arthur h. Vandenberg: From Isolation to International Engagement* (Lexington: University Press of Kentucky, 2015).

present in organized parties of the North, even for the domain of national security, even if volunteer parties showed no such alignment, and even if no one outside those parties could have been expected to believe it.

Further parallels to other policy domains could be noticed by hindsight, though none of them would have provided any obvious window on the future. The largest of these was the way that volunteer parties in the (still solidly Democratic) South anchored the ideological right on national security for the nation as a whole (Table 3.7B). Absent a countervailing national party program and in the presence of a very conservative regional base, these Southern volunteer activists did on national security what they also did on civil rights. By contrast, volunteer parties in the North were more or less the perfect picture of nonalignment, rather than actually resisting a national alignment as they did with social welfare or incubating a new one as they did with civil rights. And organized parties in the South were likewise unaligned, except for their reliably conservative active Democrats: on social welfare, civil rights, cultural values, and now national security as well.

## The Reformed World: Partisan Alignments and Party Structures

The coming of the reformed world brought the rudiments of a conventional partisan alignment to the domain of national security (Figures 3.9A and 3.9B). Nationwide, the two rank and files were clearly if still moderately polarized in the orthodox fashion, Democrats to the left and Republicans to the right. Party activists, nearly indistinguishable in the old world, were now well apart, though this was overwhelmingly a contribution from Democratic activists: Republican activists were ever so slightly to the *left* of their rank and file.[29] So those changes raised the possibility that national security would ultimately move toward a common alignment with social welfare and civil rights, though a more realistic judgment in its time would still have emphasized similarity to cultural values.

Social welfare had begun with a fully realized partisan alignment in the form that would become recognized as the modern template, an alignment

---

[29] For the larger milieu from which this impetus emerged: Charles DeBenedetti, *An American Ordeal: The Antiwar Movement of the Vietnam Era* (Syracuse: Syracuse University Press, 1990). For general successors: Michael T. Heaney, *PARTY IN THE STREET: The Antiwar Movement and the Democratic Party after 9/11* (New York: Cambridge University Press, 2015), for which Vietnam protests provided an important context.

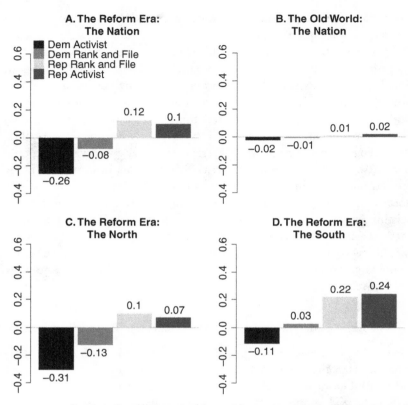

FIGURE 3.9 Partisan Populations and Issue Alignments: National Security in the Reform Era, 1970–1988

that would only become both more polarized and more symmetric during the reform era. Civil rights had begun with a pale copy of the welfare alignment, and while this acquired some greater parallels during the reform era, the familiar leftward plunge by Democratic activists was so extreme here as to sustain the possibility that this domain would end up in some other formation. Cultural values, finally, had shown no inkling of a similar alignment during the immediate postwar years, and no movement toward the conventional pattern in the reform era either, with the exception of its version of the general plunge leftward among Democratic activists.

So if national security showed more of an incipient partisan alignment than cultural values during the reform era, it was still more like cultural values than like social welfare or civil rights. What national security also had was one major development that it shared with the issue alignments that were new to the postwar period and that none of them shared with social welfare. This was that common leftward leap by Democratic activists. Yet its evolutionary implications were doubly obscure in the realm of national security. Not only was no other partisan population behaving in a fashion similar to these Democratic activists, but Republican activists were actually doing something different, staying ever so slightly to the left of their own rank and file nationally, and thus no further from the *Democratic* rank and file than those autonomously polarizing Democratic activists.

When the focus shifts to geographic regions within the nation, however, it becomes clear that the main previous difference on national security, the one that had aligned the two great regions in opposite ideological directions, had been obliterated. So one major change involved striking down those previous alignments by region, the ones that had distinguished national security from all other policy domains. Yet there was a second major change that instead introduced a familiar regional difference, into national security this time. That was an ideological difference by region as a whole rather than by party within regions, a difference that was already familiar from the domains of civil rights and cultural values. This was the tendency for all four partisan populations to be more liberal in the North and more conservative in the South. That was unequivocally the story for cultural values. It became unequivocally the story for national security too (Figures 3.9C and 3.9D).

So what was regional convergence in one aspect of their alignments became regional divergence in the other. Otherwise, Democratic activists were now the left and Republican activists were now the right on national security in both regions, wiping out the old reverse alignment while contributing yet another transformation in the politics of the South (Figures 3.9C and 3.9D). If this realignment was not as striking as the Southern transformations on social welfare and civil rights – though not cultural values, which remained essentially stable – it was still a total reversal of the old order on national security in the South. Moreover, its realization required both activist populations to travel all the way across the ideological center, with active Democrats moving right to left (+.10 to −.11) and active Republicans moving even more aggressively right (from −.23 to +.24). At the same time, the reform period saw another ideological distinction familiar to the other great policy domains being imported, stereotypically, into national security as well.

TABLE 3.8 *Party Structures and Issue Alignments:*
*National Security, 1970–1988*

| | A. North | | B. South | |
|---|---|---|---|---|
| | Org. | Vol. | Org. | Vol. |
| Democratic Activists | −.26 | −.31 | −.17 | −.12 |
| Democratic Rank & File | −.03 | −.14 | +.03 | +.03 |
| Republican Rank & File | +.16 | +.09 | +.23 | +.20 |
| Republican Activists | +.25 | +.06 | +.19 | +.31 |

That summary sets the stage for a look at the contribution of a changing party structure to the changing partisan alignment characterizing national security in the reform period.[30] The clearest element of constancy among the four moving pieces – organized and volunteer parties in the North and the South – involved organized parties in the North (Table 3.8A). What had seemed remarkably prescient in the old world, namely an alignment equivalent to those that would surface in every policy domain by the time of the modern world, was not just still present but evidently expanded in the reform period. And this was a case where appearances were not deceiving: a previously modest gap between partisan rank and files in the old world had more than doubled in its successor, from .08 to .19, while a previously clearer if still moderate gap between activist populations had nearly tripled, from .18 to .51 (Tables 3.7A and 3.8A).

By contrast, it was all change for *volunteer* parties in the North. In the old world, what had distinguished them from organized counterparts was a pattern of complete nonalignment – four partisan populations sitting more or less exactly on the national average. In the reform period, these parties drifted toward the pattern characteristic of other policy domains, abandoning their previous disengagement. The two rank and files were now clearly distinguished in the familiar left/right direction. And the

[30] For a sense of the larger environment for making foreign policy during our modern era, see Hal Brands, *Making The Unipolar Moment: U.S. Foreign Policy and the Rise of the Post-Cold War Order* (Ithaca: Cornell University Press, 2016). Two comprehensive surveys of policy conflicts in this period are Bruce W. Jentleson, *American Foreign Policy: The Dynamics of Choice in the 21st Century*, 5th ed. (New York: W. W. Norton, 2013), and Stephen W. Hook and John Spanier, *American Foreign Policy Since World War II*, 20th ed. (Washington, DC: CQ Press, 2015).

leftward plunge among Democratic activists was not just reflected but exaggerated for volunteer parties: from -.08 to -.26 among organized party activists, but from -.02 to -.31 among volunteer counterparts (again Tables 3.7A and 3.8A). So Northern Democratic activists in volunteer parties, having sat on the national average in the old world, became the most liberal partisan population in the reform period. In the process, volunteer party structure thus continued to advantage new issues at the cost of social welfare – while organized parties still did the reverse.

The South then recapitulated its previous mix of changes within the region, coupled with maintenance of differences between regions, capped off by a distinctively Southern version of the further difference between organized and volunteer parties (Table 3.8B). Within the region, both organized and volunteer parties moved toward their versions of the national alignment, left to right from active Democrats to active Republicans. At the same time, both party types retained a regional distinction by anchoring these new alignments in more conservative territory vis-à-vis the North, now in all *eight* available comparisons (Tables 3.8B and 3.8A). While this continuing effect was not so serious as to keep Southern Democratic activists on the conservative side of the national average – they were now at -.17 and -.12 – their rank and files did remain on that conservative side (at +.03 and +.03). So if Southern Democratic activists in both party types were now on the liberal side of the ideological spectrum, they were alone there by comparison to the rest of their region.

Yet in reaching this mix of new and old arrangements, the South saw the two party types end up in what would have been a stereotypical position for aligned issues in the old but not the new world. For this, Democratic activists in organized parties moved well left of any other Southern partisan population on national security. Yet Republican activists in those same organized parties were much more moderate than their volunteer counterparts – to the point of being more moderate than their own rank and file. As in the old order, so in the reform era: the policy links between partisan populations and policy preferences, as filtered by alternative models of party structure, were thus reversed in the North and the South. The North featured volunteer parties as more responsive to new issues and less interested in established party positions, with organized parties more concerned with the national party program and hence more attached to the old issues. The South instead featured organized parties skewing more toward the national picture on both old and new issues – as indeed it had for both social welfare and civil rights.

Even in its time, some of this change must have seemed a simple time lag: Northern parties had indeed come into the evolving postwar issue alignment earlier than Southern counterparts in every policy domain, just as some change was surely the response of different underlying societies: volunteer parties would skew to the left in the region that itself skewed more in that direction, just as volunteer parties would skew more to the right in the region that itself skewed that way. Either way or together, the two effects made party structure in the reform period work in an opposite fashion, North versus South.

### The Modern World: Partisan Alignments and Party Structures

The story of national security and party politics in the modern world then changed again, becoming one of symmetric partisan alignment with sharply increased polarization. A weak alignment coupled with idiosyncratic extremism by Democratic activists had characterized the reform era (Figure 3.10B). A fully symmetric and strongly polarized alignment integrating all four partisan populations now characterized the modern world (Figure 3.10A). Within this modern alignment, the distance between policy preferences among partisan rank and files had more than doubled, from .20 to .46. The distance between partisan activists had doubled as well, from .36 to .73. Though in both cases but especially within the active parties, by far the larger ideological moves had been contributed by Republicans, not Democrats, this time.

That left the two rank and files *and* the two activist populations more polarized on national security than on cultural values, though still not quite as polarized as on social welfare or civil rights. The dominant point was that differences by policy realm were no longer major. The regional story beneath this new national picture then added another embodiment of increasingly parallel – indeed converging – partisan alignments, albeit still anchored in different ideological territory (Figures 3.10C and 3.10D). On the one hand, both main measures of partisan polarization were now approaching equality as between political regions. Which is to say: the distances between partisan rank and files in the North and the South were roughly the same, as were the distances between partisan activists. On the other hand, every partisan population in the South remained more conservative in its policy preferences than its counterpart in the North.

By extension, this meant that the active Democratic Party in the North fronted the left on national security, while the active Republican Party in the South fronted the right. As we shall see, this was really a matter of

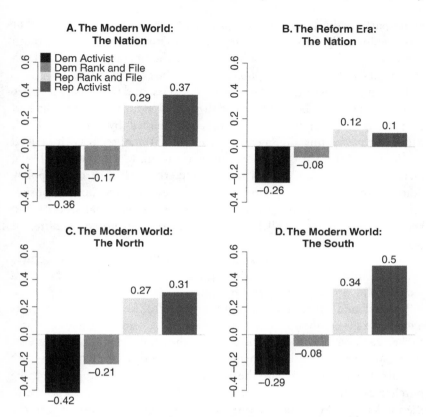

FIGURE 3.10 Partisan Populations and Issue Alignments: National Security in the Modern World, 1990–2008

volunteer party structures: active Northern Democrats in volunteer parties versus active Southern Republicans in volunteer parties as well. But first, the point is that in the three other policy domains, the ideological extremes belonged uniformly to the South, with activist Southern Democrats on the left and activist Southern Republicans on the right. So the extremism of Democratic activists in the North on national security stood out additionally – strongly off to the left of their own rank and file, far away from the Democratic rank and file in the South.

Neither similarities nor differences, however, should be allowed to mask the huge change that these new national and regional alignments collectively confirmed. In the immediate postwar years, national security was simply not a partisan matter. Every partisan population for the nation as a whole sat nearly on the national average in its policy preferences, while party activists in the regions actually showed an alignment that was ideologically opposite, North versus South (Figure 3.8). Northern Democrats and Southern Republicans were the liberals, while Southern Democrats and Northern Republicans were the conservatives.

In the modern world, all of that was gone. First and foremost, the entire policy domain had been infused with the partisan alignment that had characterized social welfare in the world shaped by the New Deal. Moreover, when this alignment surfaced on national security, it arrived not in an incipient or even an evolutionary form, but in the full-blown, increasingly polarized fashion that characterized all four major policy domains in the modern period. In the process, the old (and opposite) difference between active parties in the regions on national security had been supplanted by parallel alignments merely anchored in different ideological territory.

So that was the larger partisan framework within which party structures had to contribute any further filtering influences (Figure 3.11). National security did offer one noteworthy anomaly in the patterning of these influences, an anomaly present in no other realm. Republican activists as a whole had been notably moderate during the reform era, standing closer to their rank and file than activists in any other policy realm as well as ever so slightly out of overall alignment, standing slightly to the left of this rank and file (Figure 3.9). Beneath the surface, however, this had proved to be purely a Northern phenomenon. The overall anomaly had disappeared in the modern world (Figure 3.10A), as had its general embodiment in the North (Figure 3.10C). What survived was only a strong structural echo, in which Northern Republican activists *in organized parties* were still obviously out of sync with the modern national alignment, and now well left of their rank and file within the region (Figure 3.11A).

With this anomaly noted, however, the story of the impact of party structure was otherwise familiar. Once again, party structure made clear and autonomous contributions to partisan polarization as between the two major parties, to the representational gap within each of them, and to the behavior of specific partisan populations. As in the preceding era, party activists were further apart – more extreme – in volunteer as opposed to organized parties in both the North and the South (Figures 3.11A1 and 3.11B1 versus 3.11A2 and 3.11B2). So this fundamental difference in the representational impact of party structure was now present with national security and not just social welfare, civil rights, and cultural values.

As in the preceding era, party activists were likewise further from their own rank and file in volunteer versus organized states (Figures 3.11A1 and

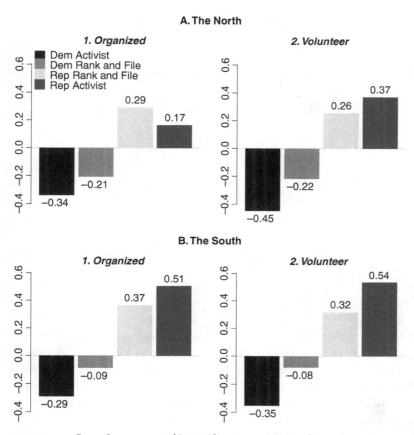

A. The North

1. Organized

Dem Activist
Dem Rank and File
Rep Rank and File
Rep Activist

0.29
0.17
−0.21
−0.34

2. Volunteer

0.37
0.26
−0.22
−0.45

B. The South

1. Organized

0.51
0.37
−0.09
−0.29

2. Volunteer

0.54
0.32
−0.08
−0.35

FIGURE 3.11 Party Structures and Issue Alignments: National Security, 1990–2008

3.11B1 versus 3.11A2 and 3.11B2). This was true of Republicans, and it was true of Democrats. It was true in the South, and it was true in the North, where that anomaly among Republican activists from organized parties actually magnified the effect.

By extension, then, Republican activists from volunteer parties in the South were still the leading hawks among partisan populations, now ever further to the right, while Democratic activists from volunteer parties in the North were still the leading doves, now ever further to the left. And the disproportionate power of party structure to shape the more emergent rather than the more established policy domains was reaffirmed in yet another policy arena.

# 4

# A Conclusion to the Long War?

## Party Structure and Policy Responsiveness

Once upon a time – and for a very long time – party structure was a central concern of those who followed American politics, both theoretically and practically. The internal structure of political parties was taken to shape what they did in a major way, and what they did was understood to be integral to American democracy. James Bryce in *The American Commonwealth* saw what we have called organized parties as the distinguishing feature of politics in the United States and viewed it as a kind of pathology.[1] Henry Jones Ford in *The Rise and Growth of American Politics* saw the same parties as instead a saving grace, the single feature of politics in America that rescued it from an unworkable Constitution and continuing policy frustration.[2]

By the time Bryce and Jones were writing, however, this intellectual battle had been joined by very practical conflicts over party structure. On the one hand, the resources that sustained machine-type parties and their organized politics had swollen. So the stakes of controlling democratic representation appeared higher than ever, while the wherewithal to filter and constrain that representation was obviously at a peak. On the other hand, there was by then an entire alternative approach to party politics, with its own representational theory and its own electoral constituency. This was Progressivism, with its ideal of enlightened citizens participating actively but voluntarily, as the spirit moved them, in party

---

[1] James Bryce, *The American Commonwealth*, 2 vols. (London: Macmillan and Company, 1888).
[2] Henry Jones Ford, *The Rise and Growth of American Politics* (New York: The Macmillan Company, 1898).

politics. This alternative model came with its own set of admirers, in a rising professional class and an associated body of political intellectuals, just as it came with its own intended differences over the policy ends of a reformed politics, a politics not just cleaner but more modern.[3]

In that sense, the major players on both sides understood that the war between the established organized parties and their rising volunteer alternatives was centrally about the transmission of public wishes into governmental institutions, along with the filtering of those wishes by the active parties along the way. These major players might not have used language that was this theoretical, but both sides saw differences not just in the way that politics was conducted but also in the ends that motivated it and ultimately in the policies that resulted. The ensuing conflict was to be both fundamental and long lasting. Organized parties might never again have the dramatic dominance that characterized them in their nineteenth-century strongholds – the trend over time was certainly toward voluntaristic reform – but the "war" was much more like World War I than World War II, a grinding combat where terrain was won or lost only incrementally and gradually.

The end of World War II diverted both scholarly analysts and active players to other concerns, including demobilization and economic reconversion at home, along with a lasting Cold War abroad. But when a handful of scholars did return to the topic in a more empirical and systematic if still impressionistic fashion, they converged on two discoveries.[4] First, organized parties had survived as a serious force in American politics for much longer than either common wisdom or scholarly lore had suggested. But second, there had indeed finally been a break point around 1970, when the long-bruited triumph of volunteer politics

---

[3] For the Progressive movement, see, among many, Arthur S. Link and Richard L. McCormick, *The Progressives* (Arlington Heights, VA: Harlan David-son, 1983); for their political theory, James W. Ceaser, *Presidiential Selection: Theory and Development* (Princeton: Princeton University Press, 1979); for a marriage of the two, Richard Jensen, "Democracy, Republicanism, and Efficiency: The Values of American Politics, 1885–1930," in Byron E. Shafer and Anthony J. Badger, *Contesting Democracy: Substance and Structure in American Political History, 1775–2000* (Lawrence: University Press of Kansas, 2001).

[4] Most especially for our purposes, James Q. Wilson, *Political Organizations* (New York: Basic Books, 1973); Alan Ware, *The Breakdown of Democratic Party Organization, 1940–1980* (Oxford: Oxford University Press, 1985); and David R. Mayhew, *PLACING PARTIES IN AMERICAN POLITICS: Organization, Electoral Settings, and Government Activity in the Twentieth Century* (Princeton: Princeton University Press, 1986).

did finally occur, later than scholars, journalists, and practitioners had initially perceived but ultimately – and structurally – triumphant.

Having saluted this victory, however, scholars once again turned away from the topic, though they hardly abandoned concerns from the realm of party politics. These were still seen as central to democratic representation. It was just that scholars turned to other aspects of the topic, like the course of issue evolution or the growth of partisan polarization.[5] Active reformers had a late, great, concentrated round of institutional success in the presidential selection reforms of the late 1960s and early 1970s, but even their attention turned elsewhere in the aftermath. So an evolving social science was never driven to generate the systematic indicators that would have commented precisely on this long war. In the absence of that inquiry, thenceforth presumed to be largely historical rather than contemporary in its implications, the impact of structural differences on policy responsiveness and democratic representation in the modern world did not come under the microscope.

That is the point at which *The Long War* and its authors entered – or really just returned to – the story. It (and they) went in search of an array of formal indicators that were widely seen to coincide with organized or volunteer approaches to party structure. These indicators proved less difficult to assemble than they would have been in an earlier period; they scaled collectively in the manner that the reform argument suggested; and the resulting scale went on to confirm the great break in the distribution of party types around 1970 (Chapter 1). That was indeed the point of triumph for the volunteer over the organized model, though as we shall note in an Afterword, the behavioral reality is once again elusive and disputed. Along the way, however, no one bothered to dig into the effects of this shift for the operational practice and policy substance of American politics.

As a result – and this has to be the real justification for the current volume – those indicators and their comprehensive scale simultaneously became available to throw a spotlight on the implications for policy responsiveness inherent in alternative party structures, both before and after the triumph of reform. Fortunately, once this link became the focus

---

[5] As with, for example, Edward G. Carmines and James A. Stimson, *Issue Evolution: Race and the Transformation of American Politics* (Princeton: Princeton University Press, 1989), and Pietro S. Nivola and David W. Brady, eds., *Red And Blue Nation?*, Vol. 1, *Characteristics and Consequences of America's Polarized Politics* (Washington, DC: Brookings Institution, 2006).

of analysis, examples of the impact of alternative structures turned up in numerous incarnations in diverse substantive domains at varying points in time. Different temporal contexts might still prime different structural impacts; that is in some sense the nature of any ongoing politics. Yet the collective essence of these structural impacts is in effect a summary of the consequences of a changing aggregate of party structures.

An effort to pull these impacts back together in concentrated form does demand that we proceed not issue by issue, as in Chapters 2 and 3, but rather as close as we can come to an integrated whole – which is the way politics in all three of our periods actually unfolded. In turn, there must be two parts to any integrated analysis, just as there were two parts to an examination of social welfare, civil rights, cultural values, national security, and the comprehensive ideologies in which they were embedded.

Step one is to begin with the substantive context within which party structure had to make its contributions. Now, though, this must involve all four major domains for policy conflict more or less simultaneously, as a collective backdrop that would evolve across the postwar years. That will occupy the first major section of this chapter. And step two is, of course, to reinsert party structure – the aggregate distinction between organized and volunteer political parties – so as to isolate the role of alternative party models in filtering and even shaping those (now collective) partisan alignments. That is the purpose of the longer second section of this chapter. A short final section can then return to the same analysis in yet a different fashion, asking this time about the *generic forms* of the contribution to this filtering process by contending party structures. Three fundamental (and fundamentally different) impacts will stand out in this final analysis.

## AN EVOLVING CONTEXT FOR STRUCTURAL IMPACTS

The route into an analysis of the impact of party structure on democratic representation runs more or less automatically through policy preferences in the major substantive domains of postwar American politics. That fact alone reinforces the need to consider the four great domains that constitute this policy context in a collective rather than just an individual manner. On the other hand, there is nothing in the simultaneous presence of policy preferences in four major domains that decrees that any (much less all) of these preferences need inherently to be aligned by partisanship, either by party attachment or activity level. The immediate postwar years were a high point in the consequences of national security, for example, yet the domain had little partisan connection, and the lesser elements of linkage that could be teased out were essentially backward looking, that is, deriving from a partisan pattern that was already fading. For good or ill, then, the nature of their collective centrality to political conflict can (and will) itself vary hugely across time.

## Partisan Alignments in the Old World, 1950–1968

Aligned or unaligned, the collective evolution of these domains needs to be revisited in the first part of this chapter to permit a comprehensive look at the filtering effect(s) of party structure within this overarching policy context. The starting point for any such collective effort is still almost inescapably the policy domain of social welfare. Social welfare was already established as the policy core of partisan politics when the post-war period began, courtesy of the Great Depression and the New Deal, bringing the welfare state to the United States. In principle, this could still have been an intense but short-run focus during that catastrophic period. In practice, we can know by hindsight that it was institutionalized as the policy core of what became known as the New Deal party system by the time of the first survey of what became the American National Election Study in 1952 (Figure 4.1A).

While social welfare was the indisputable anchor of the collective context for immediate postwar politics, civil rights was manifesting a weaker but still parallel version of the same overall alignment in these opening postwar years (Figure 4.1B). An analyst of the time might have been more circumspect about asserting this as an alleged pattern common to both domains, since every partisan population was more moderate in its policy preferences on civil rights as opposed to social welfare. On the other hand, the two main hallmarks of what was to be the common pattern were already (if incipiently) present. Thus there was a clear if modest ideological distinction on civil rights too between the Democratic and Republican rank and files. Beyond that, the active parties, in the form of two contending populations of partisan activists, were more extreme in these preferences in a parallel ideological direction.

At the same time, it would have taken some mystical foreknowledge of the subsequent evolution of this pattern – left to right from Democratic activists to the Democratic rank and file to the Republican rank and file to Republican activists – to believe that this template would ever characterize the two remaining domains, cultural values and civil rights. National security in those early years showed nary a hint of that same, parallel

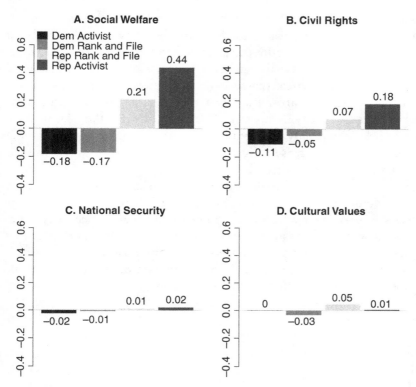

FIGURE 4.1 Partisan Populations and Issue Alignments: The Nation as a Whole in the Old World, 1950–1968

and evolving, partisan alignment (Figure 4.1C). All four partisan populations stood at essentially identical locations with regard to policy preferences on national security, effectively on the national average.

And the same could be said of cultural values (Figure 4.1D). Indeed, analysts who knew that the more educated and active members of both parties were likely to be more concerned with civil liberties might have imputed an entirely different patterning to this particular nonalignment, since both sets of activists sat in-between the two rank and files. Yet the shadowy differences buttressing this perception were not nearly large enough to sustain such a description in its own time, and issue evolution would confirm that this was not the pattern that would surface as time passed.

A different major aspect of American politics in the immediate postwar years, one that subsequent analysts could know only in a historical sense but that contemporary analysts knew all too viscerally, was that the national party system was actually composed of two sharply different regional systems, with different party balances and, especially for our purposes, different internal alignments. In this, while the North contained many individual subareas that were uncompetitive, the region as a whole was competitive in partisan terms. Yet the South was not, being overwhelmingly one-party Democratic. Moreover, these Southern Democrats, being at least implicitly representative of what would be two parties elsewhere, assumed a partisan alignment different in kind from that of their Northern fellow partisans. So it was necessary to inquire into partisan alignments in two *regions* in the immediate postwar years. And while there would be a substantial convergence of these regions across the postwar years, it remains essential to retain this focus, since party structure would continue to influence democratic representation differently by region, even as those regions converged in major regards.

The lead policy domain for demonstrating partisan alignment in the nation as a whole in these early postwar years, namely social welfare, simultaneously testified to the importance of a regional sub-focus. Seen by way of social welfare, the North showed an even stronger version of the national alignment, with Democrats to the left and Republicans to the right even in just their rank and files, and with the two sets of activists flanking those rank and files – now more clearly – in the same directions (Table 4.1A). However, the ideological placement of these Northern Democratic and Northern Republican populations was in turn heavily colored by being counterparts to a Southern regional story that was very different (Table 4.1B). The Southern portrait was distinguished by the fact that its rank and file was actually the ideological left in this regional partisan alignment. Moreover, Democratic activists were to the right of their rank and file, to the right of the national average, and hence closer to the Republican rank and file than to their own.[6]

A reconsideration of national partisan alignments on civil rights, now stratified by region, told an even more extreme version of the same story. In the North, an overall alignment parallel to that on social welfare now appeared indisputable, with a distance of .39 between activists and .24 between rank and files (Table 4.1B). Though this more-polarized alignment was different from its counterpart on social welfare in that

---

[6] The Southern Republican story in these early years was then largely one of statistical irrelevance, though this enfeebled lesser party was otherwise nearly identical to its Northern counterparts in its policy preferences on social welfare.

TABLE 4.1 *Partisan Populations and Issue Alignment: Geographic Regions in the Old World, 1950–1968*

| A. Social Welfare | | |
|---|---|---|
| | North | South |
| Democratic Activists | −.27 | +.11 |
| Democratic Rank & File | −.23 | −.03 |
| Republican Rank & File | +.21 | +.18 |
| Republican Activists | +.46 | +.46 |

| B. Civil Rights | | |
|---|---|---|
| | North | South |
| Democratic Activists | −.26 | +.31 |
| Democratic Rank & File | −.19 | +.27 |
| Republican Rank & Filer | +.05 | +.21 |
| Republican Activists | +.13 | +.46 |

| C. National Security | | |
|---|---|---|
| | North | South |
| Democratic Activists | −.06 | +.10 |
| Democratic Rank & File | −.02 | +.03 |
| Republican Rank & File | 0 | +.03 |
| Republican Activists | +.05 | −.23 |

| D. Cultural Values | | |
|---|---|---|
| | North | South |
| Democratic Activists | −.02 | +.05 |
| Democratic Rank & File | −.06 | +.06 |
| Republican Rank & File | +.03 | +.15 |
| Republican Activists | −.03 | +.20 |

Democratic activists were further from their own rank and file on civil rights, while Republican activists were far more moderate than on social welfare. By contrast, the South offered no partisan population that was even moderate, much less liberal (Figure 4.1B). Rather, all four populations were conservative, the most moderate actually being rank and file Republicans. Yet Southern Democratic activists showed the same dissidence from the national pattern on civil rights as on social welfare, standing this time not just to the right of their own (very conservative) rank and file but to the right of the national Republican Party, in both its partisan populations.

The story of regional difference was much more constricted in the two other great domains for postwar politicking. For national security, there was no real difference in the immediate postwar years within the Democratic or Republican rank and files by region, though their activists offered a noteworthy but idiosyncratic regional distinction (Table 4.1C). In the North, Democratic activists were modestly liberal and Republican activists modestly conservative. But in the South, the situation was reversed, with Democratic activists modestly conservative and Republican activists liberal – though the latter were still a very small population. Lastly, the partisan alignment on cultural values, such as it was, while looking more or less identical to national security when the focus was the nation as a whole, was mainly characterized by a uniform regional difference (Table 4.1D). Every partisan population was more conservative than its counterpart in the North (and hence the nation) on cultural values.

### Partisan Alignments in the Reform Era, 1970–1988

Two main developments would characterize *change* in nationwide partisan alignments in the reform era. One involved comprehensive alignments, where civil rights moved clearly – now indisputably – into parallel with the previous configuration on social welfare. The other main development involved a single partisan population, activist Democrats, who moved strongly off to the left everywhere, recognizably on social welfare, more impressively on civil rights, national security, and even cultural values. Though with all that said, the truly grand change involved the disappearance of the major longtime regional difference in American politics, now sharply reduced by partisan convergence across the key regions.

On its own terms, social welfare merely adjusted the alignment that had characterized this domain in the old world (Figures 4.2A and 4.1A). Net ideological distances between activists remained stable, while net ideological distances between their rank and files increased modestly. What changed within this overall stability was that both activist populations moved leftward, making Democratic activists more liberal and Republican activists more moderate. As a result, the overall alignment became considerably more symmetric, though Republican activists still

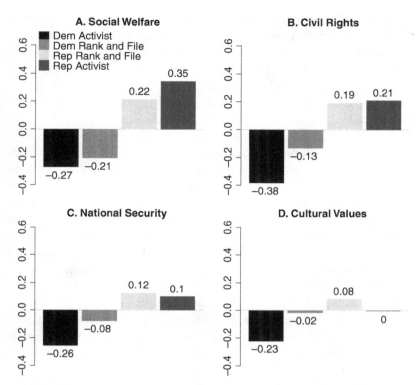

FIGURE 4.2 Partisan Populations and Issue Alignments: The Nation as a Whole in the Reform Era, 1970–1988

sat further from the national average than Democratic counterparts, and further from their own rank and file as well.

In this reform era, civil rights erased any lingering questions about an incipiently common alignment, though the four partisan populations remained capable of acting individually within a shared overall pattern (Figure 4.2B). The two rank and files were now clearly distinct, Democrats to the left and Republicans to the right. More strikingly, the modest shift leftward among Democratic activists on social welfare became a huge move left on civil rights: –.18 to –.27 on social welfare, but –.11 to –.38 on civil rights. While Republican activists remained roughly stable in their policy preferences, the active Republican Party ended up closer to its own rank and file, courtesy of a clear move rightward by the latter, so that in the end, the extreme ideological position on social welfare was (still) held by Republican activists, but the extreme position on civil rights was even more clearly held by Democratic counterparts.

National security featured its own incarnation of the leftward leap by Democratic activists, making the reform era the great period of active Democratic polarization, though this was coupled with a much more equivocal shift toward a common overall alignment (Figure 4.3C). The first change was indisputable: the active Democratic Party moved almost as far on national security as it had on civil rights during this second postwar period. At the same time, the overall result might – but only might – have been viewed as a weak incarnation of the common pattern now characterizing both civil rights and social welfare. Though absent that huge move leftward by Democratic activists, it might also have been viewed as little more than a continuing idiosyncrasy.

With cultural values, however, there should have been no confusion. One of these developments was obviously shared; the other was just as clearly nonexistent (Figure 4.2D). The leftward lurch by activist Democrats was the one that penetrated cultural values too, completing a shift whereby this particular partisan population had done the same relatively extreme thing in all four domains, though the move was more than twice as large on cultural values as it was on social welfare. Yet the general aligning development characterizing social welfare and civil rights – and possibly national security – was simply absent in the domain of cultural values. Apart from that major move leftward by Democratic activists, no one else really moved at all.

The regional story underneath this national picture then had a curious, contrary patterning to it. In two domains, a once-great regional difference in overall alignment was rapidly disappearing, though the degree of convergence still varied by policy domain. But in the other two domains, what remained was a major regional difference in the ideological point at which policy alignments were anchored, though this too varied by policy domain (Table 4.2).

The first major aspect of this regional change – and the *end* of the fundamental difference in partisan alignment that had been so central to American politics for so long – was exemplified by social welfare. On social welfare, the North was now nearly a perfect reflection of the nation as a whole in its overall alignment (Table 4.2A1). This could only be true, of course, because the old regional distinctiveness of the South had been upended: the South had come into complete alignment with the North, and hence the nation (Table 4.2B1). Where the four partisan populations had previously stood in an entirely different *relationship* to one another, North versus South, the four partisan populations were now nearly interchangeable by region. The fact that this shift was more

TABLE 4.2 *Partisan Populations and Issue Alignment:*
*Geographic Regions in the Reform Era, 1970–1988*

### A. Social Welfare

|  | North | South |
|---|---|---|
| Democratic Activists | −.27 | −.30 |
| Democratic Rank & File | −.21 | −.21 |
| Republican Rank & File | +.21 | +.24 |
| Republican Activists | +.34 | +.38 |

### B. Civil Rights

|  | North | South |
|---|---|---|
| Democratic Activists | −.39 | −.37 |
| Democratic Rank & File | −.16 | −.08 |
| Republican Rank & Filer | +.16 | +.32 |
| Republican Activists | +.19 | +.30 |

### C. National Security

|  | North | South |
|---|---|---|
| Democratic Activists | −.31 | −.11 |
| Democratic Rank & File | −.13 | +.03 |
| Republican Rank & File | +.10 | +.22 |
| Republican Activists | +.07 | +.24 |

### D. Cultural Values

|  | North | South |
|---|---|---|
| Democratic Activists | −.28 | −.05 |
| Democratic Rank & File | −.06 | +.14 |
| Republican Rank & File | +.06 | +.16 |
| Republican Activists | −.04 | +.20 |

a matter of ideological change among activists, more a matter of simple change in social composition for their rank and files, did not gainsay the degree – or the consequence – of the shift in overall alignment.

More remarkable was the same shift on civil rights. This time, there was more noteworthy change in the North as well, where the new alignment differed from the old by being both more polarized and more asymmetric, the latter courtesy of that huge move leftward by Democratic activists (Table 4.2B). But again, the titanic change came in the South, where a previously uniform partisan conservatism gave way to a regionally curious incarnation of the national pattern. The leftward jump by Southern Democratic activists was sufficiently extreme as to outpace any other partisan population in any other temporal period, moving from +.31 to −.37, from clearly conservative to clearly liberal. At the same time, the Southern Republicans finally became a regional party worthy of attention, though the fresh ideological impetus in their ranks came in the rank and file, who became more conservative. One further result was a national Republican Party that was unified around the conservative position on social welfare but split on civil rights, being moderately conservative in the North but strongly conservative in the South.

Yet when it came to national security, any definitive regional convergence was harder to find. In both the North and the South, the dominant story was still that major move leftward by Democratic activists, now reflected in both regions (Table 4.2C). On the other hand, all four partisan populations remained more conservative – and clearly so – than their counterparts in the North. Cultural values was then an even clearer version of the story of national security, with even less of an evolution toward shared overall patterns and more of an ideological difference between regions (Table 4.2D). Both North and South did feature the same strong move leftward among Democratic activists; that (and that alone) was common to all four policy domains. So Democratic activists were clearly *energized* by cultural values, and that represented a new development. Yet a powerful regional difference remained in the ideological anchor points for the two regions: every partisan population was again more conservative in the South and more liberal in the North.

### Partisan Alignments in the Modern Era, 1990–2008

The coming of the modern era would not eliminate major and ongoing differences by party structure, organized versus volunteer, as subsequent sections of this chapter will attest. The coming of the modern era would, however, simplify the larger context within which those differences operated, courtesy of an increasing convergence among major policy domains (Figure 4.3). This was by far the dominant aspect of change. All four substantive areas would acquire an increasingly parallel partisan alignment. All four areas would see growing polarization within that alignment – even cultural values, where the modern alignment managed to

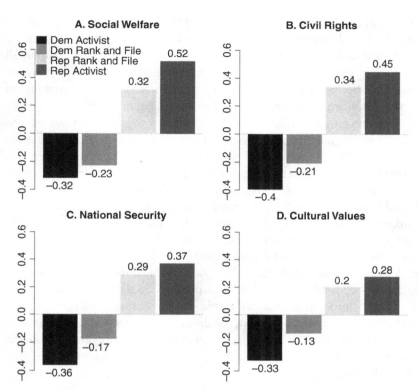

FIGURE 4.3  Partisan Populations and Issue Alignments: The Nation as a Whole in the Modern World, 1990–2008

arrive in a fully formed and substantially polarized fashion. Each policy domain would retain distinctive twists on this overall convergence, yet conformity across domains was the dominant theme of the new era.

Social welfare, the only domain with an indisputable version of the modern alignment from the first years for which we have data, still embodied the diagnostic elements of what had now become the common pattern (Figure 4.3A). There was the bedrock ideological alignment. Yet unlike its shift into the reform era, when this overall alignment had become more symmetric, social welfare shifted away in the modern era, back toward asymmetry. Even so, in this modern era, civil rights actually edged past social welfare as the most polarized policy domain within the active parties, though almost the entire increment to this activist polarization was contributed this time by a huge move to the right – effectively a doubling of their distance from the center – among Republican activists

(Figure 4.3B). The two parties' rank and files continued to be more polarized on social welfare, although there was likewise a very large move rightward within the Republican rank and file on civil rights. Despite all of that, in the modern period as in the reform era, it was Democratic activists who remained much further from their partisan rank and file on civil rights when compared to their Republican counterparts.

A bigger change arrived with national security, which finally moved into the full and regular alignment that had characterized only social welfare in the old world, and both social welfare and civil rights in the reform era (Figure 4.3C). To accomplish this shift, each of the four partisan populations had to move strongly away from the national average, while Republican activists, who had been ever so slightly to the *left* of their own rank and file in the reform era, had to shift additionally to the right. All of that did occur. Still, Democratic activists remained much further from their rank and file on national security than Republican activists from theirs, making this domain look more like civil rights than like social welfare.

Lastly, cultural values, still indisputably unaligned in the reform era, came into agreement with this shared national picture as well (Figure 4.3D). On the one hand, the domain remained the least polarized of the big four. Each of its four partisan populations was further from the national average in all three of the other policy domains. On the other hand, the more impressive fact about this new alignment was that when it made this initial appearance, it already presented a fully realized version of the modern pattern. Which is to say: it arrived not as a potential conformist nor in some "proto" version but aligned with the common overall pattern and polarized within it.

Inside these national pictures, the shift into the reform era had been characterized by declining differences in partisan alignment between the great political regions, most especially in two domains, social welfare and civil rights. In the modern era, regional convergence – and hence nationalization – became a central theme for all four of the major policy domains, though the South still mixed its previous preferences on national security and cultural values (though not social welfare or civil rights) with a more generalized Southern conservatism (Table 4.3).

When it came into conformity with the national pattern on social welfare during the reform era, this Southern realignment had been so strong as to overshoot the national picture: the South became more polarized than the North. This result was merely expanded in the modern era, with active Democrats making a further move leftward and active Republicans making an even larger move to the right (Table 4.3A). When

TABLE 4.3 *Partisan Populations and Issue Alignment: Geographic Regions in the Modern World, 1990–2008*

**A. Social Welfare**

|  | North | South |
|---|---|---|
| Democratic Activists | −.31 | −.38 |
| Democratic Rank & File | −.22 | −.25 |
| Republican Rank & File | +.32 | +.30 |
| Republican Activists | +.48 | +.60 |

**B. Civil Rights**

|  | North | South |
|---|---|---|
| Democratic Activists | −.40 | −.44 |
| Democratic Rank & File | −.17 | −.28 |
| Republican Rank & Filer | +.32 | +.35 |
| Republican Activists | +.42 | +.49 |

**C. National Security**

|  | North | South |
|---|---|---|
| Democratic Activists | −.42 | −.29 |
| Democratic Rank & File | −.21 | −.08 |
| Republican Rank & File | +.18 | +.26 |
| Republican Activists | +.25 | +.33 |

**D. Cultural Values**

|  | North | South |
|---|---|---|
| Democratic Activists | −.38 | −.20 |
| Democratic Rank & File | −.18 | −.02 |
| Republican Rank & File | +.18 | +.26 |
| Republican Activists | +.25 | +.33 |

it came into alignment with the national pattern on civil rights during that same reform era, the South had likewise overshot the national pattern, realizing a partisan polarization greater than that in the North. That old Democratic pattern stayed gone in the modern world, with the common alignment again even more polarized in the South than in the North (Table 4.3B).

What had sustained the great regional divide during the reform era, while simultaneously dividing national security and cultural values from social welfare and civil rights, was the fact that all four partisan populations in the South were more conservative than their counterpart populations in the North. That particular regional difference survived comfortably into the modern world. Yet it was now embedded in the larger change characterizing both regions, in which they came into full and parallel alignment on both national security and cultural values (Tables 4.3C and 4.3D). One other old distinction for those two domains survived this greater shift as well: Democratic activists remained noteworthy for the distance from their own rank and file in both newly aligned policy domains, with a representational gap fully three times as large on national security for Democratic as opposed to Republican activists, roughly three times as large on cultural values as well.

### The Evolution of Comprehensive Ideologies

Individual alignments apart, the presence from the start of the two domains that are most commonly used to create a multi-dimensional attitude space, namely social welfare and cultural values, also allowed an investigation of the fortunes of more comprehensive ideologies and their link to party structures. These widely recognized ideologies were Liberalism, Conservatism, Populism, and Libertarianism. The two policy domains allowed them to be isolated in a manner by which respondents and not the analyst could assign individuals to their chosen ideologies.

In the immediate postwar years, this larger ideological conflict in American politics pitted Conservatives, the narrow plurality leader, against Populists, their main challenger (Figure 4.4A). Libertarians followed, showing serious strength, while Liberals trailed, though even they were a non-negligible presence. Viewed through the lens of the preceding hundred years, a conflict between Conservatives and Populists should have seemed familiar. Seen through the lens of the contemporary world, it looks distant instead. In the reform era, Conservatism held its position as the leading ideology in American politics (Figure 4.4B). Yet Liberalism gained while Populism declined, to the point where Liberals narrowly outnumbered Populists. Libertarians declined modestly too, so the surge among Liberals caused Libertarians to fall into fourth place.

The modern world was to be different yet again (Figure 4.4C). For the nation as a whole, Liberals had become the plurality ideological grouping, challenged closely by Conservatives. Populism and Libertarianism

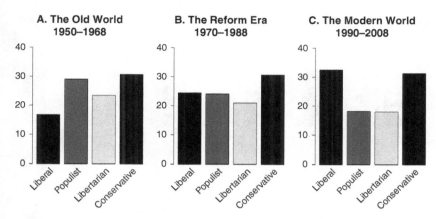

FIGURE 4.4 Partisan Populations and Political Ideologies: The Nation as a Whole across the Postwar Years

continued in retreat, with the former again suffering the greater losses. So the result was essentially a new ordering and a new balance within it. Liberals faced off against Conservatives, where Conservatives had once faced off against Populists, leaving Populists and Libertarians roughly equal but far behind the top two.

With comprehensive ideologies, however, the story of two great political regions was very different from the same story as told through individual policy domains. Moreover, the evolution of this regional story was even more consequential when the focus shifted to ideological groupings. In the old world, the two great political regions had actually evinced a parallel pattern to their comprehensive ideologies (Figure 4.5A). Moreover, here, the South was a more stereotypical embodiment of the national pattern than was the North. Though the rank ordering of ideologies was the same in both regions: Conservatives, Populists, Libertarians, and Liberals.

Rather than becoming more aligned and parallel during the reform era, however – the dominant story of individual policy domains – the distribution of these comprehensive ideologies became more varied as between regions (Figure 4.5B). So a picture of the nation as a whole became more of a formalistic sum of two great regions doing quite different things, and certainly not a picture of impending convergence. In the North, Conservatives were now challenged by Liberals. But in the South, Conservatives were still principally challenged by Populists.

Yet in the modern world and finally, the two major regions moved closer, though still not as close as they had been in the immediate postwar years

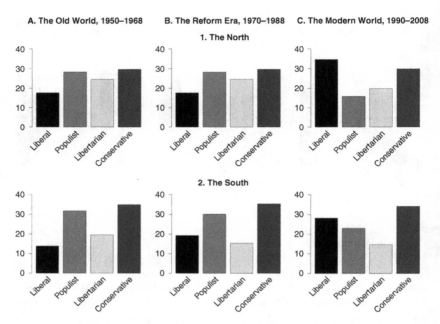

FIGURE 4.5 Partisan Populations and Political Ideologies: Political Regions across the Postwar Years

(Figure 4.5C). Leading regional ideologies were now identical: Liberals versus Conservatives, with Liberals leading in the North, Conservatives leading in the South. Otherwise, Libertarians had outpaced – really just out-survived – Populists as the leading also-rans in the North. While in the South, the opposite was true. So the South now looked more like our old world, while the North was the region most thoroughly transformed.

## THE EVOLVING IMPACT OF PARTY STRUCTURE

That is the larger context within which party structure had to – and did – exercise its influence across the postwar years. We shall argue in the concluding section of this chapter that even this larger context was partly a product of, rather than a constraint on, the filtering effect of alternative party types. If one party model helped to sustain partisan conflict in one or more of these great policy domains, and if the other party model helped to divert attention to one or more of the other policy domains – as is indeed the case – then the larger issue context that followed was itself a product of, and not just a framework for, policy impacts from party structures. Yet quite apart from that theoretical argument, party structure was constantly making detailed and specific contributions – providing individual but inescapable shaping elements – that varied by policy domain, by political region, and by temporal period.

All politics never was (and probably never could be) the same for all domains in all regions in all eras. So any concluding chapter must necessarily return to the old world of postwar politics and follow its evolution up to the modern era, period by period but now for all domains simultaneously, this time with party structure as the crucial lens. Because the larger context for American politics – especially, here, the nature of its partisan alignments – was changing over time, the contribution of party structure to this chronicle should also have changed with the times. Political parties are, after all, *intermediary* institutions, with party types as further differences in their mediating structure.

In any case, some of the most dramatic differences in this structural impact were present in our old world, the immediate postwar years. By the time the modern world arrived, this filtering effect, rather than gradually evanescing, would instead be altered, generalized, and surprisingly uniform across substantively diverse policy domains and previously determinative geographic regions. If this generalized impact was not as striking as some idiosyncratic effects at particular moments during the preceding years, it did attest to the continuing power of bedrock differences in party structure, and thus their continuing contribution to policy responsiveness and democratic representation.

## Party Structure and Policy Responsiveness in the Old World, 1950–1968

Two of the most striking instances of the power of party structure to shape policy responsiveness – that is, to make a separable contribution to democratic representation by filtering the transmission of public preferences into governmental institutions – were present from the opening point at which we have systemic evidence. We have treated this point as the "old world" of postwar American politics, and the two policy domains that already reflected a partisan alignment to policy preferences, namely social welfare and civil rights, were the two domains that were home to dramatic instances of the representational power of party structure in this opening period.

Social welfare already stood out for the degree of partisan alignment among the four main partisan populations at the beginning of the postwar years. The great regional distinction within that alignment, North versus South, likewise jumped out of the data at the time. Even within this context, itself shaping but also constraining possible further influences, party structure shone through (Table 4.4). From the start, this structure offered a diagnostic example of the power of the difference between organized and volunteer parties in reinforcing (or denying) the reach of national party positions, just as it offered an example of the power of this structural difference to work in the *same* way in two otherwise extremely divergent regions, in effect overcoming their divergence. And while it was easiest to see both effects on the Democratic side of the aisle, given the near absence of a Republican side in the South, both effects could be isolated within the Republican Party too.

In the clearest example of this structural power, the partisan alignment already characterizing social welfare nationwide in the immediate post-war years proved to be entirely the contribution of *organized political parties in the North*. Once state parties were stratified by party structure and not just by region, it became clear that even volunteer parties in the North deviated modestly from this pattern, while both party types dissented from its overall contours in the South. Said more precisely, what would become the standard partisan alignment for the nation as a whole across all four policy domains by the modern era was already evident – but solely evident – in organized parties of the North. Even volunteer Northern Democratic parties were not yet in alignment with the national party program on social welfare. Indeed, their activists not only lagged the welfare liberalism of the organized parties. They actually lagged the welfare liberalism of their own rank and file.

Being anchored in much more ideologically conservative territory, the American South looked instantly different to the eye. Yet this proved to be one of those cases where surface differences masked an underlying conformity. For within the South – and this is in some sense the ultimate testimony to the power of structural differences among political parties in these early years – the exact same filtering impacts from party structure could be observed. Which is to say: despite an ideological location that was radically different, organized parties were pulling strongly toward the national Democratic program in the South as they did in the North, while volunteer parties were in effect pulling away from that program.

Region still intruded on this structural effect in a major way: what was a simple lack of engagement by volunteer parties in the North was aggressive resistance from volunteer counterparts in the South. Yet organized parties among Democrats in both regions were pulling – and more

TABLE 4.4 *Party Structure and Issue Alignment:*
*The Old World, 1950–1968*

### A.  Social Welfare

|  | 1. The North | | 2. The South | |
| --- | --- | --- | --- | --- |
|  | Org. | Vol. | Org. | Vol. |
| Democratic Activists | −.31 | −.19 | +.06 | +.27 |
| Democratic Rank & File | −.28 | −.20 | −.06 | +.03 |
| Republican Rank & File | +.16 | +.27 | +.18 | * |
| Republican Activists | +.37 | +.49 | * | * |

### B.  Civil Rights

|  | 1. The North | | 2. The South | |
| --- | --- | --- | --- | --- |
|  | Org. | Vol. | Org. | Vol. |
| Democratic Activists | −.22 | −.27 | +.18 | +.69 |
| Democratic Rank & File | −.23 | −.16 | +.22 | +.37 |
| Republican Rank & File | +.02 | +.07 | +.21 | * |
| Republican Activists | +.10 | +.17 | * | * |

### C.  National Security

|  | 1. The North | | 2. The South | |
| --- | --- | --- | --- | --- |
|  | Org. | Vol. | Org. | Vol. |
| Democratic Activists | −.08 | −.02 | +.10 | +.17 |
| Democratic Rank & File | −.03 | 0 | 0 | +.10 |
| Republican Rank & File | +.05 | −.04 | +.02 | * |
| Republican Activists | +.10 | 0 | * | * |

### D.  Cultural Values

|  | 1. The North | | 2. The South | |
| --- | --- | --- | --- | --- |
|  | Org. | Vol. | Org. | Vol. |
| Democratic Activists | −.01 | −.05 | +.05 | +.05 |
| Democratic Rank & File | 0 | −.11 | +.08 | +.01 |
| Republican Rank & File | +.11 | −.04 | +.16 | * |
| Republican Activists | +.01 | −.03 | * | * |

* Ns too small for reliable analysis.

strongly in the South than in the North – toward the national (the New Deal) program by comparison to their volunteer counterparts. And if the active party in the South did not end up nearly as close to this national position as its Northern counterpart, that was because the region as a whole had it pulling from a far more conservative place.

That was a major structural contribution. In that long-ago time, the Republican story inside these overall contours was inherently truncated, there being little of a party rank and file and even less of an activist stratum among Southern Republicans. Yet a Republican version of the same effects – a mirror image, as befitted the opposition party – remained visible within Northern Republican ranks. While the programmatic virtues of the New Deal were still heavily contested in Northern (and national) politics, social welfare had nevertheless achieved consensus as at least the main battleground for partisan politics in the immediate postwar years.

What this meant for Republicans was that organized parties were both more able and more incentivized to try to reposition themselves within this evolving national consensus, through compromises that might return them to power at the state level. Conversely, volunteer parties were still much more seriously engaged in simple resistance. Overall, then, for both parties in both regions, it was organized parties that linked the policy preferences of party activists to the central policy concern of national politics. Just as it was volunteer parties, the reform alternative, that provided the effective dissidents from an evolving consensus on the centrality of social welfare, even if these parties continued to pitch this welfare battle in additionally different ideological territory in the North as opposed to the South.

Yet if social welfare was already the great established issue for party politics in this first postwar world, civil rights was the great emergent conflict. Nationwide, civil rights was the other main policy domain that possessed a similar alignment across the four main partisan populations, weak but apparently parallel to the one characterizing social welfare. Regionally, civil rights featured an even stronger difference in the resulting partisan alignments, North versus South. Though once again, even constraints this pronounced could not mask the power of party structure to interact with public preferences in the pursuit of governmental policy (Tables 4.4A2 and 4.4B2). This time, however, the critical further distinction was between a policy realm that was already institutionalized in national party programs, namely social welfare, compared to a realm that was clearly but still only incipiently on the rise.

With civil rights, this distinction – an established versus an emergent issue – had to remain front and center in the analysis, because it made the same structural differences between two party types work differently in a newly emergent policy domain. This was easiest to see among Democrats in the North, where partisan alignments by party structure were actually reversed as between civil rights and social welfare. With social welfare in the North, as we have just seen, organized Democratic parties pulled toward an established national program, while volunteer Democratic parties were indifferent (Table 4.4B1). With civil rights on the other hand, the story ran in the opposite direction. Here, it was volunteer Democratic parties that were engaged – grabbed – by the emergent issue, while organized parties were content to do nothing more than reflect the views of their rank and files. Not surprisingly, then, while activist Democrats from organized parties in the North contributed the left wing on social welfare, it was activist Democrats from volunteer parties in the same region who contributed the left wing on civil rights.

Remarkably, the same behavioral regularity could again be referenced in the South as well (Table 4.4B2). Among the reliably dominant Democrats in this reliably dissident region, it was activist Democrats from organized parties who were content merely to reflect the views of their rank and file on civil rights, while it was activist Democrats from volunteer parties who were strongly cathected by this new issue, pulling sharply away from their own rank and file as well as from overall preferences in the region as a whole. What made this parallel impact less immediately obvious was that its ideological effect was profoundly opposite for policy positions in the South as opposed to the North. The dominant Democratic view in the North being liberal, volunteer parties pulled additionally to the left. The dominant Democratic view in the South being conservative, volunteer parties pulled additionally – indeed wildly – to the right instead.

The story of the Republican Party in this early period was likewise different for civil rights versus social welfare, though this remained almost entirely a Northern story in the immediate postwar years. Yet in the North, where it mattered, active Republicans in organized parties were more moderate and active Republicans in volunteer parties more conservative in both policy domains. In that sense, for the Republicans as between the two domains and very much unlike the situation among the Democrats, parallel structural effects produced parallel ideological outcomes. Though an explanation for why similar structural effects could produce divergent results among Democrats but parallel results among

Republicans does require a quick detour through policy history, since it was this history that could make shared structural differences propel different ideological outcomes in the two policy domains.

For social welfare, Democrats had become the driving force behind public policy, with Republicans actively and reliably resisting. For civil rights, however, Republicans had traditionally been the driving force, with Democrats passively lagging when they did not actively resist. The result was to shape the Republican position in the two domains during the immediate postwar years in clearly different ways – anchored in more moderate territory on civil rights, anchored in more conservative territory on social welfare. With that historical context and its associated anchoring as a backdrop, then, organized parties were additionally moderate in both policy domains, civil rights and social welfare, while volunteer parties were additionally conservative in both.

While two of the four great substantive domains for policy conflict in the postwar years had come into an early partisan alignment, the other two had not. In the abstract, it might have seemed that party structure would have its greatest filtering impact in these unaligned domains, national security and cultural values, while partisan alignment in the first two would inhibit any such effect. In practice, as we have seen, neither partisan alignments in the nation as a whole nor strong further shaping by geographic regions prevented the difference between organized and volunteer parties from surfacing in social welfare and civil rights. In practice, as we are about to see, the absence of any national partisan alignment, even as regional differences continued, was to mean that party structure did not have much scope for an autonomous – or really any – further structural impact.

In the immediate postwar years, national security showed effectively no partisan alignment in the nation as a whole, with all four partisan populations sitting more or less directly on the national average. Within this nonalignment, the South was generally more conservative than the North, with active Southern Democrats the most conservative of all – more so than any Republican population anywhere. Yet both distinctions were small and not obviously predictive of a larger and more systematic subsequent evolution. So breaking this context down additionally through party structure offered only shadowy hints about what might follow – the kind of harbingers that we can recognize only by already knowing what was to come next (Table 4.4C). Northern organized parties did look most like this eventual alignment. Southern volunteer parties were furthest out of alignment with that ultimate pattern. But again, this effect was small enough, especially by comparison to civil rights, that an analyst of the time could not have assigned it much significance.

Cultural values, the final great policy domain of the postwar years and the one that would take longest to come into alignment in the nation as a whole, showed even less that could serve as so much as a distant harbinger of things to come. Like national security, cultural values was unaligned in partisan terms during the immediate postwar years. Like national security, the South was more conservative than the North in the policy preferences of its partisan populations. Yet this time, when those results were further stratified by party structure, there was just nothing further to see: nothing that could be argued to be a weak version of an eventual alignment, even among organized parties in the North, and nothing to separate organized volunteer activists in either party in either region, even among volunteer Democratic parties in the South (Table 4.D).

## Party Structure and Policy Responsiveness in the Reform Era, 1970–1988

The reform era in postwar American politics was demarcated – and named in honor of – the final triumph of the volunteer model of internal party structure, now increasingly generalized to state political parties. Yet the era also came with major changes in the partisan context for the politicking that would be shaped by this changing balance of party types. Within the four major domains for policy conflict, the reform era suggested the onward march of a common partisan alignment, albeit at different speeds and with a varying reach. Among the four major partisan populations, it was one in particular, the Democratic activists, who offered up a huge and generalized move to the left, an individualized twist that made the eventual emergence of a common template look less sure, though the greatest contextual change occurred beneath these national developments, in the striking transformation of party politics in the American South.

Nevertheless, when that larger context was further stratified by party structure, there proved to be not one but two major changes just within the domain of social welfare. First was the headline-making disappearance of a long-standing difference in partisan alignment between the North and the South, about which, more to follow later. There was a second change that came to life and operated in parallel in the two regions, involving party structure specifically.

Recall that in the North, it had been organized parties that were driving the national alignment in the old world, an alignment that had not fully penetrated even Northern volunteer parties. In the reform era, this difference was simply gone (Table 4.5A1). Volunteer Democratic parties in the Northern states had in effect "caught up" with a policy position characterizing their national party. If they had lagged at achieving conformity with national policy in the old world, they no longer lagged in its successor era. Conversely, organized Republican parties in the North surrendered their historic moderation on civil rights. And together, those two shifts, one Democratic and one Republican, demolished the old Northern difference on social welfare by party structure.

On the other hand, while the entire South was also joining this national alignment on social welfare during the reform era – a far larger change – the South was simultaneously affirming an old and not a new pattern of alignment associated with party structure, one that could be recognized only by observing change over time (Table 4.5A2). In this, in the process of coming into conformity with a national alignment that now reflected confirmed nationwide party programs, it was Southern organized parties that led the move and ended up more liberal among Democrats and more moderate among Republicans, as they had previously been *in the old world*, when these alignments were making their original appearance in the North.

Civil rights in the reform era, by offering an overall partisan context similar to that of social welfare, was the policy domain that most strongly suggested the rise of a common partisan template, one simultaneously annihilating the historic regional distinction. Yet this time, stratification by party type underlined a major and continuing difference between the two policy domains, along with an effect on temporal sequencing that was even more impressive than the counterpart development on social welfare (Tables 4.5A2 and 4.5B2). In the old world, in the North but not yet in the South, Democratic activists in organized parties had been more concerned with the established issue of social welfare, while Democratic activists in volunteer parties had been more concerned with the emerging issue of civil rights, and Republican activists had been noteworthy for their overall moderation on what was once a policy area driven largely by fellow partisans.

In the North, these distinctions could still be followed into the reform era (Table 4.5B1). Democratic activists in volunteer parties continued to be more powerfully moved by civil rights than by social welfare, thereby widening the gap with their organized counterparts and contributing the

TABLE 4.5 *Party Structure and Issue Alignment:*
*The Reform Era, 1970–1988*

### A. Social Welfare

| | 1. The North | | 2. The South | |
|---|---|---|---|---|
| | Org. | Vol. | Org. | Vol. |
| Democratic Activists | −.27 | −.27 | −.30 | −.24 |
| Democratic Rank & File | −.17 | −.21 | −.23 | −.18 |
| Republican Rank & File | +.32 | +.20 | +.26 | +.21 |
| Republican Activists | +.44 | +.33 | +.35 | +.43 |

### B. Civil Rights

| | 1. The North | | 2. The South | |
|---|---|---|---|---|
| | Org. | Vol. | Org. | Vol. |
| Democratic Activists | −.23 | −.42 | −.54 | −.24 |
| Democratic Rank & File | −.10 | −.17 | −.06 | −.10 |
| Republican Rank & File | +.23 | +.15 | +.35 | +.30 |
| Republican Activists | +.38 | +.18 | +.29 | +.28 |

### C. National Security

| | 1. The North | | 2. The South | |
|---|---|---|---|---|
| | Org. | Vol. | Org. | Vol. |
| Democratic Activists | −.26 | −.31 | −.17 | −.12 |
| Democratic Rank & File | −.03 | −.14 | +.03 | +.03 |
| Republican Rank & File | +.16 | +.09 | +.23 | +.20 |
| Republican Activists | +.25 | +.06 | +.19 | +.31 |

### D. Cultural Values

| | 1. The North | | 2. The South | |
|---|---|---|---|---|
| | Org. | Vol. | Org. | Vol. |
| Democratic Activists | −.15 | −.30 | −.06 | −.02 |
| Democratic Rank & File | +.03 | −.10 | +.15 | +.13 |
| Republican Rank & File | +.10 | +.06 | +.19 | +.14 |
| Republican Activists | +.10 | −.05 | +.17 | +.25 |

undisputed left wing in this emerging policy area. At the same time, Republican activists in organized parties came into alignment with national party positions on civil rights, effectively abandoning their historically moderate party position there, leaving only volunteer parties to continue that moderate tradition.

By contrast, movement by the South into the national partisan alignment was even more striking on civil rights than on social welfare, and this movement did characterize both organized and volunteer parties (Table 4.5B2). Yet within that movement, party structure had a further distinguishing role to play. Within the (still regionally dominant) Democratic Party, it was Democratic activists in organized parties who championed the emerging position of their national party on civil rights. Their volunteer counterparts did join this national pattern as well, yet they ended up considerably less liberal than their organized counterparts, and this could not be due to the preferences of their rank and files, for the Southern Democratic rank and file was slightly more liberal in states that possessed volunteer rather than organized parties.

At the same time, what distinguished Republican activists, newly numerous and newly energized as they were in the South, was that both party types arrived in a world where civil rights was a domain now distinguishing the two national parties in the modern (and not the historic) fashion. So there was little incentive for organized Republican parties in the South to hew to a national position that predated their own existence and that no longer characterized their national party as a whole. Instead, what distinguished this domain among Southern Republicans in the new era was that their rank and file, again within both party models, had moved strongly to the right. So while Republican activists did not have the same incentives as Democratic activists to distinguish themselves by party type, their activists, both organized and volunteer, actually lagged the growing conservatism of their own rank and file – a kind of final testament to a historic Republican moderation.

In the nation as a whole, national security offered more ambiguous signals about the coming of a shared partisan alignment. A strong embodiment of the leftward leap among activist Democrats in the reform era was evident for national security too. But it was coupled with only a weak echo of the overall alignment that now characterized both social welfare and civil rights. In that sense, national security appeared to offer less scope for a differential impact from alternative party structures. Still, among those Democratic activists who claimed the major partisan action in the reform era, now stratified by alternative party types, there were shadowy indications of what later analysts would expect from all four domains. Thus volunteer Democratic activists in the North now owned the far left on national security for the nation as a whole, while organized Democratic activists in the South were more attracted to the national party position than were their volunteer counterparts.

Cultural values was now the most distinctive of the four policy domains for the reform era, albeit for an ironic reason: it was the one that most fully resisted an incipiently common alignment. In the reform era, cultural values did experience the general move leftward by Democratic activists, a move that did not bypass the domain this time. And within this one common partisan development, volunteer Democratic activists in the North were likewise the far left on cultural values, while organized Democratic activists in the South were somewhat more liberal than their volunteer counterparts. But apart from that, stratification by party structure had little or nothing to add.

## Party Structure and Policy Responsiveness in the Modern Era, 1990–2008

The policy context for political conflict in the modern era was distinguished by two developments when the focus is partisan alignment. First, all four domains finally converged on a common overall array, the one that had once characterized only social welfare. Moreover, while all four achieved this common pattern, the move was inevitably most impressive in the previously least aligned domains, namely national security and cultural values. Second and at the same time, all four domains became additionally polarized by comparison to the preceding era, though in contrast to that reform era, the largest contribution to an increasing polarization came from Republican rather than Democratic activists this time. In a sense, the new era was also uniformly characterized by one continuing nondevelopment. The old regional division that had once caused North and South to manifest partisan alignments that were different in kind had disappeared in the reform era – and stayed gone in the modern world.

So that was the new, modern, policy context within which party structure had to exercise its filtering effects, if expanded commonalities and increased polarization had not eradicated this structural possibility. In truth, the first generic impact of party structure, the one in which different party types, organized versus volunteer, acquired partisan alignments that were actually different in kind, had not been seen since the immediate postwar years. The lone major realm with a partisan alignment in that old world, social welfare, had manifested just such a structural difference. Yet this had disappeared in the reform era, and it did not reappear in modern times.[7]

On the other hand, a second generic effect of party structure, visible in the reform era once temporal comparisons were possible, continued to surface in the modern world, albeit rising in some domains and declining in others. The main aspect of this second effect involved the way in which organized parties sustained and thereby reinforced the established partisan alignments that went with established national party positions. Conversely, volunteer parties were drawn strongly to emergent policy concerns and thereby helped push them toward inclusion in those national programs. This effect, surfacing in the reform era and continuing in the modern world, seemed theoretically consistent with fundamental differences in the alternative party models, whereby organized parties were more concerned with deliverable rewards, while volunteer parties had a perennial need for new (and usually more intense) concerns to refuel their attractiveness for volunteer labor.

Table 4.6 is the central display in the search for the continuation and modern shape of this second generic impact. To that end, it takes the four great policy domains and stratifies them by organized versus volunteer party models in the North and the South to produce the sixteen available party groupings. What results is a straightforward confirmation of this second generic effect. In the two policy realms that can be said to have already and indisputably assumed the common partisan alignment during the reform era, namely social welfare and civil rights – these become the established domains – there is very little to choose between organized and volunteer alignments (Tables 4.6A and 4.6B). Republican activists in Northern states retain a bit more moderation compared to their volunteer counterparts; otherwise among the active parties, policy preferences are nearly interchangeable.

When the focus shifts to the two policy realms that came into common alignment only in the modern era, namely national security and cultural values – these become the emergent domains – the story is noticeably different (Tables 4.6C and 4.6D). Being emergent rather than established, they would be expected to feature Democratic activists from volunteer parties who are more liberal than Democratic activists from organized

---

[7] Just as it also offered an example of the power of party structure to work in the *same* way in two otherwise extremely divergent regions, an effect that also disappeared in the reform era.

TABLE 4.6 *Party Structure and Issue Alignment:*
*The Modern World, 1990–2008*

### A. Social Welfare

| | 1. The North | | 2. The South | |
| --- | --- | --- | --- | --- |
| | Org. | Vol. | Org. | Vol. |
| Democratic Activists | −.31 | −.30 | −.42 | −.38 |
| Democratic Rank & File | −.26 | −.20 | −.28 | −.21 |
| Republican Rank & File | +.30 | +.32 | +.32 | +.28 |
| Republican Activists | +.36 | +.51 | +.57 | +.62 |

### B. Civil Rights

| | 1. The North | | 2. The South | |
| --- | --- | --- | --- | --- |
| | Org. | Vol. | Org. | Vol. |
| Democratic Activists | −.42 | −.39 | −.48 | −.48 |
| Democratic Rank & File | −.25 | −.15 | −.35 | −.20 |
| Republican Rank & File | +.30 | +.33 | +.35 | +.34 |
| Republican Activists | +.36 | +.45 | +.45 | +.50 |

### C. National Security

| | 1. The North | | 2. The South | |
| --- | --- | --- | --- | --- |
| | Org. | Vol. | Org. | Vol. |
| Democratic Activists | −.34 | −.45 | −.29 | −.35 |
| Democratic Rank & File | −.21 | −.22 | −.09 | −.08 |
| Republican Rank & File | +.29 | +.26 | +.37 | +.32 |
| Republican Activists | +.17 | +.37 | +.51 | +.54 |

### D. Cultural Values

| | 1. The North | | 2. The South | |
| --- | --- | --- | --- | --- |
| | Org. | Vol. | Org. | Vol. |
| Democratic Activists | −.29 | −.41 | −.14 | −.25 |
| Democratic Rank & File | −.17 | −.19 | −.02 | −.03 |
| Republican Rank & File | +.22 | +.17 | +.28 | +.25 |
| Republican Activists | +.24 | +.26 | +.32 | +.34 |

parties, along with Republican activists from volunteer parties who are more conservative than Republican activists from organized parties, as indeed both are, in the North and in the South. In absolute terms, those effects are impressively stronger among Democrats, whose activists were the drivers for both issues in the preceding period. In relative terms, however, Republican activists are nevertheless much further from their own rank and files in volunteer as opposed to organized states, again in both regions and on both issues as expected.

There is a different way to summarize the structural effects remaining in the modern world, however. In effect, this is the third generic filtering effect of party structure on policy preferences. Moreover, it is the one that has exploded, even while achieving commonality, in the modern world. So it is better at isolating these still-consequential impacts while making them easier to grasp. For the modern world, since all four policy domains share a general partisan alignment – but not for earlier eras, where they do not – Table 4.7 can present four simple measures that capture democratic representation in summary form:

- "Activist Range" is the ideological distance between the active parties, that is, from active Democrats to active Republicans.
- "Democratic Representational Gap" is the distance between Democratic activists and their rank and file.
- "Republican Representational Gap" is the distance between Republican activists and their rank and file.
- And "Dual Gap" is the combined distance between activists and their rank and files, for the two parties together.

These four ideological distances are then compared for organized versus volunteer parties. The best measure of partisan polarization among these four is the first, the ideological distance between the active Democratic and the active Republican parties. Two things stand out when these activist ranges are arrayed in Table 4.7A1. In the first, volunteer parties are *always* more polarized than organized parties for the nation as a whole in the modern world. And in the second main finding, the older domains for policy conflict, namely social welfare and civil rights, have a much greater commonality of policy preference between organized and volunteer parties, while the newer domains, national security and cultural values, show much greater impact from alternative party types.

For the two newer domains, this difference is huge, netting out to plus or minus 40 percent for national security ($23 \div .59$) and plus or minus 30 percent on national security ($.15 \div .50$). For the two older domains,

TABLE 4.7 *Partisan Polarization and Party Structure: The Modern World, 1990–2008*

### A. Ideological Range

| | 1. Activist Range | | 2. Democratic Gap | | 3. Republican Gap | | 4. Dual Gap | |
|---|---|---|---|---|---|---|---|---|
| | Vol. | Org. | Vol. | Org. | Vol. | Org. | Vol. | Org. |
| National Security | .82 | .59 | .23 | .12 | .14 | -.02 | .37 | .10 |
| Cultural Values | .65 | .50 | .22 | .13 | .09 | .04 | .31 | .17 |
| Civil Rights | .87 | .84 | .13 | .07 | .24 | .14 | .32 | .21 |
| Social Welfare | .85 | .81 | .11 | .07 | .23 | .15 | .34 | .22 |

### B. Ideological Increment

| | 1. Activist Range | 2. Democratic Gap | 3. Republican Gap | 4. Dual Gap |
|---|---|---|---|---|
| National Security | +.23 Vol. | +.11 Vol. | +.12 Vol. | +.27 Vol. |
| Cultural Values | +.15 Vol. | +.09 Vol. | +.05 Vol. | +.14 Vol. |
| Civil Rights | +.03 Vol. | +.04 Vol. | +.10 Vol. | +.11 Vol. |
| Welfare | +.04 Vol. | +.04 Vol. | +.08 Vol. | +.12 Vol. |

this difference is much more modest, netting out to plus or minus about 5 percent in comparative polarization for social welfare (.04 ÷ .81) as between the two party types and about 4 percent for civil rights (.03 ÷ .84). Table 4.7B1 then reinforces the same two points – greater polarization throughout among volunteer as opposed to organized parties, but a much larger effect on the new as opposed to the old partisan issues – merely by showing the absolute amount of difference between the two party types. Again, there is a similar effect even among the old issues (with +.04 with social welfare and +.03 for civil rights) but a far greater effect among the new issues (with +.23 for national security and +.15 for civil rights).

When the focus changes to the representational gap between partisan publics and their putative agents, the best measure is instead the fourth of these four, the dual gap between active parties and their rank and files. While activist polarization could in principle derive largely from polarization in those rank and files,[8] any gaps between activists and their *own*

---

[8] It does not do so here, empirically, but it could do so in principle.

rank and files are a direct measure of how much (or how little) these activists cater to themselves rather than to their putative constituents. The two parties do not necessarily move in tandem on their individual gaps. One party can outpace the other at one point in time, lag it in another (Tables 4.7A2 and 4.7A3). But when the two gaps are put back together, they do contribute what is perhaps the key measure of democratic representation here.

Seen this way, in Table 4.7A4, party structure matters in all four grand domains in terms of its impact on the representation of public preferences, though again, this difference is exaggerated on the new issues, constrained on their established counterparts. Thus active volunteer parties are almost four times as far away from their rank and files on national security (.37 versus .10), almost twice as far away on cultural values (.31 versus .17). By contrast, these same volunteer parties are half again as far away from their rank and files on civil rights (.32 versus .21) and social welfare (.34 versus .22). Table 4.7B4 once more reinforces these same perceptions through the net size of the gap itself, placing the four domains in the same order.

### FUNDAMENTAL FORMS OF STRUCTURAL IMPACT

So in the end, there have been three grand categories of filtering influence from party structure. One involves shaping the bedrock nature of partisan alignments on public policy. This is the least common form of structural influence, but the most consequential when it occurs. A second involves shaping the evolution of these partisan alignments from era to era. This is a major ongoing influence, albeit one that must change constantly in its specifics as policy domains move from emergent to established. And a third involves the representational character of the recurrent politics that results, most especially by way of the degree of interparty polarization and the size of the intraparty gap between political elites and the general public.

The first of these, shaping the bedrock partisan alignment, is the largest and most striking when it does occur. In principle, the very nature of the array of policy preferences distinguishing the two parties from each other, as well as the active parties from their own rank and files, can be heavily colored by party structure. In practice, a pointed example was already present in the immediate postwar years, in the crucial policy domain of social welfare. The New Deal, bringing the welfare state to the United States, had become the central policy realm shaping the behavior of both major parties, and national surveys confirmed that it had penetrated these parties in an ideologically straightforward fashion: Democrats to the left and Republicans to the right, with the active party to the left of its rank and file among Democrats and to the right of its rank and file among Republicans.

Yet seen through the lens of party structure, it was immediately clear that this overall alignment was not in fact truly national (Table 4.4A). Instead, it was underpinned by organized parties and not at all – indeed, it was undermined – by volunteer counterparts. There was still a huge ideological gap between the North and the South in American politics generally, so that regional alignments could be expected to inhabit different ideological territory. Yet within both regions, it was organized – and most definitely not volunteer – parties that were impelling what became known as the New Deal order, a consensus not necessarily on extension of the welfare state but certainly on the centrality of welfare concerns to party politics. Within that consensus, the two national parties had to have positions, and party structure was already shaping these positions powerfully by the time we have relevant data.

The crucial filtering role in all of this was most obvious in the numerically larger region, the North, where organized parties aligned with the national picture, while volunteer parties effectively dissented (Table 4.4A1). As between the two major parties, this common structural impetus did go on to express itself differently in Democratic as opposed to Republican ranks. Among Democrats, activists from organized parties pulled leftward on welfare policy by comparison to their rank and file, while activists from volunteer parties actually leaned rightward, away from their putative base. Among Republicans, activists from organized parties pulled back toward the ideological center, still conservative but implicitly acknowledging the power of the New Deal consensus, while activists from volunteer parties were the core of outright resistance to the welfare state, pulling very sharply to the right.

With the gift of hindsight plus survey data, however, we can see that organized parties in the South were doing essentially the same thing (Table 4.4A2). A powerful difference between regions in the partisan politics of the time could easily mask this, by anchoring regional preferences in very different ideological territory. Moreover, at this point in time, the Southern Democrats were more or less the whole story of Southern politics. Yet within their ranks, activists from organized parties were likewise pulling toward the national program by comparison to activists from volunteer parties. By contrast, these volunteer parties, dissenting more dramatically than counterparts in the North, carried on an old Southern tradition of governmental nonintervention in both society and economy.

So seen through the lens of party structure, and while the two regions centered their party struggles on very different ideological places, organized parties pulled toward a national party program, while volunteer parties demurred. On one side of the aisle in both regions, organized Democratic parties moved to extend an emergent welfare consensus, while volunteer Democratic parties were effectively disengaged. And on the other side of the aisle, in the region where the Republican Party mattered, organized Republican parties positioned themselves to address this emergent consensus, while volunteer Republican parties continued simply to confront it.

A second but similarly fundamental form of structural influence on the filtering role of political parties involved the question of receptiveness to new and different policy realms, and hence the *evolution* of policy programs and their associated partisan alignments. It was the response of the active parties on both sides of the partisan aisle that was key to this second structural impact, an impact built around the generic choice between completing an established policy program versus incubating new and aspiring policy realms. In fact, one of the behavioral differences between organized and volunteer parties across time was an institutionalized orientation toward making precisely this choice. Organized parties tended to pull toward the established national program, with the goal of completing it – and reaping the rewards from doing so. Volunteer parties, while not reliably hostile to that program, tended to have opposite priorities – pulling toward newer issues, the ones that could be more useful in mobilizing fresh volunteers.

For the nation as a whole, civil rights was already showing an incipient version of the established partisan alignment on social welfare in the early postwar years, though in truth, it is easier to be sure of this a half-century later than it was at the time.[9] Yet in the North, civil rights was otherwise very different from social welfare, in that it was volunteer and not organized parties that were driving this change (Table 4.4B1). Within the Democratic Party – now on its way to being the main impetus for policy making in the rights domain – it was volunteer parties that were leading the charge. By contrast, organized parties were less attracted by civil rights and more focused on social welfare. The policy positions of party activists

---

[9] As in Figure 2.4.

tell the tale: further from the national average on civil rights than on social welfare among volunteer parties, but further from the national average on social welfare than on civil rights among their organized counterparts (Tables 4.4A1 versus 4.4B1).

The exact same relationship appeared on the Republican side of the aisle, though this time, it was the historical positions of the two parties that threatened to mask a structural similarity. That historical record did keep all four Northern Republican populations at more moderate ideological locations than any Democratic population. Yet within Republican ranks, it was activists from volunteer parties who were moving more strongly away from the ideological center on these new issues. Even they were still only moderately conservative, but they were also clearly the most conservative Northern population on the rising issue of civil rights. Said differently, it was organized Republican parties that were holding their states in line with an established if receding party program. Conversely, it was volunteer parties that were mobilizing around what was becoming the new position of the national Republican Party, by moving away from the old program to the right.

This meant that the two volunteer party clusters, Democratic and Republican, were driven by the same structural incentives, albeit pulling in opposite ideological directions. This was an underlying structural dynamic that would continue across time: organized parties favoring established issues, volunteer parties favoring the latest alternatives. Though of course, the specific identity of the issues that were "old" and "new" would inevitably change. In this particular case and with the passage of time, civil rights would come to look more like social welfare, especially when contrasted with the policy domains yet to acquire the partisan alignment now common to social welfare and civil rights. In the eventual process of acquiring that alignment, national security and cultural values would come to look as civil rights had looked when it was the newest major policy conflict.

In the immediate successor period, our reform era, that common alignment was still far enough in the future that the main manifestation of a structural preference for old or new issues was confined to the one population that did show major ideological change in this period, namely Democratic activists. Accordingly, an analyst with foresight could have noticed that Northern Democratic activists in volunteer parties led the move away from the ideological center by comparison to their organized counterparts, clearly on national security and heavily on cultural values (Tables 4.5C1 and 4.5D1). This meant that the ideological left on social welfare was still fronted by Northern Democratic activists from organized parties, but the ideological left on both national security and cultural values was now fronted instead by activist counterparts from volunteer parties.

In the absence of a common overall alignment, however, most analysts in that time would have had no reason to make these calculations: we do them because we know where all four domains would go in the modern era. For in fact, a shared overall alignment did arrive in our modern period, 1990–2008, within which the power of this particular product of party structure – the propensity to favor established or emergent issues – would again stand out. Moreover, Democratic activists had been our bellwethers for this effect in the two previous postwar eras, and they played the same role with new issues in a new era, so strongly this time that the effect encompassed the South as well as the North (Tables 4.6C and 4.6D).

The North should by now be no surprise. On national security, the left in a newly aligned domain was contributed by volunteer Democratic activists while the right was contributed by volunteer Republican activists (Table 4.6C1). Cultural values in this period required an even larger change as a policy domain to move into the partisan alignment now common to all four policy domains. But within it, the same simple structural effect appeared: the Northern left again held by volunteer Democratic activists, the Northern right again held by volunteer Republican counterparts (Table 4.6D1).

What was genuinely novel, and all the more striking for that fact, was that the same could be said in the South: volunteer Democratic activists the regional left on both national security and cultural values, volunteer Republican activists the regional right on both (Tables 4.6C2 and 4.6D2). Within the nation as a whole, the liberal extreme on both issues was held by volunteer Democratic activists from the North and the conservative extreme on both by volunteer Republican activists from the South, but that was now just a residual regional gloss on a common (and regionally shared) impact of party structure.

So the modern world sustained this impact with regard to issue evolution, an impact that appeared in our data from the first point at which these data could plausibly produce it. Yet this modern world also brought with it the third fundamental form of widespread structural influence on the filtering role of political parties. As a result, it was to be this third generic form of structural influence that would shape a newly uniform set of partisan alignments. This third and final impact was not as striking as the first generic version, juxtaposing two opposite alignments by party type, as it did in the crucial domain of social welfare in the old world of postwar politics. Nor was this third and final impact as portentous as the second generic version, shaping the evolution of these alignments from the reform era onward, as it did with civil rights, national security, and cultural values. Yet this third generic version gained consequence from the fact that its particular shaping influence was the most generalized of all – not just an important part of the overall character of American politics in the modern era but the one most likely to continue into the future.

We closed the preceding section of this chapter with an analysis of this third basic impact, so it need only be (re)addressed in condensed form here. In the modern world and in every major policy domain, volunteer parties contributed considerably more than organized parties to *partisan polarization*. Which is to say: the active parties were reliably further apart under volunteer than under organized arrangements. Even more to the democratic point, volunteer parties contributed considerably more to the representational gap between party activists and their own rank and files, again in all four policy domains – further away in Democratic parties, further away in Republican parties, and inevitably further away when representation was considered as a product of the two parties jointly. Both effects were most striking in the domain of cultural values, still unaligned in the reform era but coming powerfully into conformity during the modern period. They were even more statistically powerful in the domain of national security, now leaving no doubt about its overall partisan alignment. Lastly, if the same effects were smaller in the older established domains of social welfare and civil rights, they remained visible there as well.

And just to close this comprehensive policy tour, everything that has been said so far still strongly understates the contribution of the triumph of the volunteer party model to partisan polarization and the representational gap, because the number of Americans doing their political business through volunteer rather than organized party structures had increased so much in recent years. In our earliest period, half of all Americans still did such business through organized parties and half through volunteer counterparts. In our time, three-quarters do their business through volunteer parties and one-quarter through organized counterparts. One-quarter of the United States of America is still a large number of political citizens. But it is also half of what it was at the beginning of this data series, and the growth of the rest has magnified every major contribution to policy responsiveness and democratic representation associated with volunteer parties.

If the entire period since World War II is considered as a single piece, then, a number of things could be said about alternative party structures, their comparative evolution, and its impact on policy responsiveness and democratic representation. The two basic alternatives for internal party structure, the organized versus the volunteer models, had been in both philosophical and intensely practical conflict for a century or so before World War II. Postwar scholars then discovered that traditional party structures, that is, the organized model, had survived well into the postwar years. Yet this model (and its adherents) really did face major battles around the year 1970, where reformed party structures, that is, the volunteer model, came out solidly – philosophically and statistically – ahead.

Yet a focus on the relationship between these alternative models and policy responsiveness confirms the suspicion that the impact of different party structures on democratic representation did not thereby disappear. Indeed, it continued to operate in familiar forms, up through the current moment. Basic party types were statistically rebalanced. That was undeniable. Presumably their aggregate impacts were rebalanced as well. But under the surface and despite an implicit scholarly consensus to the contrary, the war between them continued, in the sense that the choice of one basic model or the other continued to matter to the filtering of public preferences and hence to policy responsiveness.

This war was rarely the central aspect of politics in its time, though it came close in the late 1960s and early 1970s. As a general rule, a war between alternative party structures can rarely overwhelm fundamental aspects of social structure, nor can it simply override major issues of the day. In acknowledgment of those facts, we have tried to locate this war over party structure and its impacts within an overarching policy context and key regional distinctions at every point in time. Though please note: if alternative party structures could help shape the partisan alignments in various policy domains as well as the interaction and evolution of those alignments, they were presumably making a reciprocal contribution to the way that social structures formed around policy conflicts, as well as to the ability of policy domains to command (or lose) priority in ongoing political conflicts.

Be that as it may, and quite apart from these grand (and at least partially reciprocal) relationships, party structure continued to have three major impacts on American politics, impacts that were mixed and matched but always present in one form or another across this entire postwar period:

- The most far-reaching of these impacts involved shaping the partisan alignment of policy preferences in all four of the grand substantive domains that generated policy conflict across the postwar years. This was the least common of the three types of structural impact, but the largest whenever it occurred.
- A second such impact involved, not partisan alignment at a particular point in time, but rather the progression of such alignments across time, along with the relationship among them. Sometimes, this meant the evolution of a single policy domain as between political eras. More consequentially, it meant the comparative evolution of the mix of major policy conflicts.
- And if the third diagnostic impact of party structures on American politics was less dramatic in its individual instances, it was also the most common, the most lasting, and indeed, the most omnipresent in the modern world. This is the impact of alternative party models on interparty polarization and intraparty responsiveness, surely part of the essence of democratic representation in this – or any – time.

# Afterword

## A Newer "New Politics"? Party Structure in Modern Dress

The long war over party structure in American politics, rooted in the 1820s and joined in the 1880s, was still alive and well when postwar political science returned to its fortunes in the 1960s. Yet an array of systematic indicators of these fortunes, beginning in the 1950s and running through the 2010s, suggests that this war did indeed have a major turning point around 1970. Impelled afresh by a lesser but parallel conflict over the proper institutional forms for presidential selection, the old model of organized parties, built around a hierarchy of long-serving party officeholders, was decisively defeated by a newer model of volunteer parties, built instead around participatory networks of issue activists. That much of the existing study of this long war was mainly just confirmed by systematic contemporary measures.

Yet those measures also confirm that if the old organized model was greatly diminished after 1970, a low-grade conflict between the two party models did nevertheless continue. More to the practical point, it continued to matter: the rising volunteer parties and their declining organized counterparts retained noticeably different impacts on the filtering role that party structures inevitably play. As a result, when the modern era arrived, the active parties in volunteer states were further apart, Democrats versus Republicans, than the active parties in organized states. Moreover, and the truly consequential test, activists in volunteer parties stood further from *their own* rank and files in policy preferences than activists in organized parties. They were further from this rank and file within each party; they were even further from it when the two distances were added together.

Those differences were, of course, multiplied by the numerical triumph of the volunteer model in the 1970s. They were multiplied secondarily as well by a new overall balance in which volunteer parties became sufficiently dominant that the products of their filtering impact became in effect the essence of American politics nationwide. This second effect was not easy to measure precisely – society as a whole could not operate under a predominance of both models at the same time – but it was an implication of the first effect that was hard to escape. In that sense, the triumph of the volunteer model made a contribution all its own to the furtherance of partisan polarization and to the growing gap between the active parties and their own rank and files, above and beyond the simple fact of a numerical shift in the presence of the two party types.

And there the matter rested for on toward thirty years. The study of political parties as intermediary organizations hardly withered. There were vigorous debates over the alleged decline of partisanship within the general public, albeit measured now by party identification rather than by institutional arrangements.[1] Just as there was serious scholarly attention to the place of activists per se in the ideological polarization that increasingly characterized American politics, with activists now assumed to have greater and greater leeway in their choice of policy positions.[2] There was even some attention to the ancillary appendages of the official party, as with election committees or leadership PACs.[3] But the oldest and longest-running focus of research on political parties as institutional intermediaries, the one addressing the long practical struggle between organized and volunteer models, became effectively moribund.

---

[1] As with Martin J. Wattenberg, *The Decline of American Politcial Parties, 1952–1994* (Cambridge: Harvard University Press, 1996) versus Larry M. Bartels, "Partisanship and Voting Behavior, 1952–1996," *American Political Science Review* 44(2000), 35–50.

[2] As with Morris P. Fiorina, *Disconnect: The Breakdown of Representation in American Politics* (Norman: University of Oklahoma Press, 2009) versus Alan I. Abramowitz, *The Disappearing Center: Engaged Citizens, Polarization, and American Democracy* (New Haven: Yale University Press, 2010).

[3] A wide-ranging survey, coming to many conclusions parallel to ours, is Raymond J. LaRaja and Brian F. Schaffner, *Campaign Finance and Politcial Polarization: When Purists Prevail* (Ann Arbor: University of Michigan Press, 2015). See also Robin Kolodny, *Pursuing Majorities: Congressional Campaign Committees in American Politics* (Norman: University of Oklahoma Press, 1998), and David W. Rohde, *Parties and Leaders in the Post-Reform House* (Chicago: University of Chicago Press, 1991).

## THE GHOST RISES

That is until it was radically if somewhat accidentally reinvigorated by a new strand of research, implicitly arguing that this generalized conclusion about political intermediation was premised not on a decline in the operative power of internal party structures, in the way that these had been formalized by Wilson and investigated by Ware and Mayhew. Rather, the widely perceived decline was rooted only in a widespread theoretical misunderstanding. Twenty-first-century parties did not *look like* their nineteenth- (or even twentieth-) century predecessors. That much was true. Yet these new parties had re-secured the critical resources and re-solidified the operational arrangements appropriate to a vigorous intermediary role in the twenty-first century. Along the way, they had restored a modern counterpart to the internal structure that had allowed historic predecessors to shape the process of electoral politics and influence the rewards of public policy, largely to the exclusion of their own (putative) rank and files.

The opening shot in this alternative interpretation was fired by Marty Cohen, David Karol, Hans Noel, and John Zaller in *The Party Decides*.[4] In this provocative modern opener, the changes that had been the focus of Wilson, Ware, and Mayhew had indeed occurred. Moreover, those changes were acknowledged to have the direct *institutional* impacts ascribed to them. Yet what had looked like a terminal disruption of the filtering power of political parties was now argued to have been merely an anarchic interregnum, before active party players adjusted their resources, networks, and behavior so as to reassert the coordinating power of the official party:

> To summarize: the reformers of the 1970s tried to wrest the presidential nomination away from insiders and to bestow it on rank-and-file partisans, but the people who are regularly active in party politics have regained much of the control that was lost. Control rests on their ability to reach agreement on whom to support and to exploit two kinds of advantage – control of campaign resources and the persuasive power of a united front of inside players.[5]

This opening version of a revisionist argument was still focused on the mechanics of presidential selection, the most easily accessible window on party structure nationwide but never more than a corollary, a derivative,

---

[4] Cohen, Karol, Noel, and Zaller, *The Party Decides: Presidential Nominations before and after Reform* (Chicago: University of Chicago Press, 2008).

[5] Ibid., 6–7.

of the larger filtering power of alternative party models. While developed for quite autonomous purposes, a serious attempt to put operational detail into this argument and, more importantly, to drive it through the entire party system was then Seth Masket, *No Middle Ground*.[6] Beginning with the ideological polarization of the modern political world, Masket attempted to work backward to the new but recurrent elements of party politics that had produced it:

Nominations are made in primaries that typically have low turnout, little advertising, no rival party labels among which to choose, and virtually no media attention until they are over. For these reasons, nominations are often easily controlled by political insiders, including legislative leaders, interest groups, activists, and others. I call this collection of actors the *informal party organization*, or IPO, and I argue that these IPOs are the heart, soul, and backbone of contemporary political parties. Since activists are a prominent and energetic component of these organizations, IPOs tend to seek the most ideologically extreme candidate they feel they can get elected in a general election. And, since most general elections are not seriously contested today, winning at that stage is often not much of a constraint.

My claim, then, is that the parties control the public behavior of their office-holders by acting as gatekeepers to public office. Just as it is nearly impossible to win office without the nomination of a major political party, so it is nearly impossible to win the nomination of a major political party without the backing of a local IPO.[7]

Said differently, the traditional party organizations (TPOs) of the Mayhew analysis, widespread and vigorous into the 1960s but shrinking and withering from the 1970s onward, had indeed declined on their own terms. But along the way, they had acquired an informal modern variant, every bit as behaviorally muscular, every bit as effectively closed to random participants, and every bit as directive – probably even more directive – in shaping public policy. In pursuit of his demonstration of a renewed intermediary role for political parties that were now built around purposive incentives, Masket found its critical operative element in the modern incarnation of another classical notion, namely political ideology:

Although the shape of the modern party is more of a network than a machine hierarchy, the function is essentially the same: a small group of people operating only barely within the law manages to control elections and thereby the

---

[6] Seth E. Masket *No Middle Ground: How Informal Party Organizations Control Nominations and Polarize Legislatures* (Ann Arbor: University of Michigan Press, 2014).

[7] Ibid., 9. A speculative precedent from the authors of *The Party Decides* was Kathleen Bawn, Martin Cohen, David Karol, Seth Masket, Hans Noel, and John Zaller, "A Theory of Political Parties: Groups, Policy Demands, and Nominations in American Politics," *Perspectives on Politics* 10(2012), 571–597.

government. The major difference between these modern informal party organizations (IPOs) and their machine forebears is the existence of ideological activists. Machines distrusted ideologues; IPOs rely on them. The result is extreme candidates and highly polarized politics.[8]

Stable and coordinated ideological parties of this sort might prove stronger than not just the reformed volunteer parties but even the old organized parties, stronger, that is, if the standard is augmenting partisan polarization and widening the gap between rank and file preferences and the goals of party activists. Regardless, the notion that political parties that had been informally resurrected in this ideologized modern model were not having a powerful filtering impact on the transmission of public preferences seemed very unlikely – if the strategic behavior associated with party structure did indeed adhere to this new, revised, nationwide model.

As provocative as such propositions can be made to sound, however, none of these authors went on to forge the ultimate link between their modern revisionism and its classical predecessor, though the latter was always lurking in the background. In this classical view, almost as long-lived as the war over party structure, institutional reforms were often just procedural tinkering. They surfaced in occasional eruptions of reformist zeal. And social forces might be channeled differently in their aftermath. But that was all. The active agents of those social forces still ordinarily found a way to adjust their resources and strategies to a reformed environment, most especially if changes were essentially procedural. This adjustment might require time, but it would occur:

> The governing elite is always in a state of slow and continuous transformation. It flows on like a river, never being today what it was yesterday. From time to time, sudden and violent disturbances occur. There is a flood – the river overflows its banks. Afterwards, the new governing elite again resumes its slow transformation. The flood has subsided; the river is again flowing normally in its wonted bed.[9]

### STRUCTURAL MEASURES FOR A REVISIONIST ARGUMENT

Proponents of volunteer structure had certainly never argued that reformers intended a powerful autonomous contribution to partisan polarization,

---

[8] Ibid., 19.

[9] Vilfredo Pareto, *Compendium of General Sociology*, abr. Giulio Farina, trans. Elizabeth Abbott (Minneapolis: University of Minnesota Press, 1980), 279, originally published as Pareto, *Trattato Di Sociologia Generale*, 3 vols. (Florence: Barbera, 1916).

much less to distancing the active party from the wishes of its rank and file. For many, that would have been a bitterly ironic result of their reforming efforts. What they did promise – and what most aspired to produce – was a more open and fluid party politics, one that would be more accessible to a broader array of persons and preferences; one where party programs – both of them – would change more rapidly across time; and one that would, by this logic, be more democratically responsive.[10] The behavioral truth of these theoretical considerations has been at the center of the preceding chapters. Yet these were precisely the arguments that were now being denied, more and more explicitly, by the newest look at the interaction of institutional reform, party structure, and political behavior.

In any case, the point for an Afterword is that these arguments too can be slipped easily into the analytic framework used here, and given a preliminary test. This will hardly produce a "Volume II" to our analysis. That would require developing full-fledged scales of party structure specialized to the modern world, then retrofitting them as far back as they would go. But if there are a couple of key indicators that seem particularly well suited to a modern revisionist era, and if these indicators hang together in empirical terms, then it should be possible to offer a preliminary test – a kind of intellectual teaser – for the post-reform argument about the impact of party structure. So an Afterword should surely make the attempt.

Fortunately, the revisionist argument does contain two implicit but simple and direct indicators of the alleged internal power of contemporary, as opposed to historical, political parties. One of these involves career paths in partisan politics. The other involves geographic locales for partisan fund-raising. Together, they contribute a preliminary means of testing the relationship between the historic premises of the long war and their purported translation to the contemporary world.

Those who write about what we might call *restabilized* parties emphasize the degree to which nominations to public office have been reclaimed

---

[10] Perhaps the clearest statement of these aspirations can be found in the report of what became known as the Hughes Commission, the informal body proposing the resolution that became a reform mandate at the Democratic National Convention of 1968, and even more critically in the report of what became known as the McGovern Commission, the formal body tasked with operationalizing these goals. Commission on the Democratic Selection of Presidential Nominees, *The Democratic Choice* (New York: Self-Published, 1968), and Commission on Party Structure and Delegate Selection, *Mandate for Reform* (Washington, DC: Democratic National Committee, 1970).

as an internal party prerogative. In the structural dichotomy following from this premise, stronger parties are once again able to build political careers from within, while weaker parties are not. More specifically, stronger parties will have nominees who possess prior careers in partisan politics, while weaker parties, the ones that continue to be truly participatory, will remain fluid and open, to the point of embracing enthusiastic novices not just as participants but even as candidates.

Those who write about these restabilized parties likewise emphasize the ability to raise funds from indigenous and recurrent sources, rather than relying on financial transfers from outside bodies. More specifically – and again structurally – stronger parties can promise at least the rudiments of the funding that makes a candidacy possible, while weaker parties, being genuinely fluid, need to generate the necessary funds from individualized candidacies and policy currents of the moment – which encourages them to turn to outside bodies to help defray the costs of state party business.

Accordingly, we have collected both measures for our modern period, 1990–2008.[11] For political careers, this means the record of major political offices held by all successful gubernatorial candidates, where governorships were taken to be the premier elective office at the state level and where major positions were defined as state-level executive or legislative offices, plus mayoralties.[12] States can then be scaled according to the share of the prior careers of elected governors that had been spent in partisan politics. For party finance, this approach means the record of contributions from nonlocal party bodies to state parties for the same period, where the national party committees plus the congressional campaign committees are the key out-state financial donors.[13] Here, too, states can be ranked according to the share of total receipts coming from these external bodies.

---

[11] There was a huge shift in the partisan outcomes of American politics in 1994, suggesting yet another 'new world' thereafter, so we have actually used the 1994 election as the cut-point for this preliminary inquiry.

[12] The entry for "Former Governors' Bios" on the website of the National Governors Association (www.nga.org) was sufficient for most such records. Excluding other local offices like school board membership was intended to create a hard test of the role of prior political careers in the selection of the Governor, the major state-level elective office.

[13] Data can be found under the entries for Republican and Democratic state party committees on the FEC website (www.fec.gov/data/). Funds listed under "transfers from affiliated committees" were divided by the total amount of funds available and averaged across time periods.

Note that the two rankings are inverse. It is longer political careers and lesser external funding that are the signs of strength, while shorter careers and greater outside funding are signs of weakness. Fortunately, the two measures prove to be strongly (if inversely) correlated for the fifty states across the entire modern period, with a standard correlation coefficient of $-.74$. This allows the extraction of a common factor for the contemporary translation of restablized versus participatory political parties, along with individual state loadings on this common factor. Moreover, the distribution of these loadings proves to have a relatively natural break point, effectively the empirical divide between modern party types – the divide at the center of the revisionist argument.

With these measures and this classification in hand, it is a straightforward process to assign ANES respondents once again to populations of Democratic and Republican activists plus their rank and files. The analysis to follow thus presents the policy preferences of four key partisan populations in four major policy domains through the lens of a revised definition of modern party structure. To avoid analytic confusion, it is worth clarifying the nomenclature for this. *Organized parties* remain defined by the traditional model, as they have been throughout the preceding chapters, and *volunteer parties* the same. To test the revisionist argument, those that continue in the volunteer tradition, but now as redefined by the revisionists – drawing their elected officials from outside the party and raising their funds from outside state-based ranks – will be called *participatory parties*. Those that have retained a continuity with the organized tradition, again as redefined by the revisionists – limiting public office-holders to those with official party support and offering them indigenous financing – will instead be called *restabilized parties*.

## PARTISAN ALIGNMENTS AND PARTY STRUCTURES IN A POST-REFORM WORLD

This distinction allows us to compare a pair of aggregate indicators for the contemporary revisionist argument with the larger matrix of systematic indicators from the historic long war. And the result is instantly provocative. On the one hand, the representational impact of the rise of party activists as opposed to party officialdom continues to work in a modern revisionist world: activist-dominated parties continue to show greater interparty polarization in ideological terms along with greater intraparty distances between activists and their own rank and files. On the other hand, what drives this effect under updated measures of party structure is

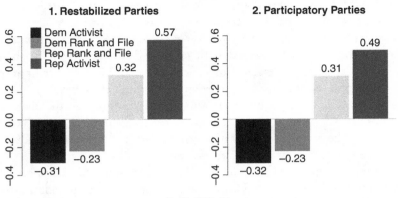

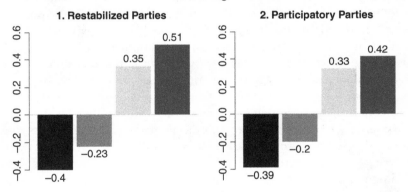

FIGURE A.1 A Newer "New Politics"? Partisan Alignments under a Revised Measure of Party Structure

the ability of some of these activists to reassert older prerogatives informally, thereby regaining the old ability – so harshly criticized during the great reform surge forty years ago – to center power on internal party mechanics while distancing themselves from the preferences of their putative rank and files.

As a result, using revisionist indicators in the most recent years, it is restabilized parties, those where party activists have indeed succeeding in reasserting their traditional prerogatives informally, that now appear as more polarized than participatory parties, those that continue in the mode that most reformers intended (Figure A.1). Moreover, the activists in those restabilized systems likewise stand further away from the policy

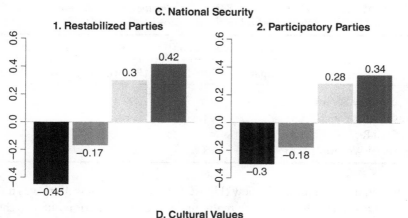

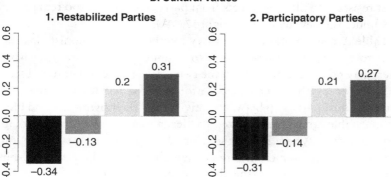

FIGURE A.I (cont.)

preferences of their ostensible rank and files than activists in participatory systems. So the initial test of a revisionist structural argument passes its opening test. And it is the more practically *closed* parties, not the more genuinely open ones, that are now driving the relationship among party structure, policy responsiveness, and democratic representation.

All four policy domains in fact attest to this development. Indeed, the substantive ranking of these effects has not even changed. Thus, the difference between organized and volunteer parties as conventionally defined was largest in the realm of national security, and it is largest for national security under revised definitions too (Figure A.IC). Those differences were next largest in the other late-aligning realm, cultural values, and they remain next largest under this alternative classification of party structures (Figure A.ID). Civil rights came next under the old definition

TABLE A.1 *Party Structure, Policy Responsiveness, and Democratic Representation in the Revisionist Argument*

| | Activist Polarization | | Representational Gap | |
|---|---|---|---|---|
| | Participatory | Restabilized | Participatory | Restabilized |
| 1. National Security | .64 | .87 | .18 | .40 |
| 2. Cultural Values | .58 | .65 | .23 | .32 |
| 3. Civil Rights | .81 | .91 | .28 | .33 |
| 4. Social Welfare | .81 | .88 | .27 | .33 |

and remains next under the new (Figure A.1B). And social welfare was not only the longest-aligned policy realm under the old definition but also the most resistant to filtering effects from party structure. It too remains that way under the new definition (Figure A.1A).

Table A.1 assembles the summary numbers for revisionist classifications to specify the same points. Now, under contemporary measures, interparty polarization between the two active parties on national security is .87 for restabilized parties, .64 for their participatory counterparts, while the intraparty gap between activists and their own rank and files is a remarkable .40 for restabilized parties, a mere .18 for their participatory opposites. Where it was the triumph of party activists under longstanding traditional measures that originally created these relationships, they are now driven by the division between states in which those activists have managed to re-close politics within their own circles, as opposed to states that still work more as the volunteer model intended. A look back at the bar graphs for the revisionist measure of partisan alignment makes it clear that the impressive size of this internal party gap between the rank and file and their ostensible representatives on national security is disproportionately due to Democratic activists in restabilized parties (Figure A.1C).

Cultural values tells essentially the same story, in a more modest way and absent the peculiar contribution of those restabilized Democratic activists (Table A.1). Thus interparty polarization for the two active parties in the domain of cultural values is .65 for restabilized parties and .58 for participatory counterparts, while the dual intraparty gap is .32 for restabilized parties and .23 for participatory parties. A quick return to Figure A.1D reveals that the larger part of this intraparty representational gap is contributed this time by Democratic activists in both party types, through the effect is less striking than with national security.

Civil rights conforms to all those patterns, but in a less intense way (Table A.1). Ideological polarization between the two active parties remains greater in restabilized than in participatory parties. The representational gap is likewise greater under the restabilized as opposed to the participatory models, being more than a quarter larger. Though another return to the bar graphs shows that in this policy realm, the two activist populations, Democratic and Republican, make more equal contributions to these numbers (Figure A.1B).

The final domain, social welfare, longest aligned and previously most resistant to structural differences, again shows the most modest effects from those differences when they are redefined in revisionist fashion, though both impacts (on partisan polarization and on the representational gap) still surface (Table A.1). Thus interparty polarization is .88 for restabilized parties, .81 for participatory counterparts. In turn, intraparty representational differences are .33 for restabilized parties, .27 for participatory counterparts. Though here, a return to the bar graphs (Figure A.1) shows that, in this domain, it is Republican activists in both party types who make the larger contributions to a dual representational gap.

In the end, though, we would want to call this preliminary revisionist test provocative rather than decisive. Chapters 1 to 4 have a strong and consistent story to tell about the power of party structure to filter policy responsiveness and shape democratic representation. This is a story that emerged from a hundred years of impressionistic observation by analysts who often disliked what they saw yet nevertheless shared with their opponents a common set of overall perceptions. That story could then be elaborated by sixty years of data stratified by clusters of multivariate indicators that follow directly from the theoretical argument. So that is the one between these two stories that is well grounded and richly defended.

The revisionist story, as given a very preliminary test in a short Afterward, with exactly two horseback indicators, can make none of these overarching claims. What the sharpness of the apparent difference within the latter should provide is a goad to further research. These alternative indicators are less consensually central, there are far fewer of them, and they cover a much shorter period of time. Yet their result is suggestive enough about the evolution of party politics after the triumph of the volunteer model that their implications cannot be dismissed out of hand. In that light, what this Afterword has really attempted is to remind students of policy responsiveness and democratic representation that the role of party structure in shaping both was hardly completed in 1970 and is hardly finished today.

# Bibliography

Abramowitz, Alan, *The Disappearing Center: Engaged Citizens, Polarization, and American Democracy* (New Haven: Yale University Press, 2010).

Baer, Kenneth S., *Reinventing Democrats: The Politics of Liberalism from Clinton to Reagan* (Lawrence: University Press of Kansas, 2000).

Baldassarri, Delia & Andrew Gelman, "Partisans without Constraint: Political Polarization and Trends in American Public Opinion," *American Journal of Sociology* 114(2008), 408–446.

Banfield, Edward C. & James Q. Wilson, *City Politics* (New York: Vintage, Books, 1963).

Bardes, Barbara A. & Robert W. Oldendick, "Public Opinion and Foreign Policy: A Field in Search of Theory," *Research in Micropolitics* 3(1990), 227–247.

Barone, Michael, *Our Country: The Shaping of America from Roosevelt to Reagan* (New York: Free Press, 1990).

Bartels, Larry M., "Partisanship and Voting Behavior, 1952–1996," *American Political Science Review* 44(2000), 35–50.

Bawn, Kathleen, Martin Cohen, David Karol, Seth Masket, Hans Noel, & John Zaller, "A Theory of Political Parties: Groups, Policy Demands, and Nominations in American Politics," *Perspectives on Politics* 10(2012), 571–597.

Berard, Stanley P., *Southern Democrats in the U.S. House of Representatives* (Norman: University of Oklahoma Press, 2001).

Berkowitz, Edward D., *America's Welfare State: From Roosevelt to Reagan* (Baltimore: Johns Hopkins University Press, 1991).

Berkowitz, Edward D., *Something Happened: A Political and Cultural Overview of the Seventies* (New York: Columbia University Press, 2006).

Berry, Jeffrey, *The New Liberalism: The Rising Power of Citizen Groups* (Washington, DC: Brookings Institution, 1999).

Black, Earl & Merle Black, *The Rise of Southern Republicanism* (Cambridge, MA: Harvard University Press, 2002).

Brands, Hal, *Making the Unipolar Moment: U.S. Foreign Policy and the Rise of the Post-Cold War Order* (Ithaca: Cornell University Press, 2016).

Brewer, Mark D. & Jeffrey M. Stonecash, *Split: Class and Cultural Divides in American Politics* (Washington, DC: CQ Press, 2006).

Browning, Robert X., *Politics and Social Welfare Policy in the United States* (Knoxville: University of Tennessee Press, 1986).

Brownlee, W. Elliott & Hugh Davis Graham, eds., *The Reagan Presidency: Pragmatic Conservatism & Its Legacies* (Lawrence: University Press of Kansas, 2003).

Bryce, James, *The American Commonwealth*, 2 vols. (London: Macmillan and Company, 1888).

Campbell, Angus, Philip E. Converse, Warren E. Miller, & Donald E. Stokes, *The American Voter: An Abridgement* (New York: John Wiley & Sons, 1964).

Carmines, Edward G. & James A. Stimson, *Issue Evolution: Race and the Transformation of American Politics* (Princeton: Princeton University Press, 1989).

Carmines, Edward G., Michael J. Ensley, & Michael W. Wagner, "Political Ideology in American Politics: One, Two, or None?" *The Forum* 10(2012), Issue 3, Article 4.

Carmines, Edward G., Michael J. Ensley, & Michael W. Wagner, *Beyond the Left-Right Divide: Conditional Mass Polarization and the Future of American Politics* (in manuscript and forthcoming).

Carsey, Thomas M. & Geoffrey Layman, "Changing Sides or Changing Minds? Party Identification and Policy Preferences in the American Electorate," *American Journal of Political Science* 50(2006), 464–477.

Ceaser, James W., *Presidential Selection: Theory and Development* (Princeton: Princeton University Press, 1979).

Ceaser, James W., *Reforming the Reforms: A Critical Analysis of the Presidential Selection Process* (Cambridge, MA: Ballinger, 1982).

Ceaser, James W., Andrew E. Busch, & John J. Pitney Jr., *Defying the Odds: The 2016 Election and American Politics* (Lanham, MD: Rowman & Littlefield, 2017).

Claggett, William & Philip H. Pollock III, "The Modes of Participation Revisited, 1980–2004," *Political Research Quarterly* 59(2006), 593–600.

Claggett, William & Byron E. Shafer, *The American Public Mind: The Issue Structure of Mass Politics in the Postwar United States* (New York: Cambridge University Press, 2010).

Claggett, William, Pär Jason Engle, & Byron E. Shafer, "The Evolution of Mass Ideologies in Modern American Politics," *The Forum* 12(2014), Issue 2, Article 2.

Clark, Peter B. & James Q. Wilson, "Incentive Systems: A Theory of Organizations," *Administrative Science Quarterly* 6(1961), 129–166.

Cohen, Marty, David Karol, Hans Noel, & John Zaller, *The Party Decides: Presidential Nominations before and after Reform* (Chicago: University of Chicago Press, 2008).

Commission on Party Structure and Delegate Selection, *Mandate for Reform* (Washington, DC: Democratic National Committee, 1970).

Commission on the Democratic Selection of Presidential Nominees, *The Democratic Choice* (New York: Self-Published, 1968).

Converse, Jean M., *Survey Research in the United States: Roots and Emergence, 1890–1960* (Berkeley: University of California Press, 1987).

Council of State Governments, www.ncls.org.

Council of State Governments, *The Book of the States: 2016 Edition* (Lexington, KY: Council of State Governments, 2017).

Council of State Governments and American Legislators, *The Book of the States* (Chicago: Council of State Governments and American Legislators, 1935).

Crotty, William J., *Political Reform and the American Experiment* (New York: Thomas Y. Crowell, 1977).

Crotty, William J., *Decision for the Democrats: Reforming the Party Structure* (Baltimore: Johns Hopkins University Press, 1978).

Davies, Gareth, *From Opportunity to Entitlement: The Transformation and Decline of Great Society Liberalism* (Lawrence: University Press of Kansas, 1996).

DeBenedetti, Charles, *An American Ordeal: The Antiwar Movement of the Vietnam Era* (Syracuse: Syracuse University Press, 1990).

Divine, Robert A., *The Illusion of Neutrality* (Chicago: University of Chicago Press, 1962).

Ehrman, John, *The Eighties: America in the Age of Reagan* (New Haven: Yale University Press, 2005).

Elazar, Daniel J., *American Federalism: A View from the States* (New York: Thomas Y. Crowell, 1966).

Fiorina, Morris P. & Samuel J. Abrams, *Disconnect: The Breakdown of Representation in American Politics* (Norman: University of Oklahoma Press, 2009).

Flynn, Edward J., *You're the Boss: My Story of a Life in Practical Politics* (New York: Viking Press, 1947).

Ford, Henry Jones, *The Rise and Growth of American Politics* (New York: The Macmillan Company, 1898).

Gaddis, John Lewis, *The United States and the Origins of the Cold War, 1941–1947* (New York: Columbia University Press, 1972).

Gaddis, John Lewis, *Surprise, Security, and the American Experience* (Cambridge, MA: Harvard University Press, 2004).

Gerring, John, *Party Ideologies in America, 1828–1996* (New York: Cambridge University Press, 2004).

Gillespie, Ed & Bob Schellas, eds., *Contract with America* (New York: Times Books, 1994).

Gitlin, Todd, *The Sixties: Years of Hope, Days of Rage* (New York: Bantam, 1993).

Hamby, Alonzo L., *Man of the People: The Life of Harry S. Truman* (New York: Oxford University Press, 1995).

Hamby, Alonzo L., *The Imperial Years: The United States since 1939* (New York: Weybright & Talley, 1976).

Hamby, Alonzo L., *For the Survival of Democracy: Franklin Roosevelt and the World Crisis of the 1930s* (New York: Free Press, 2004), 344–346.

Heaney, Michael T., *Party in the Street: The Antiwar Movement and the Democratic Party after 9/11* (New York: Cambridge University Press, 2015).

Hinckley, Ronald H., *People, Polls, and Policymakers: American Public Opinion and National Security* (New York: Lexington, 1992).

Holsti, Ole R., *Public Opinion and American Foreign Policy* (Ann Arbor: University, of Michigan Press, 1996).

Hook, Stephen W. & John Spanier, *American Foreign Policy since World War II*, 20th ed. (Washington, DC: CQ Press, 2015).

Hunter, James Davison, *Culture Wars: The Struggle to Define America* (New York: Basic Books, 1991).

Hurwitz, Jon & Mark Peffley, "How Are Foreign Policy Attitudes Structured: A Hierarchical Model," *American Political Science Review* 81(1987), 1099–1120.

Hyman, Herbert H., *Taking Society's Measure: A Personal History of Survey Research* (New York: Russell Sage Foundation, 1991).

Inglehart, Ronald, *The Silent Revolution: Changing Values and Political Styles among Western Publics* (Princeton: Princeton University Press, 1977).

Jentleson, Bruce W., *American Foreign Policy: The Dynamics of Choice in the 21st Century*, 5th ed. (New York: W.W. Norton, 2013).

Johnston, Richard, Michael G. Hagen, & Kathleen Hall Jamieson, *The 2000 Presidential Election and the Foundations of Party Politics* (New York: Cambridge University Press, 2004).

Jones, Charles O., *The Republican Party in American Politics* (New York: Macmillan, 1965).

Kaplan, Lawrence S., *The Conversion of Arthur H. Vandenberg: From Isolation to International Engagement* (Lexington: University Press of Kentucky, 2015).

Katznelson, Ira, *Fear Itself: The New Deal and the Origins of Our Time* (New York: W. W. Norton, 2013).

Keech, William R., *The Impact of Negro Voting: The Role of the Vote in the Quest for Equality* (Chicago: Rand McNally, 1968).

Kennedy, David M., *Freedom from Fear: The American People in Depression and War* (New York: Oxford University Press, 1999).

Kleppner, Paul, *The Cross of Culture: A Social Analysis of Midwestern Politics, 1850–1900* (New York: Free Press, 1970).

Kleppner, Paul, *The Third Electoral System, 1853–1892* (Chapel Hill: University of North Carolina Press, 1979).

Kolodny, Robin, *Pursuing Majorities: Congressional Campaign Committees in American Politics* (Norman: University of Oklahoma Press, 1998).

Ladd, Everett Carll, Jr., *Negro Political Leadership in the South* (New York: Atheneum, 1969).

Ladd, Everett Carll, Jr., with Charles D. Hadley, *Transformations of the American Party System: Political Coalitions from the New Deal to the 1970s* (New York: W. W. Norton, 1975).

LaRaja, Raymond J. & Brian F. Schaffner, *Campaign Finance and Political Polarization; When Purists Prevail* (Ann Arbor: University of Michigan Press, 2015).

Layman, Geoffrey, *The Great Divide: Religious and Cultural Conflict in American Party Politics* (New York: Columbia University Press, 2001).

Layman, Geoffrey C., Thomas M. Carsey, John C. Green, Richard Herrara, & Rosalyn Cooperman, "Activists and Conflict *Extension in American Party Politics,*" *American Political Science Review* 104(2010), 324–346.

Leege, David C., Kenneth D. Wald, Brian S. Kreuger, & Paul D. Mueller, *The Politics of Cultural Differences: Social Change and Voter Mobilization Strategies in the Post–New Deal Period* (Princeton: Princeton University Press, 2002).

Lindeman, Kara & Donald R. Haider-Markel, "Issue Evolution, Political Parties, and the Culture Wars," *Political Research Quarterly* 55(2002), 91–110.

Link, Arthur S. & Richard L. McCormick, *The Progressives* (Arlington Heights, VA: Harlan Davidson, 1983).

Lipset, Seymour Martin & Stein Rokkan, eds., *Party System and Voter Alignments: Cross-National Perspectives* (New York: Free Press, 1967).

Masket, Seth E., *No Middle Ground: How Informal Party Organizations Control Nominations and Polarize Legislatures* (Ann Arbor; University of Michigan Press, 2011).

Mason, Robert, *The Republican Party in American Politics from Hoover to Reagan* (Cambridge: Cambridge University Press, 2012).

Mayer, William G., *The Changing American Mind: How and Why American Public Opinion Changed between 1960 and 1988* (Ann Arbor: University of Michigan Press, 1992).

Mayhew, David R., *Placing Parties in American Politics: Organization, Electoral Set-tings, and Government Activity in the Twentieth Century* (Princeton: Princeton University Press, 1986).

McClosky, Herbert, Paul Hoffman, & Rosemary O'Hara, "Issue Conflict and Consensus among Party Leaders and Followers," *American Political Science Review* 54(1960), 406–472.

McCormick, Richard L., *The Party Period and Public Policy: American Politics from the Age of Jackson to the Progressive Era* (New York: Oxford University Press, 1986).

Miller, Warren E., "An Organizational History of the Intellectual Origins of the National Election Studies," *European Journal of Political Research* 25(1994), 247–265.

Miller, Warren E. & J. Merrill Shanks, *The New American Voter* (Cambridge, MA: Harvard University Press, 1996).

Miroff, Bruce, *The Liberals' Moment: The McGovern Insurgency and the Identity Crisis of the Democratic Party* (Lawrence: University Press of Kansas, 2007.

Morgan, Iwan W., *Beyond the Liberal Consensus: A Political History of the United States since 1965* (London: Hurst, 1994).

National Governors Association (www.nga.org).

Nivola, Pietro S. & David W. Brady, eds., *Red and Blue Nation?* Vol. 1, *Characteristics and Consequences of America's Polarized Politics* (Washington, DC: Brookings Institution, 2006).

Norpoth, Helmut, Andrew H. Sidman, & Clara H. Suong, "Polls and Elections: The New Deal Realignment in Real Time," *Presidential Studies Quarterly* 43(2013), 146–160.

Page, Benjamin L. & Robert Y. Shapiro, *The Rational Public: Fifty Years of Trends in American Policy Preferences* (Chicago: University of Chicago Press, 1991).

Pareto, Vilfredo, *Compendium of General Sociology*, abr. Giulio Farina, trans. Elizabeth Abbott (Minneapolis: University of Minnesota Press, 1980), 279, originally published as Pareto, *Trattato di Sociologia Generale*, 3 vols. (Florence: Barbera, 1916).

Pastor, Robert A., *Congress and the Politics of U.S. Foreign Economic Policy, 1929–1976* (Berkeley: University of California Press, 1980).

Patterson, James T., "The Failure of Party Realignment in the South, 1937–1939," *Journal of Politics* 27(1965), 602–617.

Patterson, James T., *Brown v. Board of Education: A Civil Rights Milestone and Its Troubled Legacy* (New York: Oxford University Press, 2001).

Patterson, James T., *Restless Giant: The United States from Watergate to Bush v. Gore* (New York: Oxford University Press, 2005).

Polsby, Nelson W., *Consequences of Party Reform* (New York: Oxford University Press, 1983).

Polsby, Nelson W. & Aaron B. Wildavsky, *Presidential Elections: Strategies of American Electoral Politics* (New York: Charles Scribner's Sons, 1964).

Popkin, Samuel L., *The Reasoning American Voter: Communication and Persuasion in Presidential Campaigns* (Chicago: University of Chicago Press, 1991).

Rae, Nicol C., *Southern Democrats* (New York: Oxford University Press, 1994).

Ranney, Austin, *Curing the Mischiefs of Faction: Party Reform in America* (Berkeley: University of California Press, 1975).

Rohde, David W., *Parties and Leaders in the Postreform House* (Chicago: University of Chicago Press, 1991).

Scammon, Richard M. & Ben J. Wattenberg, *The Real Majority: An Extraordinary Examination of the American Electorate* (New York: Coward-McCann, 1970).

Schickler, Eric & Devin Caughey, "Public Opinion, Organized Labor, and the Limits of New Deal Liberalism, 1930–1945," *Studies in American Political Development* 25(2011), 162–189.

Seagull, Louis M., *Southern Republicanism* (Cambridge, MA: Schenkman, 1975).

Shafer, Byron E., *Quiet Revolution: The Struggle for the Democratic Party and the Shaping of Post-Reform Politics* (New York: Russell Sage Foundation, 1983).

Shafer, Byron E., *Bifurcated Politics: Evolution and Reform in the National Party Convention* (Cambridge, MA: Harvard University Press, 1988).

Shafer, Byron E., *The American Political Pattern: Stability and Change, 1932–2016* (Lawrence: University Press of Kansas, 2016).

Shafer, Byron E. & Anthony J. Badger, eds., *Contesting Democracy: Substance and Structure in American Political History, 1775–2000* (Lawrence: University Press of Kansas, 2001).

Shafer, Byron E. & William J. M. Claggett, *The Two Majorities: The Issue Context of Modern American Politics* (Baltimore: Johns Hopkins University Press, 1995).

Shafer, Byron E. & Richard H. Spady, *The American Political Landscape* (Cambridge, MA: Harvard University Press, 2014).

Sides, John & Lynn Vavreck, *The Gamble: Choice and Chance in the 2012 Presidential Election* (Princeton: Princeton University Press, 2013).

Silbey, Joel H., *The American Political Nation, 1838–1893* (Stanford: Stanford University Press, 1991).

Steward, Frank Mann, *A Half-Century of Municipal Reform: The History of the National Municipal League* (Berkeley: University of California Press, 1950).

Sullivan, Denis G., Jeffrey L. Pressman, & F. Christopher Arterton, *Explorations in Convention Decision Making: The Democratic Party in the 1970s* (San Francisco: W. A. H. Freeman, 1976).

Summers, Mark W., *The Era of Good Stealings* (New York: Oxford University Press, 1993).

Sundquist, James L., *Politics and Policy: The Eisenhower, Kennedy, and Johnson Years* (Washington, DC: Brookings, 1968).

Tate, Katherine, *From Protest to Politics: The New Black Voters in American Elections* (New York: Russell Sage Foundation, 1993).

Van Buren, Martin, *Inquiry into the Origin and Course of Political Parties in the United States* (New York: Hurd & Houghton, 1867).

Viguerie, Richard A., *The New Right: We're Ready to Lead* (Falls Church, VA: The Viguerie Company, 1981).

Valelly, Richard M., *The Two Reconstructions: The Struggle for Black Enfranchisement* (Chicago: University of Chicago Press, 2004).

Walton, Hanes, Jr., *African American Power and Politics: The Political Context Variable* (New York: Columbia University Press, 1997).

Ware, Alan, *The Breakdown of Democratic Party Organization, 1940–1980* (Oxford: Oxford University Press, 1985).

Ware, Alan, *The American Direct Primary: Party Institutionalization and Transformation in the North* (New York: Cambridge University Press, 2002).

Washington, George, "Farewell Address," collected in James D. Richardson, ed., *A Compilation of Messages and Papers of the Presidents* (Washington, DC: Bureau of National Literature, 1897–1913), Vol. 1, 205–216.

Wattenberg, Martin J., *The Decline of American Political Parties, 1952–1994* (Cambridge, MA: Harvard University Press, 1996).

Wilson, James Q., *Political Organizations* (New York: Basic Books, 1973).

Vann Woodward, C., *The Strange Career of Jim Crow* (New York: Oxford University Press, 1955).

Wurgler, Emily & Clem Brooks, "Out of Step? Voters and Social Issues in U.S. Presidential Elections," *The Sociological Quarterly* 55(2014), 683–704.

# Index

9 781108 718868